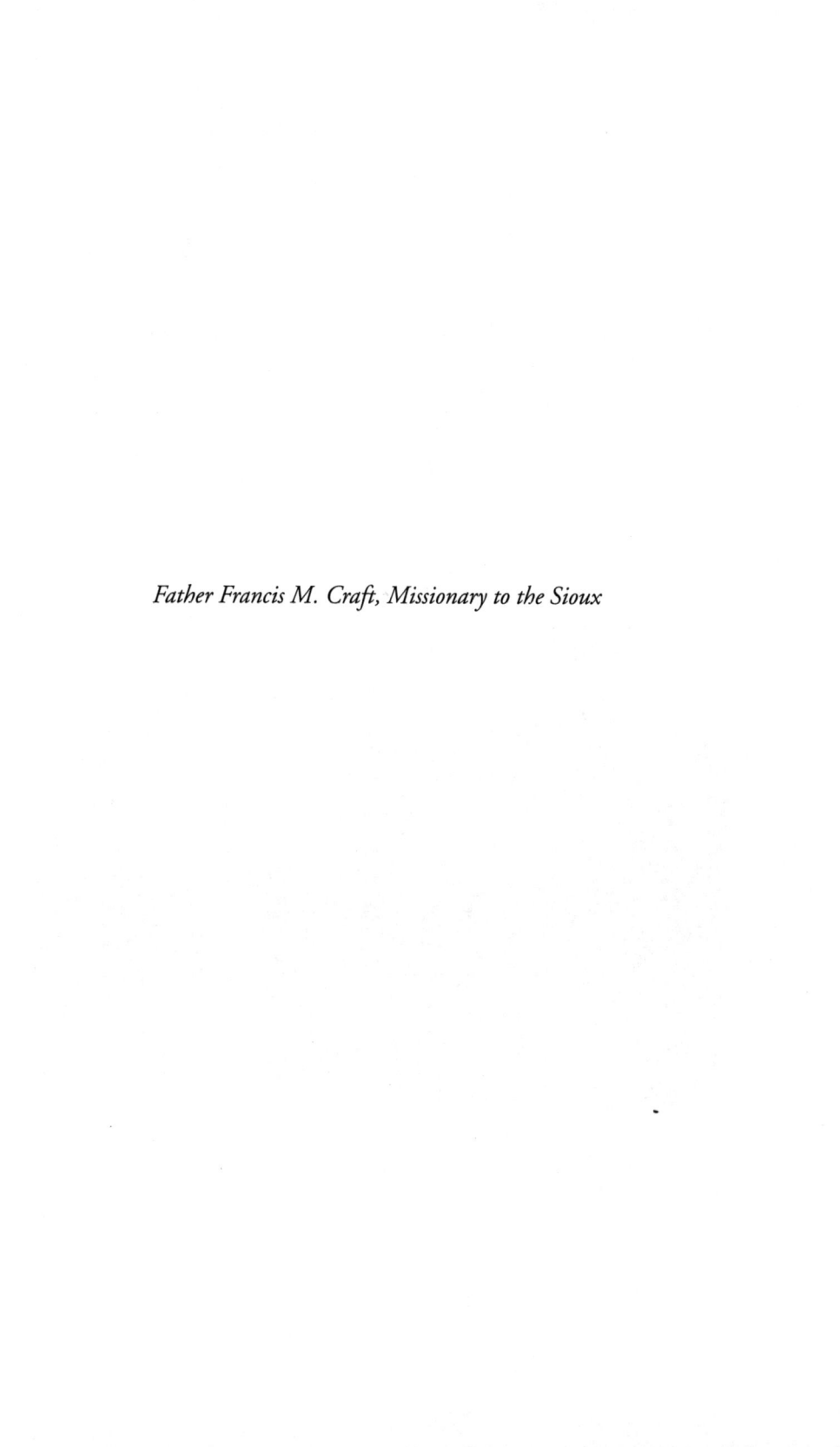

Father Francis M. Craft, Missionary to the Sioux

Father Francis M. Craft, about 1905–10, when serving as a pastor of St. Matthew's Church, East Stroudsburg, Pennsylvania. Photographer unknown. Author's collection.

FATHER
FRANCIS M. CRAFT

MISSIONARY TO THE SIOUX

THOMAS W. FOLEY

UNIVERSITY OF NEBRASKA PRESS

LINCOLN AND LONDON

Publication of this book was assisted by a grant from
The Andrew W. Mellon Foundation.
Portions of this book appeared in earlier form in "Father Francis Craft and the Indian
Sisters," *U.S. Catholic Historian* 16, no. 2 (spring 1998): 41–55, and "Prominent Priests of
the Hoban Years," in *Envisioning Faith: The Pictorial History of the Diocese of Scranton,*
ed. James B. Early (Devon PA: William T. Cooke, 1994), 185.

Library of Congress Cataloging-in-Publication Data

Foley, Thomas W., 1931–
Father Francis M. Craft, missionary to the Sioux / Thomas W. Foley.
p. cm.
Includes bibliographical references and index.
ISBN 0-8032-2015-4 (cl.: alk. paper)
1. Craft, Francis M.   2. Catholic Church — Clergy — Biography.   3. Missionaries — West
(U.S.) — Biography.   4. Dakota Indians — Missions — History.   I. Title.
BV2765.5.C74 F65   2002
266′.2′092 — dc21
[B]   2002017971

To my wife, Ruth,
and to our children, Eileen, Tom, and John

CONTENTS

ILLUSTRATIONS

Maps

ACKNOWLEDGMENTS

In 1944, rummaging around my Aunt Mame's Chicago apartment, I found a shoe box stuffed with a collection of old letters, newspaper accounts, three small handwritten volumes, and a single photograph. The three volumes were the journals of Father Craft, written during a twenty-six-month period on Standing Rock Agency in 1888–90. The letters included correspondence from bishops, cardinals, Civil War generals, the secretary of war—even a message from Sitting Bull. As a teenager, I was fascinated with my find and asked my aunt if I could have these "Indian papers." She agreed to pass them on to me, and on the back of the lone photo, she identified the subject as Father Francis M. Craft, noting that he had "passed away in the arms of Robert R. Foley, your Daddy."

Father Craft, my father, and my aunt, Mary B. McCarthy, had become close friends while he served as pastor of St. Matthew's Catholic Church in East Stroudsburg, Pennsylvania; they were especially instrumental in the building of St. Mark's Mission Church in Delaware Water Gap, Pennsylvania, shortly before Father Craft died in 1920. First and foremost, then, I am grateful to my father and aunt for having conserved the priest's papers for that first quarter century.

Since retiring in 1990, I've researched Father Craft's life and the events that influenced it using sources ranging from frontier abbeys to the Vatican Museum; from Marquette University in Milwaukee to the Katholieke Universiteit Leuven in Belgium; historical societies from the Dakotas to Florida, Pennsylvania, and New York; diocesan archives from the Dakotas to Philadelphia, Scranton, and New York; and the National Archives in Washington DC.

One of the more gratifying aspects of this project has been the generous cooperation and encouragement I have received from historians and archivists across the country. My first visit was with Mark Thiel, assistant archivist at Marquette University, who introduced me to the country's largest collection of material on the Bureau of Catholic Indian Missions. Mark also introduced me to Sister Mary Ewens, O.P., who had done considerable research on Craft and his Congregation of American Sisters. In addition to writing numerous studies on the history of the American nun, Sister Mary Ewens's past achievements included terms as associate director of the Cushwa Center for the Study of American Catholicism at the University of Notre Dame and as president of Edgewood College in Madison, Wisconsin.

Harvey Markowitz, a scholar with the D'Arcy McNickle Center for the History of the American Indian at the Newberry Library, Chicago, translated the Lakota entries in Father Craft's journals.

In the Dakotas I met present-day Benedictines, whose heroic predecessors played a major role in Craft's life. Sister Verena Kaiser, O.S.B., archivist at Sacred Heart Monastery in Richardton, North Dakota, was most helpful, as was Rev. Denis Fournier, O.S.B., archivist at Assumption Abbey in Richardton, North Dakota. Rev. Terrence G. Kardong, O.S.B., former editor of the *American Benedictine Review* and author of *Catholic Life at Fort Berthold, 1889–1989,* commiserated with me on the daunting task of describing the complexities of Craft's life.

Other Benedictines who supported this project include Rev. Regis Probstfield, O.S.B., pastor of the Catholic Indian Mission at Standing Rock Indian Reservation, Fort Yates, North Dakota, and Rev. Cyprian Davis, O.S.B., archivist at St. Meinrad Archabbey, St. Meinrad, Indiana. Especially valuable were the insight and sage counsel of Rev. Quentin Kathol, O.S.B., archivist at Conception Abbey, Missouri, who helped me unravel the conflicts in Craft's relationships. Father Quentin also provided the English translation of some letters that were written in German script.

I am particularly indebted to Michael F. Steltenkamp, S.J., professor of anthropology at Wheeling Jesuit University, Wheeling, West Virginia, who encouraged me to persevere through a long and difficult course to publication. My sincere thanks go also to Christopher J. Kauffman, editor of the *U.S. Catholic Historian,* who provided much-needed encouragement by publishing an article of mine on Father Craft and the Indian sisters a few years ago.

A crucial resource was the New-York Historical Society, repository of the James Edward Kelly Papers. Despite severe budget constrictions, Margaret Heilbrun, library director and curator of manuscripts, ably assisted by Megan M. Hahn, manuscripts assistant, and Alan Balicki, senior conservator, provided critical documents.

The National Archives in Washington DC was blessedly user friendly owing to the professional efforts of Michael T. Meier of the Military Reference Branch, Timothy Wehrkamp and Richard Fusick of the Bureau of Indian Affairs Branch, and Reginald Washington of the Reference Services Branch.

I am grateful also to Sister Maria E. McCall of the archives of the Sisters of the Blessed Sacrament in Bensalem, Pennsylvania, for allowing access to the Katharine Drexel Papers.

This book's documentation reflects the broad range of its resource contributors. I can't list them all, but some deserving of special recognition are Msgr. John A. Bergamo, V.F., pastor of St. Matthew's Church, East Stroudsburg, Pennsylvania; Wm. Kevin Cawley, associate archivist at the Archives of the University of Notre Dame; Nancy Merz of the Jesuit Missouri Province Archives; Jon K. Reynolds, archivist, Lauinger Library, Georgetown University; and Sister Ann Kessler, O.S.B., and Sister Victorine Stoltsz, O.S.B., at Mount Marty College, Yankton, North Dakota.

INTRODUCTION

In July 1888 a young Catholic priest brought his horse to a halt in front of Coles's General Store on Standing Rock Agency, Dakota Territory. He dismounted, tied Pinch's reins securely to the hitching rail, and stepped quickly into the store. His purchase that day was four arrows.

A few days earlier he had been confronted by Hóthąka, a local Sioux headman who had fraudulently represented the parentage of a girl who had failed to attend the agency school. The youngster was an orphan, but Hóthąka had claimed her aunt was her mother in order to keep her in the camps rather than send her off to school. The priest had presented the actual state of the case despite Hóthąka's strenuous objections. The argument escalated until Hóthąka, whose name translates "Big Voice," threatened to kill the priest.

Hóthąka picked the wrong man to threaten: the Reverend Francis M. Craft responded by summarily pitching the Indian headlong down the small hill where the dispute took place. In retaliation, Hóthąka's tribesmen petitioned to have the cleric removed from the reservation.

Four separate bands inhabited the agency confines at the time, led by Gall, Grass, Mad Bear, and Big Head. As he made his way into each of the four camps, Craft called for a council meeting. Presenting an arrow to each band, he told them in their own language: "If you want to get rid of me, use this, instead of your lying tongues."[1]

This scene of a lone priest riding into a Sioux encampment in 1888 to throw down the gauntlet befits the dramatic style of a man who is little remembered today but was one of the most remarkable, flamboyant, and controversial figures of that time and place. His priestly garb was probably topped off by either a pith helmet or a wide-brimmed black felt hat adorned with eagle feathers. His ploy succeeded, since he was not killed, nor was he removed from the reservation—at least not then.

With the zeal of Saint Paul, the idealism of Don Quixote, and the flair of Cyrano de Bergerac, Francis M. Craft strode across the American panorama quite unlike any others of his time. He was hero and villain, soldier and statesman, doctor, journalist, priest, and prophet, a visionary and an eccentric crank, an eastern white man who became an Indian chief.

Denied his quest for a soldier's death on such diverse battlegrounds as Gettysburg, Sedan, and the eastern provinces of Cuba, he tried instead to storm heaven for the cause of the American Indian. Through it all, he came nearest his goal of martyrdom on the frozen, bloody field at Wounded Knee.

Recovering from nearly fatal wounds, he embarked on a ten-year odyssey that took him from the arid plains of Dakota to tropical Cuban hillsides. His quest: a desperate but doomed attempt to establish an order of Native American nuns to labor for the spiritual and temporal welfare of their own troubled race. Ironically, his valiant efforts in this undertaking were thwarted not by steel and lead but by his superiors' unwillingness to see the great potential in his vision.

Father Francis M. Craft, Missionary to the Sioux

I

THE FORMATIVE YEARS

Francis M. Craft was forged of a unique mix of Native American blood, military heritage, and a medical legacy that profoundly affected the course of his adventurous career. The Indian blood came from Rebecca Basset, his paternal grandmother. Rebecca's parents were an immigrant Welshman and the full-blood daughter of a Mohawk chief who had sided with New York troops in the Revolutionary War.[1] She married William Craft, who also served in the rebellion as a private in the Second Regiment, Westchester County Militia, and had spent the summer of 1779 as a British prisoner of war.[2]

Isaac B. Craft was the second son of Rebecca Basset and William Craft. Born in 1808, he apprenticed in medicine and surgery under various New York physicians, eventually establishing a practice as a surgeon at Bellevue Hospital in New York City.[3] At age nineteen he had been commissioned a captain in the same New York regiment his father had served in. In August 1851, at age forty-three, Isaac married twenty-one-year-old Sarah Phillips, a direct descendant of Nathanael Greene, also of Revolutionary War fame.

The first child of Dr. Isaac Craft and Sarah Phillips Craft, Francis was born in New York City on 23 September 1852. The family attended St. Luke's Episcopal Church, just down the block from the Craft home at 495 Hudson Street.

In his early years Craft attended local public schools in his New York neighborhood, but as the Civil War engulfed the nation, Isaac Craft was apparently swept up in the emotional fervor of the times. Lee's Army of Northern Virginia had advanced beyond Chancellorsville and pushed northward as townspeople throughout Pennsylvania prepared for Confederate attack. Recruiting was rife in the New York City area even as the Lincoln administration made plans for the first military draft in 1863. Partly for preparedness and partly out of his own martial inclinations, Dr. Craft arranged for his young son to learn the manual of arms: to hone his skills as a marksman with "musket, carbine, and pistol."

The minimum age for enlistment was eighteen, but recruiters often ignored this limitation. Moreover, for musicians, drummer boys, and those small and quick enough to scamper across a battlefield with messages in their sacks, there were no age restrictions. The Twenty-first Indiana may have established a record when a young musician joined up at age nine, but a precocious Francis Craft was not far behind. On 1 May 1863 Dr. Craft wrote a note "to any officer of the U.S. Army" giving his ten-year-old son "permission to enter the military service of the United States." The note was impressively official. It was written on the back of Dr. Craft's own commission as a captain of the Second Regiment of Artillery, signed by New York Governor De Witt Clinton.[4]

Armed with his father's authorization, Francis traveled to Gettysburg in time for the pivotal battle of the Civil War. The officer who discovered him wandering around the grounds near the command tent of the First Army likely was unimpressed with the lad's potential as a picket or rifleman. As a messenger, however, he could free up others for the more grueling requirements of combat.

Young Francis Craft's introduction to nineteenth-century warfare was mercifully brief. During the first day of the battle, after Maj. Gen. John F. Reynolds was killed in the fight at the Stone Wall, a Confederate charge drove Northern troops in full retreat across the battlefield. Scrambling through the smoke and confusion, Craft was struck a glancing bayonet blow to the forehead that knocked him senseless. Regaining consciousness, he found an abandoned federal unit battle flag, wrapped it around his shoulders, and stumbled toward the rear. Some soldiers of a Massachusetts regiment brought him to safety.[5] Having survived this first attempt to emulate his heroic heritage, Craft returned home, a bit bloodied but still determined to reach beyond the bounds of ordinary conduct.

In search of a healthier climate, in 1865 Dr. Craft moved his family to northeast Pennsylvania's Pike County. They settled in a backwoods region called Red Ridge, about five miles beyond the town of Milford. By then

Francis had a younger brother, Walter, and a sister, Alice. The last of the Craft children, Fanny, was born in 1867.

Dr. Craft constructed an access road to the Erie Railroad, and at the edge of a pond fed by a stream that came to be called Craft Brook, he built a home and outbuildings. In addition to the tools of his profession — surgical instruments, scales, pharmaceutical paraphernalia — the doctor brought with him from New York a collection of rare books, an assortment of musical instruments, and a gallery of select paintings. In sharp contrast to the rural surroundings, a high sense of culture and style flourished in the Craft household.

Young Francis was keenly interested in the area's history. He first searched out the Schocopee Trail used so many years earlier by Delaware tribesmen as they traveled from Woodtown to Minisink Island. Decades later he and an uncle concluded that the nearby Shohola River derived its name from the French *chaud haut lieu,* (warm high place), called thus by early Jesuit Fathers and later spelled to fit an Indian pronunciation. The local stream called the Santantine, he reasoned, was originally "Saint Antoine," again a phonic corruption that found its way into common usage.[6]

Craft's initial attempt to rival the military exploits of his ancestors only whetted his appetite for more. Temporarily stymied as a warrior, at age twelve Craft entered Columbia University to follow the medical profession of his father. From there he went to Belgium, where he studied surgery at the University of Louvain, completing his curriculum just as the Franco-Prussian War broke out in July 1870.[7] Inherently drawn toward conflict and still too young to practice medicine, Craft became a mercenary for France in this brief and savage conflict. After an initial victory at Saarbrücken, the French were routed at Spichern and Weissenburg, effectively splitting the French forces as German troops penetrated the French countryside. As French forces under Marshal François Achille Bazaine remained under siege at Metz, Marshal Maurice de MacMahon maneuvered his troops to a small fortress at Sedan, not far from the Belgian border. There, in the great Battle of Sedan, heavy losses from German assaults forced a quick surrender. Napoleon III was among the more than eighty thousand prisoners taken that day. It was the end of the Second Empire in France, the beginning of German reunification, and it set the stage for World War I four decades later.

It is unclear where the freelancing Craft entered the fray, but he re-

portedly took part in a final desperate charge at Sedan. As apparently
was the case at Gettysburg, a battle brewing anywhere within a hundred
miles proved irresistible. He joined with remnants of the French cavalry,
which he later described as the Marquis de Gallifet's "mixed squadron . . .
Chasseurs d'Afrique, Chasseurs a cheval, Hussars, Dragoons, Cuirassiers,
Lanciers" as a few hundred broke through to the Belgian frontier. With
no officers left to direct them, the Germans, he recalled, let them escape
rather than suffer the losses "necessary to annihilate them."[8]

The hostilities concluded, Craft returned home to join his father in
practicing medicine at Red Ridge. But the life of a rural physician offered
little to sustain the interest of a teenage veteran of two wars. Another campaign beckoned, this time in Cuba. The Cuban War for Independence
from Spain (Ten Years' War), which had begun in 1868, soon drew the
nineteen-year-old warrior. In 1871 he recruited 250 mercenaries, "all Irish-
men except four," and sailed with them from Tampa, Florida, to Cuba,
where they offered their services to the Cuban flag. They were called the
American division of the Cuban army.

The mercenaries he recruited were veterans of Confederate or federal
armies, "all expert cavalry or artillery men." Craft himself held a military
command and rose to the rank of brigadier general, his exploits earn-
ing him the sobriquet "the American devil." In a 1902 interview Craft is
quoted: "Was I wounded? Slightly, several times. . . . Bullets grazed me
and bayonet and sabre cuts were frequent, but none were sufficient to keep
me out of the saddle."[9]

He described his Cuban adventure as guerrilla in nature and reported
that his contacts in the action included "Maceo, [Antonio] Gomez, Garcia,
and Bandera."[10]

The newspaper accounts these early adventurous excursions were reconstructed from could be neither confirmed nor disproved. There are no
records proving that Craft was at Gettysburg or that he studied medicine
at Columbia University or surgery at Louvain. His father, Isaac, is listed as
a student at the New York College of Physicians and Surgeons in 1827–28,
but there are no records of his ever receiving a degree from this predecessor
of Columbia University's medical school. Nineteenth-century American
medical education had yet to make the full transition from homegrown,
doctor-owned schools and apprenticeship programs to formal curriculums
at the university level. All the medical schools in New York in the late
1860s, when Francis Craft would likely have attended, were faculty-owned

institutions where tuition payments were often made directly to the principals at the conclusion of each seminar or series of lectures. Records were sporadic and incomplete. The University at Louvain, whose archives were largely destroyed in two world wars, is unable to verify his attendance before 1870, but Jesuit records there confirm his presence in 1879. And of course there are no exhaustive records identifying every combatant in the Franco-Prussian War or in Cuba.

Craft converted to Catholicism in the mid-1870s. The first Catholic church he entered was Our Lady of Mercy, in Brooklyn, New York. The year was 1874.[11] Exactly what prompted his religious conversion is unclear; perhaps he was influenced by the Jesuit fathers at Louvain or by the Irish-Catholic filibusters in Cuba. Mary Sharp, a housekeeper of Father Craft, recalled that he had become "interested in the Catholic faith through a group of Irish soldiers that he knew."[12] His Mohawk Indian blood was certainly a critical factor in his decision to enter the priesthood, a vocation to which he felt "called . . . by God."[13] He "became an Indian to save the Indian"[14] and often avowed that he would not have endured the trials of a religious profession for any other purpose.

II

PATH TO PRIESTHOOD

Craft was not a typical candidate for the priesthood, and he was especially unsuited for the structured environment of a disciplined order like the Society of Jesus,[1] which he entered at West Park, New York, in January 1876. He was somewhat older than his contemporaries and certainly more worldly. No impressionable youngster just out of secondary school, he was twenty-three when he joined the Jesuit order. By then his character had been framed and tempered by forces and experiences that few nineteenth-century novices could match. Of 103 candidates who entered the order in 1876, only eleven were as old as Craft or older. The average age of the entrants that year was nineteen.[2]

The transition from Episcopalianism to Catholicism was difficult enough, but it was the move from physician and soldier of fortune to Jesuit priest that especially frustrated him and exasperated his Jesuit advisers. He immersed himself in the writings of Ignatius Loyola, Socrates, Marcus Aurelius, and assorted Platonists and Stoics as he struggled with Jesuit philosophy and teachings. On 12 April 1877, fifteen months after joining, he made his "vows of devotion,"[3] a freewill, nonbinding, informal pledge to persevere in the novitiate, generally made during a candidate's second year. After three years at West Park he was sent to the College of Louvain, Belgium, for additional studies in philosophy. In the interim, the New York–Canada Mission of the Jesuits was merged with the Maryland Province, so on his return late in 1879 he was transferred to Woodstock College, the Jesuit theologate near Baltimore.[4] A letter to an adviser at West Park speaks to his perplexities regarding the Jesuit pursuit of perfection and reveals the intensity he could bring to a rather abstract subject:

> Here I am in religion; called there, I am sure, by God; bound under sin, I am told, to aim at perfection; my rules, and the commentaries of superiors and spiritual fathers upon those rules, the lives of our saints, and of all other saints, and in short, everything in the shape of instruction that is given to members of our order—all cry out—"*perfection!*"
>
> Very good, it must be the will of God, and therefore I wish to attain to this thing called perfection. I know very well that I can't fly or jump, even in these days of rapid transit, to a state of perfection; nothing that becomes what the world calls perfect is made so but by time and labor. However, I must get there in some way, and as God wishes me to get there, there *is* a way. Now I am really in earnest about the matter, and wish to begin. "Well," you may say, "go on, what is there to prevent you?" Now that is precisely what I would do if left to myself; but in spiritual things, I am told, it is impossible to advance without a guide. Very good, I go to my spiritual guides, and say, "What and where is perfection, and by what means can I attain it, or, at the very least, advance towards it?" The good fathers are sorely puzzled, and their looks and manner seem to say, as plainly as natural language can speak, "'Why, what a madcap hath heaven lent us here!' This fellow, forsooth, talks of perfection. Can't he see that perfection is for the favored few?" Well—it may be so, I remark, that those born and educated in the Church, grasp, and even put in practice, truths which I can reach only by painful and long-continued efforts. Not, as I would be compelled to do, by reflection, and step by step, but at once and almost instinctively. . . .
>
> I can see now the truth of what you once told me when speaking of Catholics. "They never examine those questions; they act with simplicity." It must be so. I would willingly imitate them; but experience has taught me that if I wait for such light and grace as they receive, I may wait in vain. It might even be presumption. They have an infallible guide, who, unless resisted, will lead them safely. I have *not*,—at least not in the same way—and yet I must reach the same end as they. We both fight our way; but they strike surely, while I often "beat the air." I am placed as it were between two fires; on one side is the obligation to aim at perfection, and on the other is obedience. If I stand, which means, of course, falling back, I am guilty; if I advance it is without orders, and is in some way against obedience, and again I am guilty. It's the old story. "You shall and you shan't, you will and you won't, you'll be damned

if you do, and damned if you don't." *N'importe* [It's no matter], I can't help it. All I can do, is, to study my position as well as I can, and try to find the most vulnerable point in the enemy's lines. If I can cut my way out, so much the better; if I can't, "*non omni moriar*" [I shall not wholly die], I hope."[5]

This dichotomy between the convert and those born in the church remained with Craft, causing personal conflicts throughout his life. In 1888, five years into his priesthood, he complained:

> The Church is Divine, but the ulcer that is sapping the vitality of its temporal part, is the want of charity, confidence, sympathy, Christian esprit de corps, and energy among those consecrated to God. Here am I, the least of all, a convert, and by no means holy, know at least that much, while the spoiled, petted, children of the Church, who have lived in the light of the Holy Spirit from their cradles, can't be made to see it. It proves, it is true, that I am enough outside of God's Church, to take an outside glance at its workings, and therefore, so much the worse for me, but that I can't help. It also proves how much more easily than I, the more favored ones should see the weak point in their line, but they won't try to see it, and, therefore, so much the worse for them. It would be well for all of us if the convert had more of their innate, though not practical, sanctity, and if they had more of his practical, though worldly, ways of looking at things.[6]

A much later message to James Edward Kelly in 1906 also provides insight into Craft's aristocratic view of himself; clearly, he was not a candidate for the structured environment of a religious order.

> Gentlemen led, as they always did, in every age, where all depended on the trained and educated knight, who did all the *leading,* and, in earlier times, nearly all of the actual fighting. Gentlemen also did all the suffering and sacrificing, while the rank and file embarrassed the leaders by clamoring for *pay.*
>
> It is the same even in the Church. The peasantry produced few or no epoch-makers, even among Saints, while the knightly class produced Loyolas, Xaviers, Assisis, etc., while the rest of the clergy wanted to persecute them for their heroism, because they had ideas above bread and beer and beef and "boodle."[7]

Although intellectually brilliant, Craft was unable to conform to the constitution of a religious congregation such as the Jesuits or Benedictines.

He was too independent, too much of a maverick, too challenging. There was no common ground on which he could meet his brother novices. "I am as much alone as if I were in the midst of a desert," he wrote.[8] The tragedy of Francis Craft is that he would never find common ground—not in the military, not on the reservations, not in his personal relationships, and especially not in the church.

Unable to adjust to the ascetic ideals of the Jesuits, Craft left the order in 1880 to pursue another dream. A wound to the head at Gettysburg and cavalry charges and saber cuts in France and Cuba temporarily satisfied an innate challenge to share in the glory of his rebellious forefathers. But he had yet another ancestral force at work: the Indian blood of his grandmother, Rebecca. His medical background remained a grand complement to a religious vocation; he needed only to follow a more independent path.

Woodstock College, the source of most Catholic missionaries to the Northwest and Rocky Mountain missions, was the route that brought the young cleric to work as a catechist among the Kalispels[9] and at other missions in the Idaho–western Montana area.[10] Along with the Flatheads, Pend d'Oreilles, and Spokans, the Kalispels spoke dialects closely related to the Salishan tribal group.[11] No further references to Craft's experiences among these tribes could be found, but other, strangely connected events during this period would shape the rest of his life.

SPOTTED TAIL'S QUEST

The year 1876, when Craft entered the Jesuit order, was a watershed for the Plains tribes. Sioux, Cheyennes, and Arapahos joined forces to defeat General Crook at the Battle of the Rosebud as Custer's Seventh Cavalry rode toward annihilation at the Little Big Horn. These victories, however, failed to slow the relentless advance of a civilization that brushed aside Native groups who sought to retain their rightful domain. Although the Black Hills and the Great Sioux Reservation in Dakota Territory had been set aside for the Sioux in the Treaty of 1868, Crook and Custer returned just eight years later to open this ceded territory for settlement. Indians won the ensuing battles but lost the war (along with much of their land).

The Sioux Nation in the nineteenth century comprised three basic tribal groups loosely allied by language and culture. They ranged from the headwaters of the Mississippi River in Wisconsin on the east to the Black Hills and beyond on the west. A group of northern woodland Sioux (Mdwakantons, Sissetons, Wahpekutes, and Wahpetons), who spoke a dialect called Dakota, occupied the eastern portion of the territory to the plains of Minnesota and eastern North and South Dakota. More or less centrally located in this vast expanse were the Yankton and Yanktonai Sioux, often referred to as Nakotas. Farther west the Teton Sioux, who spoke Lakota, formed the third facet of the Sioux Nation. Together the four subtribes of the Dakotas, two Nakotas, and the Lakota-speaking Tetons were called Oceti Sakowin, the Seven Council Fires, by the Indians themselves. The Teton

Sioux, in turn, embodied seven subtribes (Hunkpapas, Itazipcos, Miniconjous, Oglalas, Oohenunpas, Sicangus[1] and Sihasapas).[2]

The Agreement of 1876 fragmented the territory of the Teton Sioux. Red Cloud's Oglala Sioux had been shunted about by the military since Nebraska was declared a state in 1867 and were relocated to Pine Ridge Agency, just north of the state line. Directly to the east, Spotted Tail's Sicangus were removed to the Rosebud Agency, while Sihasapas (Blackfeet), Miniconjous, Itazipcos (Sans Arcs), and Oohenunpas (Two Kettles) drew their rations at the Cheyenne River Agency. Sitting Bull's Hunkpapa band had fled to Canada after the Custer defeat but by 1881 were settled at the Standing Rock Agency on the Grand River.

In 1870 President Grant had introduced the government's "Peace Policy," intended to civilize Native Americans through what was then considered to be a calming, enlightened, and benevolent influence brought about by Christian religious groups. Grant also hoped that by depoliticizing the Department of Indian Affairs he could bring an end to the massive graft and corruption that infected the Indian service at the time. In practice, the policy provoked a decade of bickering among religious groups as they debated perceived inequitable distribution of the Indian agencies. Agents assigned to run these agencies were often woefully unprepared to manage the politics and realities of an Indian reservation. The Catholics reasoned that their previous missionary activities among Native Americans warranted their exclusive appointment to thirty-eight of the seventy-two agencies then in existence. Instead, they were assigned only seven. The Methodists, with little record of Indian missionary effort at the time, received double that number; Orthodox Friends and Presbyterians got ten and nine, respectively, and other reservations were assigned to various Protestant denominations such as Episcopalian, Congregationalist, and Lutheran. In an effort to strengthen their position and reverse the distribution of reservation assignments, Archbishop J. Roosevelt Bayley of the Archdiocese of Baltimore appointed Gen. Charles Ewing, a lawyer and Civil War veteran, to lobby for Catholic interests in 1874. He was assisted by Father John Brouillet, an Indian missionary from Oregon Territory who developed the office into the Bureau of Catholic Indian Missions and became its first director. The Third Plenary Council of Baltimore approved it as a permanent institution of the church in 1884. Bishop Martin Marty, O.S.B.,[3] was named the first president of the commission. Among

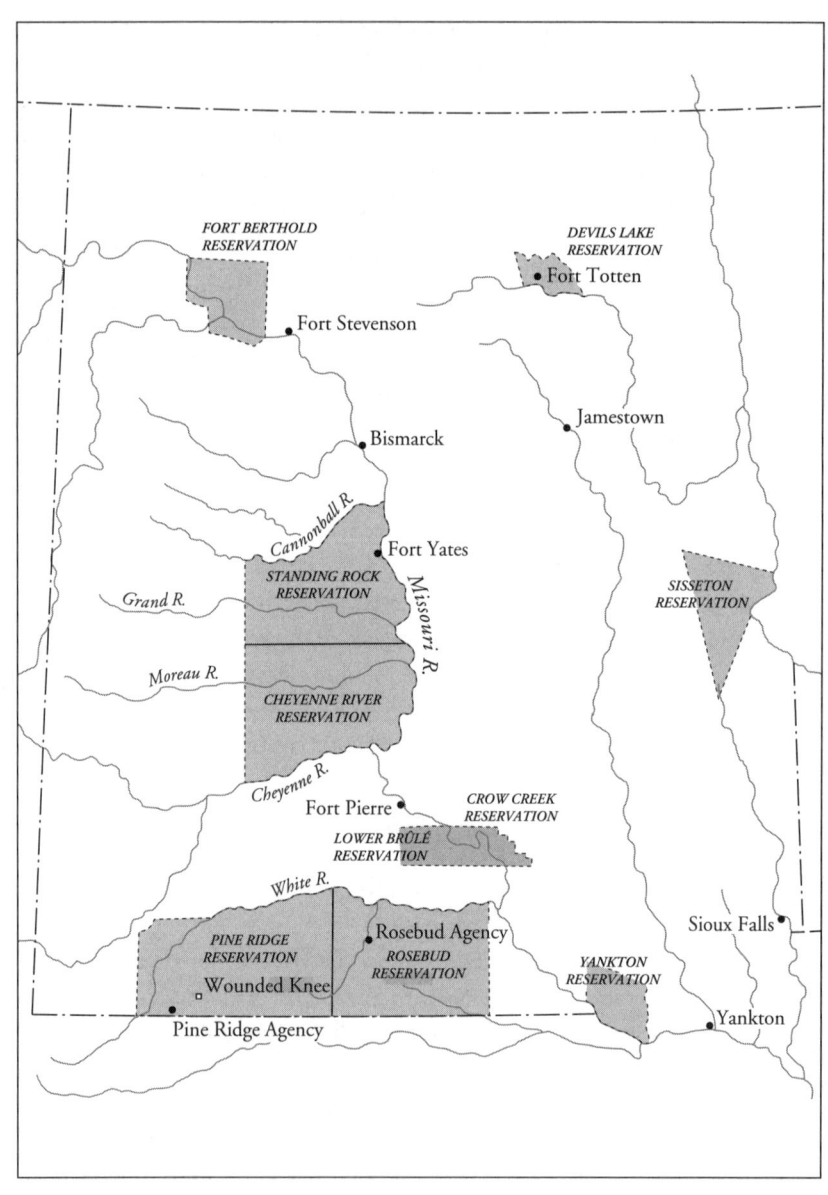

1. Dakota Territory, late nineteenth century

the reservations that would eventually feel the presence of Father Craft, the Pine Ridge and Rosebud Agencies were assigned exclusively to the Episcopal Church, while Standing Rock was designated a Roman Catholic enclave.[4]

Pierre J. DeSmet, S.J.,[5] the noted Jesuit missionary, was the first Catholic priest to visit the Sioux (in the 1840s), and sporadic follow-up sojourns were undertaken by Christian Hoecken, S.J. Later, several diocesan priests (Augustine Ravoux, Jeremiah Trecy, and J. M. Ryan) evangelized the people, but it was left to the arrival of Benedictine monks, led by Abbot Martin Marty in the mid-1870s, to offer any realistic hope for a permanent Catholic mission.[6]

Martin Marty transferred in 1860 from the Benedictine monastery in Einsiedeln, Switzerland, to St. Meinrad Abbey in southern Indiana. In 1876 he traveled to Dakota Territory, exploring its missionary potential, envisioning another monastery, farther west, to serve both the Indians and the German settlers who were moving into the area. Standing Rock Agency had been a "Catholic" reservation for some six years, and still no Catholic missionary activity was evident. With two volunteers from St. Meinrad's, Marty founded in 1876 what would become St. Benedict's Mission near Fort Yates. He returned again the next year to Pine Ridge and Rosebud, where he met with Red Cloud and Spotted Tail. Both chiefs asked him to send priests to educate their people, but the abbot's resources were limited.[7] Moreover, the Peace Policy restricted his options to the "Catholic" reserve at Standing Rock. Red Cloud's and Spotted Tail's people, at Pine Ridge and Rosebud, remained under the auspices of the Episcopalians.

A practical chief, Spotted Tail reasoned that if white civilization was destined to overwhelm his people, they had better learn to deal with it. And basic to this goal would be to learn the white man's language. However, the chief was unable to find any students who could read or write English at reservation schools operated by Episcopalians. Backed by most of the lesser chiefs at the Rosebud Agency, he presented Agent W. J. Pollack a petition in 1879 asking that the Episcopalian White Robes be replaced with Black Robes.[8] His request was denied.

Spotted Tail then took another approach. In October that same year, he sent several of his children and grandchildren to Carlisle, Pennsylvania, as part of the first group of students in Capt. Richard H. Pratt's Indian school. The next summer, the chief and some of his headmen were brought to Washington, DC on a government-sponsored promotion designed to placate Sioux leaders (negotiations were then under way to acquire large portions of Indian territory).

Stopping at Carlisle, he found a harsh, oppressive military environment that bullied his children and broke their spirits but failed to instill an understanding of basic English. Spotted Tail was furious. He confronted Pratt and demanded that the thirty-four Rosebud students be returned home. At the capital, Spotted Tail again bitterly denounced the Carlisle school.

There were substantial elements at Rosebud who opposed any cooperation with federal or religious efforts toward civilization, and Spotted Tail had put his status and his life at risk among his people by supporting the government's educational efforts. This cooperation, though, was not producing positive results. Nonetheless, pressure from Secretary of Interior Carl Schurz weakened the resolve of other Sioux chiefs, and Spotted Tail soon found himself alone in his objections over the ineffectiveness of both church- and government-backed schools.

En route home by way of Carlisle, he took seven of his young relatives out of the school and returned with them to Rosebud.[9] This move alienated the administration and, by extension, the new agent on the reservation, John Cook. It also strengthened the hand of Crow Dog and his followers on Rosebud, who opposed Spotted Tail's progressive ways.

When Secretary Schurz abated Grant's Peace Policy in February 1881, the reservations were opened to all religious denominations. Except where rival factions would be detrimental to peace and order, or where treaties would be violated, all faiths became free to preach their version of the gospel on any of the nation's reservations.[10]

Spotted Tail promptly resumed his campaign for Catholic priests. In a confrontation on 4 July 1881, Crow Dog pressed the muzzle of his rifle to Spotted Tail's chest, threatening an abrupt end to the chief's conciliatory efforts. He stood his ground, and Crow Dog backed down.

A month later, Agent Cook arranged for a tribal council to select representatives for another Washington trip. Spotted Tail, chosen to lead the delegation, announced at the council that he also intended to visit Bishop Marty to seek Catholic priests from the East. He told his tribesmen that his life had already been threatened and that if he died the first Black Robe sent by Bishop Marty should be named chief in his place. Reportedly, no objections were voiced.[11]

Spotted Tail left the council on horseback and headed toward his camp beyond the two-story house the government had built for him. He rode on, slightly ahead of Two Strike, He Dog, and Ring Thunder, who followed on foot. Probably more by design than by chance, Crow Dog was on the trail, coming toward the agency with a wagonload of wood. As Spotted Tail approached, Crow Dog passed the reins of the team to his wife, dropped to one knee at the side of the trail, and swung his rifle into position. The force of the bullet as it slammed into the chief's chest hurled him from his mount. He struggled to his feet, grabbed for his pistol, and fell back dead.[12]

Spotted Tail's assassination left the Sicangus without a clear successor to the chieftainship. Crow Dog, charged with murder and sentenced to hang, was unable to claim the title. His appeal to the United States Supreme Court, however, resulted in a landmark decision that the Dakota court had no jurisdiction over a dispute between Indians that took place on an Indian reservation. Crow Dog eventually went free, but crucial time had been lost, and with it the chieftainship.

Black Crow, Hawk Dog, and Medicine Bear vied for the position of chief along with the younger Spotted Tail (one of the chief's many children). However, none of them wielded significant influence, and the Bureau of Indian Affairs was not particularly interested in seeing *anyone* surface to provide strong leadership for the band. As a policy matter, the government preferred to split the tribes into small units that could be more easily controlled by the agent in charge. For eighteen months after Spotted Tail's death, the Rosebud Sioux could not name his successor.

Abbot Marty had been appointed the first bishop of Dakota Territory in February 1880, and when Secretary Schurz opened the reservations to all religions the next year, he intensified his search for missionary candidates. It was during this period that Craft's aspirations coincided with the bishop's needs. In June 1882 Marty wrote to the Bureau of Catholic Indian Missions that he had several teachers who were "at a moment's notice ready to work in a Dakota school." Craft's name was listed among them.[13]

Bishop Marty was well aware of Craft's résumé as a Jesuit seminarian, characterizing him as "not flexible enough for that vocation although good natured."[14] He sent him temporarily to Conception Abbey, where, along with several Benedictine candidates, Marty ordained him to the subdiaconate and diaconate in the weeks before Easter 1883.

Craft entered the priesthood, however, not as a Jesuit or a Benedictine but as a secular priest unencumbered by monastic vows or rules. Bishop Marty ordained him a secular, or diocesan priest in Omaha, Nebraska, on Holy Saturday, 24 March 1883, and sent him directly to the Rosebud Indian Reservation. He was the first Catholic priest assigned to what had been the exclusive turf of the Episcopalian Church.

IV

CONSPIRACY ON ROSEBUD

Craft in his prime was an impressive, commanding presence. Sculptor James Kelly's artist's eye saw him "over six feet tall, and as keen, sinewy and powerful as a stag. His face was very strong in structure, fine in feature, and spiritual in expression. His voice was clear and cultivated, and his complexion weather-beaten, as were his shapely, refined, and very powerful hands."[1] The arrival of the bold and spirited Black Robe, already an experienced horseman and expert marksman, was enthusiastically greeted by the Rosebud Sioux. Spotted Tail's family, especially, regarded him as the fulfillment of their fallen patriarch's prophetic request. As the first Black Robe to appear in response to their long-standing requests, Father Craft was adopted into the family as a relative through the Lakota rite of *hukápi*. One of the sacred rites of Sioux beliefs, *hukápi* creates a bond between people that is stronger than a biological kinship; those connected by this relationship are obliged to die for each other should the need arise.[2] It was a matter of some significance to his acceptance on the reservations. With four wives, three dozen children, and a multitude of brothers, sisters, nephews, nieces, and in-laws, the slain chief's family extended into every part of the old Great Sioux Reservation. At least that would be Craft's position on the matter.

Given the honorary rank of chief and the name Wąblí chįcá agláhpaya (The eagle covers its young, or Hovering Eagle), the priest called Spotted Tail's wife "'ina,' mother, and her children brother and sister."[3] The Indians provided him with a hat trimmed with shell and wampum work and a dalmatic made from two deerskins, embroidered with porcupine quills and embellished with a drawing of an eagle hovering over its nestlings. In keeping with Lakota tradition, locks of hair from his new relatives fringed the sleeves.[4] His acceptance was so complete that he soon took up residence in Spotted Tail's abandoned mansion on the reservation.

Craft cherished his adoptive relatives and was revered by the Sicangus in return. His popularity with the Rosebud Sioux, however, was at the expense of favorable acceptance by whites on the reservation. As a disciple of Roberto De Nobili, the seventeenth-century Jesuit who had pioneered the method of missionary adaptation in southern India, Craft immersed himself in the native culture in order to gain the trust and friendship of his flock. He wore feathers in his hat and learned to speak the Lakota language, encouraging and defending the Omaha dance as "common to all Dakotas, Poncas, Omahas, Winnabagoes, etc., just as we ourselves have many different dances common to many nations."[5] Conversely, though, he adamantly opposed activities he viewed as demoralizing, such as polygamy and gambling.

He also was protective of Indian rights and was quick to criticize and expose government corruption wherever it existed. Consequently he was singularly unpopular with the Indian agent and reservation bureaucrats. *"Every single trouble I had,"* he wrote, "was started, not by Indians, but by *whites* on the Agency."[6]

Two whites who struck first were James G. Wright and Rev. William J. Cleveland. Wright was the United States Indian agent in charge of Rosebud; Cleveland was the Episcopalian missionary who had enjoyed exclusive access to the Rosebud Sioux until Craft appeared on the scene. The agent's report to the Indian Bureau that year signaled his suspicions regarding Craft's missionary activities and proclaimed his high personal regard for the Reverend Mr. Cleveland.[7]

Craft approached his missionary assignment on Rosebud with all the verve, passion, and discretion he manifested on the battlefields of France and Cuba. High on his list of priorities was establishing the Catholic religion in an Episcopal stronghold.

Major Wright, the Indian agent, was a member of Cleveland's Episcopal mission, so Craft, a former Episcopalian himself, began his proselytizing right at the top. The agent didn't respond well to Craft's assertion that the "Church of England is not the Church of Christ."[8] Craft, though, acknowledged Wright's temporal authority on the reservation as he also lent

FIGURE 1. Sketch of Father Craft in full "Hovering Eagle" regalia, by James E. Kelly. *Irish World,* 16 August 1890 and 3 January 1891. Marquette University Archives.

support to the agent's efforts to reform Indian culture. Some of the Indians even complained to Bishop Marty about the severity of Craft's positions regarding gambling and polygamy. Wright, on the other hand, accused the priest of baptizing dead bodies, including those who "had been previously baptized by the Episcopal Clergyman," and would not permit him to administer the sacrament of matrimony to anyone the agent had already married.

Once, when an Indian groused to Wright about some damage that had been done to his garden, the agent ordered him out of his office, kicking the Indian in the leg when he refused to leave. When the Indian made a move toward his belt, as if to draw a knife or gun, he was immediately apprehended by the agent's police and thrown in the guardhouse. Outraged, other Indians gave Wright the name Mathó wanáȟtaka (Kicking Bear), sharpened their hatchets, and prepared to break open the jail, release the Indian, and replace him with the agent. The priest managed to quiet them on this occasion and others as well.[9]

Craft, for his part, was equally audacious and impolitic in his missionary zeal. As early as August 1883, Cleveland complained to Wright that Father Craft had told the Indians that it was his "first duty . . . to reclaim the sheep who had been led astray by the white-robed wolf, as they were in a worse case and further astray from the road of life than those who had never yet heard of the Gospel."[10]

In November 1883, Capt. Richard H. Pratt visited Rosebud to obtain students for his school at Carlisle, Pennsylvania, and promptly leagued with Wright and Cleveland, criticizing Craft's activities in reports to the secretary of Interior. Pratt, a Civil War veteran and a well-known Indian reformer with Protestant ties, was an outspoken critic of Catholic missions. He considered Catholic educational efforts contrary to the nation's best interests and viewed Catholic schools on the reservations as unnecessary and undesirable.[11] The situation continued to deteriorate over the winter, when another schoolmaster arrived seeking students for a new government academy at Genoa, Nebraska.

There was intense competition to recruit Indian children to fill government boarding schools such as those at Carlisle, Genoa, and Hampton, Virginia. The Indian families, however, were understandably reluctant to part with their children, often claiming that their offspring were already attending religious schools to avoid their removal to distant government facilities.

Major Wright sent Craft a note on 14 January 1884, asking the priest to attend a meeting in the agency council room. Several chiefs and headmen would be there, along with S. F. Tappan, superintendent of the Genoa Industrial School. Craft went, expecting to be asked to help obtain children for the new school. The agent, however, stormed into the room scowling angrily at Craft, his every look and gesture expressing his displeasure with the priest's presence. He referred several times to "the priest" and the "priest's school," adding bitter emphasis to the words as he accused Craft of dissuading the children from attending government schools. A dissenting undertone of Lakota conversation filled the room as Craft shook his head in denial of the accusations. Wright exclaimed: "The priest shakes his head, but what I say is true." Craft cut him off as the Indians became increasingly annoyed at the rancorous display. They had no intention of giving up their children anyway.

"Major," said Craft, "this is doing no good . . . you are cutting your own throat." Wright responded that he had "said all I want to say, and I want the *priest* to speak." Although fluent in Lakota, Craft elected to speak through an interpreter. He felt, perhaps naively, that expression in both languages would prevent anyone from misrepresenting what he was about to say:

"My friends, the Agent asks me to speak to you. When I came here I intended to speak to you if I was asked to do so. The Agent does not understand me, and, as you see, speaks to me, and treats me unkindly. I am sorry, but it does not matter. It will not make me change what I wanted to say to you when I came here. When I speak, I hope you will hear me and believe me, for you know I speak for your good only. You know the Black Robe. You have always trusted him, because he has never lied to you. I have no reason to deceive you. It is my interest to tell the truth. I have nothing to hope for from man, but only from God. He will be pleased with me only so far as I speak the truth, and will be angry if I should lie. I am one of those men whom God has taken from the world and consecrated to Himself. I do not belong to the whites nor to the Indians, although I live among you, and you regard me as one of you. I do not belong to the Great Father (President), to the Department, to the Agent, to the white men, to the red men, to the black men, or to any men on earth. I belong to God alone. I fear no one but Him, and, therefore, must necessarily speak the truth.

Remember what I have always told you about schools, for you will hear me say the same thing now. It is a good thing to send your children to the Government Schools among the whites, to learn quickly their language and customs, so that they can be prosperous and happy, and make their people so. I have always advised this, and always say the same whenever I hear of a good school for your children. You know I would not ask you to send them away if I thought they would be injured by going. As to the school at Genoa in particular, I am very much in favor of it. Although I have not yet heard very much about it, what I *have* heard is very good. It is what you have asked for long ago. You say you want your children to live and be near you, and not die far from you. That too is my wish, and the wish of the Great Father (President) and that is what you will obtain for them if you send them to the school at Genoa. It is a very healthy place, and very near you. You know the place. You call it Shell Creek. You have often hunted there. I think you would do well if you would send your children there.

An Indian named Turning Bear suddenly rose and launched into an oration that quickly brought the meeting to a close. Clamorous applause greeted Turning Bear's emphatic rejection of the government's plan as he turned and stormed from the room, followed by all the others. Father Craft tried to call them back, but the agent's surly conduct proved too convenient an excuse for them to keep their children in the camps.[12]

On 16 January 1884, Wright gave his version of the meeting and other events in a letter to the commissioner of Indian affairs, concluding that Craft's conduct had "become . . . imprudent and prejudicial to good government and . . . constituted authorities."[13]

The formal charges alleged that Craft had taken a number of Indians to Valentine, Nebraska, where the Indians "danced the Omaha dance, in the public street, where there are liquor saloons on all sides; that the priest took off his own hat to receive contributions . . . [in which] he wore an eagle feather [as an] insignia [of the] Omaha Dancing Club."[14]

The charges were seriously misleading. A group of Indians had accompanied Craft to a sawmill near Valentine, Nebraska, to haul lumber for his church and school. As usual, they had to wait a day or two while the lumber was loaded on wagons. The Indians camped outside the town, but a few of them went to a local storekeeper they knew from earlier visits. In fact the storekeeper kept a drum on hand to encourage the Indians to dance and trade with him and the other merchants. The Omaha dance was an important expression of Native American social and tribal pride featuring dancing, oratory, public distribution of gifts, ritual drama, and feasting.[15]

Craft had just baptized a child who was dying of inflammation of the brain in a house near the stores; the last thing he wanted was the racket of an Indian dance nearby. As more Indians reached the first corner of the town, the priest admonished them to return to their camp. By now, several townsfolk had appeared, tossing coins at the dancers to urge them on. Craft finally coaxed the Indians back to their camp, reminding them that when they gave him the eagle feathers to wear they had also given him the right, as one of their nation, to provide counsel on their customs and actions.

The more frivolous charges, however, were accompanied by the grave allegation that the priest had "held himself and his church above all civil law or the authority, wishes, or other instructions of the President, honorable Secretary of the Interior, or any other constituted authority."[16]

Without the formality of a hearing, the commission summarily banished Father Craft not only from the reservation, but from "Indian Country" as well. In February he moved out of Spotted Tail's house and went to Bishop Marty's residence in Yankton to prepare his defense. Almost five months passed before he was able to see the allegations that had been brought against him. His lengthy, eloquent defense was only partially effective. In September the commissioner of Indian affairs revoked his order expelling Father Craft from Indian Country. Part of the agreement, though, was "that it was neither the intention nor the desire of Bishop Marty to send you back to the Rosebud Agency."[17]

This experience marked Father Craft with a paranoia that was shared by most everyone who worked in the malicious spoils system that permeated the reservations. No one—Indian or white, agent or missionary, Catholic or Protestant, soldier or settler—absolutely no one, was safe from the threat of removal. Bishop Marty next reassigned Father Craft to Standing Rock Agency, where the likes of Agent James McLaughlin and Sitting Bull held forth.

V

CONFLICTS ON STANDING ROCK

Father Craft would have preferred reassignment to his adoptive family on Rosebud Reservation, but he was, after all, a soldier. Dutiful soldiers—and priests—obey. Unaware of the deal Bishop Marty had struck to effect his reinstatement to Indian Country, Craft thought he had been totally exonerated. The bishop, however, agreed that it was best not to return his headstrong missionary to the role of usurper on Episcopalian Rosebud, regardless of the modifications in Grant's Peace Policy.[1]

Standing Rock Agency, about a hundred miles to the north of Rosebud, had been a Catholic agency for several years. A German-born priest of Irish and Greek extraction, Joseph A. Stephan, was assigned to the position of agent in October 1878. Stephan had originally intended to pursue a career as a soldier but was temporarily struck blind in military school. When his sight returned, he apparently experienced a religious conversion that led him to the seminary. Ordained in March 1850, he served parishes in Ohio and northern Indiana, and for four years he was a Union chaplain during the Civil War. He returned to northern Indiana after the war, then embarked on a missionary career among Native Americans.[2]

Stephan was an ineffective agent, given to mean disputes with the commander of troops at the agency post at Fort Yates. He believed the military was a disruptive presence on the reservation, accused the commandant, W. P. Carlin, of plotting his removal, and delayed his departure from Standing Rock to fight charges that had been brought against him.[3]

Stephan's obstinacy and quick temper also adversely affected his relationship with the Benedictine missionaries on the reservation.[4] In 1881, in poor health and clearly frustrated by it all, Stephan relinquished the position. He sent his resignation to Gen. Charles Ewing, commissioner of the Bureau of Catholic Indian Missions, the administrative body that directed Catholic Indian relief efforts from Washington DC. As was often the case on Dakota reservations, Stephan's difficulties stemmed more from whites than from Native Americans: "The Indians here are peaceable and good, with few exceptions," he wrote. "Our mutual relations are of the most amicable and friendliest kind—only the 'whites' are the trouble-some element and the constant harping, backbiting, and lieing [sic] from those men, makes me disgusted with the place and I hope you will do me the favor to help me get out of it."[5]

Ewing got Stephan out of it by replacing him with James McLaughlin in September 1881. From 1882 to 1884 Stephan served in various responsibilities at Fargo, Jamestown, and Yankton, including a stint as vicar general and adviser to Bishop Marty. On the recommendations of Marty and Bishop James O'Connor of Omaha, he replaced John Brouillet as director of the Bureau of Catholic Indian Missions in 1884. Father Stephan was instrumental in negotiating Father Craft's reinstatement to Indian Country.[6]

McLaughlin was a Catholic layman who had begun his career with the Indian service as a blacksmith some ten years earlier at Devils Lake Agency in Dakota Territory. Long before Father Craft arrived, McLaughlin was well established as the government's official representative on Standing Rock. His wife, Marie Louise, the daughter of a full-blood Indian mother, was equally accepted in both white and Native American cultures. She had been educated in convent schools in Wisconsin and was fluent in the Sioux language.[7]

McLaughlin governed with an authority born of a magisterial approach to the plight of the Indians; he was generally held in awe by his wards on the reservation. Politically, he was one of few agents who could expect to survive a change of administration in Washington or the appointment of a new commissioner of Indian affairs. In his autocratic style, he had established an Indian court and maintained absolute control over an Indian police force of about forty handpicked warriors who kept the others in line.

Major McLaughlin juggled his religious connections so well that both Catholic and Protestant missionary groups supplemented his $1,700 annual salary from the government.[8] Bishop Marty often gave the agent as

FIGURE 2. Sitting Bull and Agent James McLaughlin (center) at the dedication of the Standing Rock, about 1880. D. F. Barry photo. Denver Public Library, Western History Collection.

much as $100 to dissuade him from leaving the Indian service.[9] It is not surprising, then, that when the commissioner's office revoked the order expelling Father Craft from Indian Country, a place for the controversial cleric could be found on Standing Rock.

Not all was religious harmony on the reservation, however. Just as Craft had encroached on the Episcopalians at Rosebud, Congregationalists and Presbyterians were making inroads on Standing Rock. From his new post in Washington DC, Father Stephan complained that the Presbyterian minister and mission board acted "like the Kuckoo bird, who lays his eggs in other nests. . . . When Sitting Bull and his hostile tribe were masters of the situation you could not find a protestant to show his face at Standing Rock . . . now since we have subdued . . . them . . . the gospel peddlers run in to drive us out. . . . Should they get additional land, I shall ask for more too and the Methodists and Baptists will do the same and Standing Rock will be a worse religious battlefield [than] Sitting Bull's and Genl. Custer's."[10]

McLaughlin also corresponded regularly with Herbert Welsh, secretary of the Indian Rights Association, a Protestant amalgam supporting religious and educational efforts to civilize Native Americans. Welsh was an upper-class career reformer from Philadelphia. At the behest of William Hobart Hare, Episcopal bishop of Niobrara, Nebraska, he had a major role in founding the Indian Rights Association after a visit to the Dakota reservations in 1882.[11]

Welsh's relationship with McLaughlin was such that he considered the agent a staunch supporter of the association's goals; in fact he believed McLaughlin was an ally in a movement to diminish Catholic influence on the reservations.[12] Among his many notable contacts and supporters were Rev. William J. Cleveland, Craft's competitor on Rosebud, and Capt. Richard H. Pratt, founder of Carlisle School, the priest's nonresident competitor on Standing Rock.

All this competition for native souls, of course, only confused the Sioux, increasing their suspicions of *wašíchu* religions and buttressing their reluctance to abandon traditional ways. The religious conflicts on Standing Rock were aggravated by the unscrupulous rapacity of a small army of federal bureaucrats, traders, land boomers, settlers, and assorted hangers-on, all seeking a share of the public and tribal funds being allocated for the acculturation of the Indian. There was little attractive or noble about an Indian reservation in the 1880s, especially the one called Standing Rock.

Craft soon found that the Standing Rock Sioux were not receptive to the friendly, family-oriented approach he had used among the Sicangus. The Standing Rock tribes were notoriously more bellicose than those at Rosebud. They included the Hunkpapa band that fled to Canada after the Custer fight and were gradually rounded up or grudgingly returned to the reservation, choosing that option over starvation. About 1,800 Hunkpapas, along with lesser numbers of Upper and Lower Yanktonais, Blackfeet, and mixed-bloods numbering 4,385 in all, were spread in small settlements throughout five districts on the reservation: Cannonball, Big Head, Central, Farm School, and Grand River.[13] McLaughlin had them well under control. He partially neutralized Sitting Bull's influence by promoting the chieftainships of Gall, Grass, Mad Bear, Big Head, Cottonwood, and some of the other lesser headmen.

McLaughlin also had problems with his predecessor on Standing Rock, Father Stephan, director of the Bureau of Catholic Indian Missions. Stephan not only evinced a talent for aggressively defending Catholic missions on the reservations, he also displayed a vindictiveness that even the agent found difficult to handle. The latest episode had begun in 1883, when Stephan asked McLaughlin to allow Sitting Bull to travel to Jamestown, Dakota Territory, to be displayed at a church fair. McLaughlin refused to do so, but Stephan persisted and in 1884 obtained permission from Secretary of Interior Henry M. Teller to take the chief on an eastern tour. McLaughlin diverted the trip to a shorter version that never got farther east than St. Paul.[14]

However, Sitting Bull's appearance the next year in Buffalo Bill Cody's Wild West Show angered Father Stephan, who McLaughlin believed was the source of eight anonymous charges brought to block his reappointment to the position of agent. While never referring to the priest by name, he was more than direct in his response:

The other . . . charges could only be concocted for a base purpose by a perverted and designing scoundrel, who is well known to me as a hypocrite, and, although the name of my accuser is not given in the charges, I know but one individual capable of such contemptible slander and I can read his name in every charge. . . .

The character of my accuser is shown by the absurdity of the charges, and the animus prompting it is principally from his disappointment in not securing the Indian Chief Sitting Bull to exhibit in the East in the Summer and Autumn of 1884 for his so called *church purposes*. . . .

He gave scandal as a clergyman, was a fraud and a failure as an Indian Agent, and a disgrace to those who know him in the position he now occupies, and as I do not tolerate his interference in the educational work that is being done at this agency . . . he has sought revenge by trying to injure me.[15]

Harsh words to describe the director of the Bureau of Catholic Indian Missions! It would not be long, however, before Father Craft would echo the same sentiments about both Stephan *and* McLaughlin, since the only issue that would eventually bring the director and the agent together again would be their shared opposition to Father Craft.

McLaughlin's reappointment was approved, but now Sitting Bull weighed in against Craft by bringing "filthy charges" against him with Inspector E. W. Bannister of the Department of Indian Affairs.[16] No record of these charges could be found, but they probably involved allegations of moral turpitude. Drunkenness, adultery, and other lascivious conduct were common charges brought against priests on the reservations. Sitting Bull's allegations probably involved the priest's recruitment of young girls for the Benedictine convents. Craft suspected McLaughlin was behind the sordid attack but was never able to prove it.

Although Craft's unorthodox and impolitic conduct would scarcely engender a defense from most quarters on the reservation, he was cleared of the charges through the support of Josephine Crowfeather, the twenty-year-old daughter of Hunkpapa chief Joseph Crowfeather.[17] Josephine's Indian name was Ptesą wąyákapiwį (They see a white buffalo woman).[18] A central figure in Sioux religious traditions, White Buffalo Woman was the legendary being who delivered the sacred pipe and bundle to the Sioux Nation, pointing the way to the right path of life. Appearing miraculously in a beautiful vision, dressed in white buckskin, she vanished after being transformed into a white buffalo. The Indians believed she would return again at the end of the world.[19] So Josephine was imbued with the spirit of Wakhą́ Thą́ka (The great mysterious), even from birth. Her hallowed origins were enhanced when her father carried her on horseback, still an infant, in a battle with United States troops. When father and daughter both came through the skirmish unharmed, the tribe ascribed great powers to the child.[20]

Craft considered Josephine part of his extended Rosebud family, a sister with whom he would form a sacred bond that would dominate a critical decade of his life. Whether it was the sacred nature of her past that intrigued him, or her own religious calling, or that she alone stood by him in the Sitting Bull affair — or perhaps for all of these reasons — Josephine's successful vocation and eventual salvation became an obsession. He had placed several young women in the care of the Benedictine sisters' school at Fort Yates, but Josephine was clearly his favorite. Fiercely protective of her welfare, he once met Josie and her sister Lucy on the way to visit their parents on the day of a big dance. Concerned for their safety that evening, he sent word "that it would be best for any Hobu [a wild young man] who thought of annoying Josephine, to get a coffin first, and settle his affairs, as she has a brother who will inflict summary punishment upon anyone annoying her."[21]

Craft's braggadocio served to protect Josephine and also to foster occasional camp legends that appeared in contemporary historical accounts. Word of the priest's reputation was spreading throughout not only the reservation but the nation, as in a work by W. Fletcher Johnson, an eastern author who in 1891 compiled a biography of Sitting Bull from news accounts and interviews. Father Craft, he reported, "had many bitter opponents, and his life was often threatened. But he was a formidable opponent. He was one of the best shots with rifle or revolver in all the country, and on several occasions when men wanted to fight him he satisfied them amply by drawing his revolver and with unerring aim planting bullet after bullet in chips that were floating far out in the river." [22]

The author offered no documentation for this story, and there are no entries in the Craft journals that would support such a romanticized account, but the image of the priest demonstrating his skill as a marksman is easy to envision. In April 1888 Craft ordered a Remington revolver and "drop shoulder holster" from Montgomery Ward. "Night rides are getting unsafe," he mused. "I have but little of the spirit of the martyr, and knowing the motives of the rascals here, feel sure that death would not be martyrdom. Therefore I wish the best next to martyrdom, viz. a soldier's death, and I will take care that the soldier dies hard, and—not alone." [23]

VI

SETTLING IN ON STANDING ROCK

The Benedictine priests and brothers who staffed the Catholic mission and schools on Standing Rock Reservation were Swiss immigrants, most of whom came from Conception Abbey in Missouri. In addition to Father Martin Kenel and Father Bede Marty (no relation to Bishop Marty), there were Father Bernard Strassmaier and Brothers Meinrad Widmer and Nicholas Enz. Most of the Benedictine sisters who taught at the boarding school were also of Swiss or German extraction. There was one Irish nun, Sister Gertrude McDermott, and in 1890–91 an Irish priest named James McNally was assigned to Fort Yates. However, a feud soon broke out between the Irish and German factions, and the Irish were reassigned to other missions.

Adopting a more conservative approach to civilizing the Indians, the Benedictines trod the narrow ground carefully, avoiding any action that might alienate the agent or agitate the chiefs. Craft, conversely, often antagonized both sides. His impatience with Indian duplicity (an artful balance of the appearance of progressive behavior while clinging steadfastly to traditional ways) and his propensity to challenge the agent's authority were worrisome to Father Martin and Father Bede. The family relationships the priest nurtured among the tribes seemed at best unconventional to the Benedictines and a dangerous aberration to most whites on the reservation.

Father Craft arrived at Fort Yates, site of the agency headquarters, in November 1884. Initially he boarded with the Wells family at Cannonball.

FIGURE 3. Father Craft and Benedictine missionaries at St. Benedict's Mission, Standing Rock Reservation, about 1886–88. Left to right: Father Martin Kenel, O.S.B.; Father Craft; Father Bernard Strassmaier, O.S.B.; Brother Meinrad Widmer, O.S.B.; Brother Nicholas Enz, O.S.B.; district farmer William Whitsell. Photographer unknown. Conception Abbey Archives.

Aaron C. Wells and his wife, Josephine, conducted a school for some sixty students about twenty-five miles north of the agency, just below Parkins Ranch.

Other schools and missions were scattered throughout the reservation as well. Protestant schools had been established at St. Elizabeth's Episcopal Mission, the Marmot Day School, and the Dakota American Missionary Association's site, all situated along the Grand River about thirty-five miles south of the agency. In 1886 Craft opened a day school in the midst of this Protestant enclave, locating a mission in Flying By's settlement on Grand River at the confluence of Oak Creek, about thirty miles south of the agency. The building was financed by the Bureau of Catholic Indian Mis-

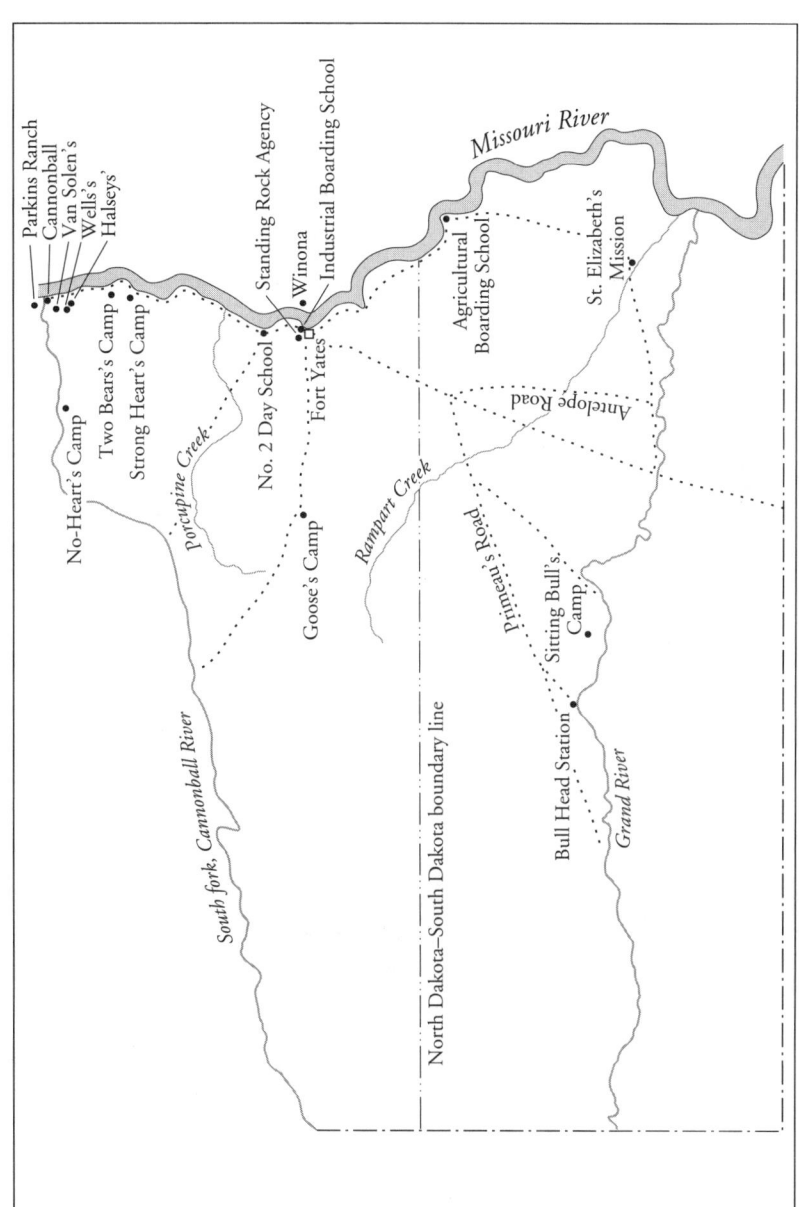

2. Standing Rock Reservation, late nineteenth century

sions through a $1,200 donation from Katharine Drexel. About twenty-five students were enrolled, and Craft was assisted by Emeran White Boy, a full-blood who had studied for three years at St. Paul's Industrial School at Clontarf, Minnesota.[1] Bishop Marty apparently intended to send Father Joseph B. Wilhelm, another diocesan priest, to assist in Craft's missionary work, but his exact arrival date is unknown.[2]

Father Craft regularly visited eleven mission stations or Indian camps, each circuit taking him 300 miles through the perilous and desolate Dakota landscape.[3] Daily trail rides often exceeded 50 miles; once he rode 110 miles in two days.[4] He made his rounds on a spirited cow horse named Pinch, a bay stallion disposed to jarring gaits, sudden rearing, and occasional prancing and backing in response to the bit. Pinch's stamina and reliability, though, more than compensated for these shortcomings.

The conditions Craft operated under were unimaginably difficult. Howling "blazing blue blizzards" with snowdrifts up to Pinch's chest; subzero temperatures that froze humans, cattle, and the thermometer itself; summer droughts and thunderstorms with hail big enough to knock a rider off his horse; smallpox, measles, and tuberculosis decimating the Indian population. The winter of 1886–87 was especially harsh as blizzards continuously coursed across the plains from Montana to Texas. In the "great die-up," some said as many as 90 percent of all free-range cattle perished in the storms. "In this country," Craft once lamented, "we get all things—good or evil—in real bonanza style, rather too much than too little."[5]

Sparse vegetation on the broad Central Plains dried and shriveled through the summer months, only to be followed by monstrous thunderstorms that set prairies ablaze on both sides of the Missouri River. Shell King and another Indian were killed when a lightning bolt struck their tent during a storm in June 1888. Miraculously, a child in Shell King's arms survived.[6] A winter storm claimed the life of Rose Daly, who froze to death as she tried to reach her parent's camp in February 1890. Before setting out on his winter rounds, Craft would wash his face with snow to prepare for the journey. In midsummer, mosquitoes often became unbearable. The occasional rattlesnake the priest encountered was always summarily dispatched.

Always willing to start at the top, with Agent McLaughlin already in the Catholic fold one of Craft's earliest assignments was to convert Sitting Bull to the Catholic faith. Bishop Marty wrote in December 1884 that he was going to Rome that next Easter and wanted to "bring to the Holy Father the news that Sitting Bull is a member of the Church. He might prepare a buffalo robe, on which he could represent the reception they gave me in their camp on Frenchmen's Creek in May 1877. I would take it along to Leo XIII."[7]

Father Craft was never able to gather in the soul of the obdurate chief, but he did get the robe. In April 1885 Marty personally delivered the magnificent artifact to the pope.[8]

Craft often distributed crucifixes and other religious articles in the course of his missionary work. He presented crosses (Craft used the terms "cross" and "crucifix" interchangeably) to the founding members of the St. Joseph's Society on Standing Rock in April 1888 and awarded medals and holy cards to the schoolchildren. Scapulars and pictures of the Sacred Heart, obtained from the Apostleship of Prayer's League of the Sacred Heart, were also freely dispensed to adult Indians as well as whites.

Belly Fat, Flying By, Gray Eagle, Long Dog, Long Feather, and Sitting Bull were each photographed by D. F. Barry wearing missionary crucifixes, probably received from Father Craft. Indeed, the photos may well have been made to accompany the buffalo robe.

Belly Fat, according to the priest, was a "good old 'gent chief'" who, although he attended mass regularly and supported Craft's efforts among the young people, never approached the sacraments himself.[9] Along with the crucifix, Belly Fat wears an 1871 Ulysses S. Grant peace medal.

Craft described Flying By's camp, where he built his first school and chapel on the reservation, as the "only decent place on Grand River."[10] Gray Eagle, on the other hand, apparently tried to follow both Sitting Bull and the Black Robe at the same time. In a chance meeting at Coles's general store, after Sitting Bull had brought charges against him, Craft gave Gray Eagle the cold shoulder and threatened to knock him down if he persisted in speaking at all.[11] Presumably Gray Eagle was not wearing the crucifix at the time.

Long Dog was another tribesman who had a conflicted relationship with Craft. Arrayed in full Indian costume and paint, he generally carried a three-knife war club on his left arm. In 1885, as Long Dog lay desperately ill, hemorrhaging from nose and mouth, Father Craft knelt and anointed him. He seemingly recovered instantly, took a smoke from the priest's pipe, and walked off "perfectly well." Long Dog was a vocal supporter of Sitting Bull's accusations against Craft in the fall of 1887 and, like Gray

FIGURE 4. *(above left)* Belly Fat, 1880s. D. F. Barry photo. Denver Public Library, Western History Collection.

FIGURE 5. *(above right)* Flying By, 1880s. D. F. Barry photo. Denver Public Library, Western History Collection.

FIGURE 6. *(right)* Gray Eagle, 1880s. D. F. Barry photo. Denver Public Library, Western History Collection.

FIGURE 7. *(opposite, top)* Long Dog, 1880s. D. F. Barry photo. Denver Public Library, Western History Collection.

FIGURE 8. *(opposite, left)* Long Feather, 1880s. D. F. Barry photo. Denver Public Library, Western History Collection.

FIGURE 9. *(opposite, right)* Sitting Bull, 1880s. D. F. Barry photo. Denver Public Library, Western History Collection.

Eagle, a victim of Craft's strategic neglect policy in 1888. "When the devil was sick, the devil a monk would be," wrote Craft, "but when the devil got well, the devil a monk was he."[12] "[Long Dog] is a thorough and paced rascal, and, though he probably has almost as much faith as Satan himself, he is a clear case of unmitigated 'witkotko' [craziness]."[13] Perhaps Long Dog got his crucifix from Father Bede or Father Martin after all. In any event, the distant buildings in the photo of Long Dog on horseback are the Catholic church and fenced priest's house near Fort Yates.

Long Feather was also photographed with Father Craft and two young Indian women. One of the young ladies is Josephine Crowfeather, the founder of Craft's Congregation of American Sisters. The other young woman, who bears a strong resemblance to Long Feather, appears to be his daughter. She may have entered the religious life along with Josephine. Since Craft considered himself a brother of Josephine and other members of her generation, he also referred to Long Feather as his "uncle." When Long Feather died during a visit to Pine Ridge Agency in fall 1888, Craft lamented the loss: "I hear that Long Feather is dead. . . . Died of hemorrhage of lungs. . . . Though he was a treacherous wretch, I grieve to think he died so." Craft blamed others for instigating Long Feather's reluctance to accept Catholicism. "May God forgive him and not visit on the poor tool the vengeance due those who set him on. I shall be satisfied if God forgives me as freely as I forgive poor uncle Long-feather."[14]

The sixth of the Indians to be photographed adorned with a crucifix was Sitting Bull himself.[15] Nothing in Father Craft's papers indicates that Sitting Bull ever did more than tolerate or, more likely, manipulate efforts to Christianize him. Legend or not, the story is that the Hunkpapa chief told Bishop Marty he would never give up any of his wives as he would be required to do if he converted to Christianity.

Craft countered Indian obstinacy with a stern missionary strategy. When Cottonwood and Red Fish persisted in practicing what he perceived as devil worship, he not only pressured McLaughlin to break them from their positions as chiefs but struck Red Fish's son, Frosted, a "heavy blow with his fist." Wary of the priest's aggressive conduct, the solicitous agent expressed concern to Bishop Marty: "If Fr. Craft would only manifest a more kindly spirit towards them and treat them in a more christian like manner, I think it would be much more in keeping with his calling, but he does not speak to any of them whom he imagines have injured or wronged him."[16] McLaughlin, however, did not ask the bishop to take any spe-

FIGURE 10. Father Craft with Josephine Crowfeather, Long Feather, and Long Feather's daughter, 1880s. D. F. Barry photo. Denver Public Library, Western History Collection.

cific corrective action other than passing on "some friendly advice" on the matter.

If Marty made any sustained effort to rein in his contentious missionary, his attempts bore little fruit. The priest's daily journals, which he began in March 1888, reveal several such physical confrontations. He once warned Sitting Bull's son-in-law, Andrew Fox, not to advance toward him beyond a certain fence post, and when Andrew transgressed the limit, he hurled him over the fence into the middle of the road. In another instance he rode a would-be rapist down with his horse, leaving the mark of his quirt across the offender's shoulders. In still another case he threw a young Indian lad off the porch when he caught him spying on young girls at the mission's boarding school. For emphasis, he told the young voyeur that if he "ever insulted a girl whom I claimed as a relative (meaning especially my sister Josephine) I would send a pair of bullets through his brain."[17]

When a young girl named Agnes Comes Last tried to tear up a holy picture of the Blessed Virgin Mary, Craft was infuriated:

> I gave her a "blasting" such as she, probably, never got before, and won't care to get again. Had anything in the shape of a male Indian or white had done it, I would have left him but very little life, and very many broken bones. Miss Agnes prefers the white blanket of the "Ho-bu" to the white robe of innocence, and hence a picture of Mary Immaculate excites her deviltry, as a red rag excites a mad bull. . . .
>
> It is not well to "cast pearls before swine," and swine, lower, viler, filthier, more completely debased, and fonder of wallowing in filth, than these vile beings, I never yet saw or heard of. . . . It would be well if a Jew, or some other swine-hater could be made Agent here. Speaking of Jews, the history of these Indians, as one who knows them could write it, would be merely a reprint of the history of Jewish perverseness, as Holy Scripture gives it, merely changing Hebrew names to Indian, and somewhat intensifying the malice, brutality, and pig-headedness of the Jews to suit their worthy descendants, who have still further degenerated from most execrable ancestors. Moses got temporal punishment as a reward for his loyalty and affection for the Jews, but he would have been pretty sure to lose his soul into the bargain, had he done the same for these reprobates.[18]

Craft's journals and other writings often reveal an elite arrogance that betrays a lengthy inventory of his own deeply held prejudices: Jews, Protestants, nonprogressives and other Indians who happened not to meet his standards, Catholic "pharisees," and most foreigners. The Jesuit father who wrote an article opposing Craft's views on Indian vocations was described as "a very funny Teuton, whose great soul expands itself upon the rearing of pigs and chickens." These contemporaries, and Father Stephan especially, were branded as "foreign tuft-hunters . . . gilded dignitaries of foreign peasant origin and coarseness and narrowness, but aristocratic cravings" who asked that he "forget faith, chivalry, and honor . . . to desert [the] helpless ladies" under his care.[19] The hierarchy of the Roman Catholic Church, including the apostolic delegate, would be lambasted by Craft as "base-born foreign scoundrels,"[20] "Dagoes who pose as friends of monks and other disciples of Machiavelli."[21]

Other passages in the journals provide insight into the source of Craft's belligerent attitude. Ironically, he echoes the sentiments of the first Standing Rock agent, Father Joseph A. Stephan:

A fine Catholic Agency, this. . . . the Agent and all the whites stand ready to oppose all done to civilize or convert. If any noise is made, they all blame the priest. A Priest must do his duty, and if Satan opposes him, Catholic Pharisees all unite to misrepresent his conduct, and injure his work. A fine time I am having. God's herder, riding day and night on the range, rounding up the best ones of the herd of Israel. Wild cattle they are: stampedes, charges of mad bulls, obstinate brutal yellowness of Sitting Bull,[22] wheeling, plunging and bellowing like demons around me. . . .

I have to defend myself against the wolves that attack my herd, against my mad herd that join the wolves against me, and against the hirelings who draw pay for watching God's herd, and at the same time try to help the wolves devour it, and kill or drive away the herder who is too active and vigilant in guarding it. . . . It is the old story. False brethren, low born and low bred; incapable of understanding the work of God and His priests, desirous of gratifying their "stinking pride" or vanity by ruling and degrading beneath them those to whose standard they will not try to rise, turn against the Church that gave them all they have and hope for, and try to bend it to suit their depraved and worldly tastes. James the blacksmith is a worthy successor to Alexander the coppersmith.[23]

A fine thing, truly, if priests—who have in the world stood high above such reptiles, and who have forsaken the world and its honors, and trampled upon its false teachings, for the sake of gaining the eternal glories of heaven by following and teaching here the truth of Christ—should be found so mad, and so blinded, and so wretchedly and foolishly base as to fall down and worship a creature of their own making, and after eating unlimited mud and swallowing unlimited insults, find in the end that they had "Forfeited to be his slave," "All here, and all beyond the grave."

I have fully determined that this must end here and now. The history of our failures here, since McLaughlin became Agent, is exceedingly mortifying. I have checked the stampede of our herds, and mean to turn them back to the ranges of the Church, and, of course, this hireling tries to drive them over me. Now comes the crisis—such as it must be in every mission managed as this has been. If the Bishop and my brother priests do not turn against me, I shall succeed, and I am sure that they see the case in its true light now. McLaughlin has the cunning of Satan. He has tried in every way to misrepresent me to Bishop, priests, and seculars since he found I was determined to do my duty. Failing in this, he tries now to turn the Indians against me, beginning with Sitting Bull and the bad element, and extending his efforts to others who are not so bad. Some he tries to move by open means; others by quietly letting them see that their allegiance to me will be regarded as treason to him. He thinks to cause some disturbance which he can lay to my charge, or so annoy me that I will yield or leave. He has sadly mistaken his man. He could not possibly do worse than he has now done without giving me a legal hold, which I would at once take up. When he, either by active instigation or silent consent, caused the outrageous accusations of Sitting Bull to be brought against me, I laid out my course and, Deo volente, I shall carry it out to the end. I will not yield my principles, and I will not leave to give the enemies of the Church a triumph. I will remain here and fight it out until the last enemy of our faith has been crushed and the mission is at peace.

I have informed the Bishop of his designs and have now so arranged matters here that he is placed in the dilemma of either undoing the evil he has done, and letting the Church alone, or being crushed down under the stampede he has raised.

I have temporarily, and perhaps, if necessary, permanently changed my plan of action with the Indians, withdrawing from aiding them in any way that could divert my attention from the enemy's movements. I have notified the Agent to control Sitting Bull and other opponents, and seldom go near their camp—never, except when absolutely necessary, so as to give no chance to anyone to accuse me of beginning a fight. The Indians deserve, for their cowardly supineness, that I should neglect them awhile. I avoid, carefully, doing anything different from what is done by other priests, except, of course, the care of distant missions, and even that not too actively, and in the meantime, both here and at Washington, I put in motion every possible means to discover the enemy's plans and to defeat them. I will soon, I think, succeed and then I may without danger begin my active work again.[24]

For all his personal frustrations and private reflections on his lonely missionary presence in an unfamiliar culture, Father Craft remained a vigorous advocate for the often misunderstood and misrepresented Native American. "It must be remembered," he advised his eastern readers, "that Indians are not fools, but men of keen intelligence."[25]

Craft was literally fearless in his dealings with the often fierce and superstitious Sioux. While the Indians were circulating a petition to have him removed for throwing Hóthąka to the ground in July 1888, he responded by riding into their camps alone to offer an arrow as an alternative means of removing him. A few weeks before, as he made his rounds on Pinch, he encountered a small band of mounted Indians from Sitting Bull's camp. The Indians reined in their horses and stayed almost motionless at the side of the trail, staring insolently at the lone priest as he slowly rode by. Pausing, he coolly moved his horse in a backward arc, gradually maneuvering a full 360 degrees around them as he asked what they meant by their unfriendly actions. "They were frightened, and 'took water,' and I warned them to be more careful, wheeled my horse round them, and left them."[26]

Agent McLaughlin, however, was considerably more subtle and efficient in controlling troublesome Indians, especially medicine men like the one named Frosted. As a shifting wind swept away a light snow one evening in April 1888, the crisp night air pulsated with a strange drumbeat from Cottonwood's camp. A rhythmic beat, similar to the *waphíyapi* (curing ceremony) beat, but on a large drum, followed by the monotonous cadence of the *hąwácipi* (night dance) beat, but much more rapid and more sharply struck. The drummer was Frosted, using the *iníkağapi* (the sweat lodge ceremony) drum in "some of his infernal incantations—literally raising the devil."[27]

The following autumn, when Frosted boasted that he was invulnerable to bullets, Craft "wanted him to give me a shot at him." He ridiculed the absurdity of the conjurer's claim when Frosted declined to "stand fire."

That same month, Frosted emerged from a sweat-induced trance with the alarming prophecy that sixteen Crow Indians were on the warpath, headed toward Standing Rock. The entire Yanktonai camp bristled with sharpened hatchets and knives as other warriors uncovered cached fire-arms, mounted their ponies, and rode off to meet their mortal enemies. Craft interceded, telling them "not to listen to that devil-dreamer," and explained the consequences if the Sioux were to cross into the white man's country armed. He advised them to send out scouts instead and even offered to go himself.

Ignoring the priest's warnings, more than two hundred braves crossed the Cannonball River, intruding almost ten miles beyond the northern boundary of the reservation. Agent McLaughlin, away from his post at the time, had left George Faribault in charge of the agency. It would have been useless for Craft to alert McLaughlin's Indian police, since most of them had already joined in the search for the Crow aggressors. He knew also that if he told Faribault about the pending trouble, the acting agent would simply target him as the instigator of the disturbance. A district farmer in the area telegraphed news of the impending "attack" from Parkins Ranch to Fort Yates, where two troops of the Eighth Cavalry set out to intercept the Indians and prevent panic among white settlers. The troops reached Cannonball on the night of 22 October, camping at Parkins Ranch. Be-fore they could strike their tents the next morning, Crazy Walking, cap-tain of the Indian police, reported that most of the renegades had quietly returned during the night after hearing about the arrival of the troops. The commanding military officer ordered Crazy Walking to bring in the stragglers and place Frosted under arrest. Thus ended the "Crow War of 1888."

On his return, Major McLaughlin, furious over the need for federal military encroachment into his jurisdiction, had Frosted transferred to the agency guardhouse. He had worked hard to counter the influence of one troublesome medicine man on his reservation—Sitting Bull—and did not relish the rise of another.

The Indian police interrogated Frosted, who played into McLaughlin's hands by predicting that he and his singers could mystically transport the "standing rock" from its pedestaled location on the agency grounds to the guardhouse itself. The boulder-sized rock, looking vaguely like a woman and child, was the namesake for the reservation. Agent McLaughlin said they could try if they wanted, and if they were successful, he would set Frosted free. If the rock stayed put, though, Frosted would be returned to the military guardhouse with ball and chain.

FIGURE 11. Frosted in irons, 1880s. D. F. Barry photo. Denver Public Library, Western History Collection.

Frosted sent for his singers, who appeared in full dance regalia, including bells, beads, and headdresses. D. F. Barry, who was working in the area at the time, photographed Frosted and his entourage before the ceremony began. "Frosted sang, and tried to move the rock, but failed," Craft wrote. "He will be ironed."[28]

After the event, photographer Barry snapped a picture of a solitary, permanently diminished Frosted in prison garb, wrapped in ball and chain. His status among his people would never be the same.

In spite of these onerous assaults from man and nature, Craft had considerable success during these early mission years. Eight hundred baptized Sioux had been counted at Rosebud,[29] and now Craft was making similar inroads on Standing Rock.

Two Bears, a son of the famous Yanktonai Sioux chief of the same name, Mathó núpa, who had befriended Father Pierre J. DeSmet years earlier, lent his support to Craft's mission. When Two Bears died on 24 November 1885, Craft leveraged the chief's passing to enhance his own influence among tribal members. The priest wrote the last will of Two Bears, a document obviously designed to sway others to the Catholic faith.

Though I die, or rather, though I go to the G[reat] Spirit, still Chief Two B[ears] does not die. I shall live with the Great Spirit, and on earth I shall live again in my son. I wish him to take my name and rank. I wish him to visit the Great Father [the President] as I did last summer. I wish him to be the friend of the Black Robes, and the friend of the whites, as I was, and to obey and help the Agent. . . .

As soon as they hear that I have gone to the Great Spirit, I wish [my people] to make a feast and rejoice, and from the country of the Great Spirit I will see them and rejoice with them. My people, I will talk with the Great Spirit for you, and He will give you life. . . . I have friends in the country of the G. Spirit. I will shake hands for you with them—with the Son of the G. Spirit—with Mary the Mother of our people—with all the Indians whom we knew here—and with all the angels, the soldiers of the Great Spirit. We will all remember you and Chief Tamaheca [Bishop Marty]. . . .

I wish my people to bury my body near the B.R.'s church at the Agency. I do not wish them to paint my face. Though I know that the wa-se [wasé, red] signifies the blood of the Son of the G. Spirit that washes away our sins and gives us life—still I feel that my soul has been made red and good by that blood, and therefore I need nothing on my body to represent it. That is all I wish to say. For the last time here, I shake hands with you all. Now I will talk with the Black Robe and prepare to go.

This is I Chief Two Bears

Thus I say.[30]

Craft sent a copy of Two Bears's will to the *North Western Chronicle*, emphasizing that when the chief was about to die, "he said that he wished to teach his people how to die, as he had taught them how to live, as good Christians."[31]

It was not the first time Father Craft used a written document to charm the Sioux. Among his papers is a letter in his own hand dated 16 March 1871. Under the heading of St. Louis University, the message states that "two Black-gowns will soon arrive in your midst, with the sole intention of devoting themselves to the welfare of all and particularly of your dear little children, as soon as means can be obtained for the erection of school houses." Purportedly signed by P. J. DeSmet, S.J., it is directed "to the Chiefs and Braves," including such notables as "Two Bears, Grass, Bear's Rib, Running Antelope, Log, The Black All Over, Spirit Ghost, Burning Cloud, Sitting Crow, and 'a great number of other chiefs and braves whose memory shall be always dear to me.'"[32]

Father DeSmet's travails in this life had ended in St. Louis in 1873, but his carefully selected and recorded words eased the path walked by Father Craft and Father Wilhelm on Standing Rock in 1885.

VII

MISSIONARY LABOR AND SACRIFICE

Craft generally started his day by celebrating mass at 6:30 or 7:00. On Sundays he usually said two masses: the first at 9:00 for the Indians and the second, often a high mass, at 10:30 for the whites. He preached in Lakota to the Indians, instructing them on the gospel story of the day. Interspersed were themes on the Holy Family, imitations of the life of Jesus, the communion of saints, marriage, and the sacraments. Obedience to God and his church and respect for self and family were also major topics of his homilies. He did not often preach to the whites, preferring to defer to one of the Benedictine fathers. In his opinion, whites were the bane of the reservation who spent every day but Sunday undermining the work of the priests and sisters, and he would as soon not waste his breath on them. On "Catholic" Standing Rock, of course, this did not endear him to that element of reservation life.

He would tolerate no disorder or disturbance during mass and was quick to remove anyone who dared to distract the congregation. Also, he was always on guard against those who would present themselves for communion right after a healthy breakfast or other leftovers from the previous night's dance feast.

Father Craft promoted the growth of St. Joseph's and St. Mary's Societies, intended to supplant Indian ways and encourage the transition to civilized life. The rules he established for these groups included a marked abandonment of tribal customs and superstitions. He restricted attendance at dances, required young braves to cut their hair, and condemned polygamy and gambling. He adamantly opposed summer vacations for children attending boarding schools, fearing that even so brief a return to camp life would negate their progress. After the children reached age twenty-one, Craft believed they could safely return to help in their parents' transition to civilization. This, of course, was unpopular with both the young *and* the old.

Still, Craft saw a commonality between Catholic and Sioux traditions that gave him a special insight into many of their rituals. He eventually developed a regular theme on the subject that he used in lectures and in articles for the eastern press.

The Sioux, he said, told a story of a "chief of Black Robes" who had come from the East about seven hundred winters earlier. This would have placed the date around A.D. 1100, too late for Saint Brendan, abbot of Clonfert, Ireland, whom Craft and others claimed was the first missionary to the New World about 540. Eric Upsi, however, the bishop of Greenland who visited the Norse settlement at Vinland on the East Coast, was a distinct possibility. He supposedly stayed and traveled inland until 1121 and may have met or instructed the descendants of inhabitants of the Great Lakes region.

In any event, Craft was sure that the symbol of the cross had a long-standing history in Indian design and ornamentation. Moreover, he saw similarities between the seven Catholic sacraments and several religious rites of the Sioux. Baptism echoed *ḥuḳápi,* the making of relatives—his own entrée into the Sioux Nation. Both the purification rite and the ritualistic incantations preceding the smoking of the pipe were likened to Catholic confession in the sacrament of penance; fasting and sacrifice of the Sun Dance in the Holy Eucharist; and the sacrament of confirmation in the *ḥablécheyapi* (vision quest). Rounding out the seven, the Sioux recognized their marriages, ordained their shamans, and painted their dying. And in *wanáǧiyata,* the four passages of departed spirits, Craft saw the Way of Souls.[1]

Despite the obstacles the priest often placed in his own way, the sheer momentum of his aggressive, audacious approach contributed to the growth and well-being of the mission. The societies he promoted for teaching the basics of Catholicism to Indian men and women not only flourished but attracted the support of agency personnel. Agent McLaughlin's wife, Marie Louise, directed one of these religious entry groups for Indian women, the St. Mary's Society. Participants showing progress moved into

St. Joseph's Societies, where they were expected to give up Indian ways and follow rules similar to Catholic sodalities in the East. There were two branches of the St. Joseph's Society; one met at the agency itself and another at St. Benedict's Mission. The St. Aloysius Society for boys met at St. Francis Xavier's Mission near Cannonball, as did the Holy Angels' Society for girls. For more advanced young women, a Sodality of the Immaculate Conception was formed at the agency boarding school. With upward of five hundred members, these groups often filled the small chapels at the agency and at St. Benedict's Mission. The procession to mass on Sundays, on horseback with banners unfurled and crosses aloft, was a source of pride to Father Craft.[2]

Occasionally, when sacramental wine was unavailable, he would substitute "homegrown" wine. Cedar boughs replaced palm fronds during Easter week observances. Often he would say mass at the home of Mr. and Mrs. Wells or at other temporary quarters in the outlying school districts he visited. Unlike most of his contemporaries, who tended to stay close to their home base at a mission or school, he often traveled with Indian bands as they roved across reservation lands. In 1886 Sitting Bull left a message for him at Standing Rock Agency: "Myself and people are anxious to have you go with us to Crow Agency—will wait two days . . . please send me word if you cannot go."[3] Once, in response to a request from an artist, Craft sketched a scene of a mass celebrated in an Indian camp and provided this description:

> A large tent, the front thrown open. An altar made of a canvas stretched over a frame of sticks. Two young Indians lay aside their blankets, from the right arm, to serve mass. They drop the blanket from the right shoulder, and wrap it round the body, and hold it with the left arm, leaving the right free. The others kneel wrapped in the blankets and buffalo robes. Some have plain robes, some robes painted with the figure of the sun in the centre. Robes worn with the hair inside.
>
> Four chiefs in front wear the long war-bonnet of eagle feathers. The men are in front and on the gospel side; the women in the rear, and on the epistle side of the altar. Beyond those in front, and extending far to the rear, are many hundreds ranged in the same order as those in front. The altar and its shelter tent are set up on a plain in the centre of the camp. The tents are ranged in a circle, with the plain in the centre. Beyond the tents the horses are scattered over the prairie grazing. The mass was said at sunrise. The Indians wear the

FIGURE 12. Father Craft's sketch of a mass at sunrise. New-York Historical Society.

longer feathers standing erect. The young Indians, serving mass, wear the short plumes of soft white "down," or soft breast-feathers of the eagle, hanging down or floating in the wind.[4]

On the prairie, Father Craft would fashion an altar out of four crotched sticks and two rifles. The four sticks were driven into the ground forming a rectangle, and the rifles were laid between the crotches of the front and back pairs of sticks. A tent canvas folded across this framework provided the base over which he draped an altar cloth. Two number six candles placed on either side of his own nine-inch missionary crucifix, hung from a center stick at the back of the makeshift altar, completed the arrangement.[5] Building an altar of sticks and rifles fit Father Craft's style.

The priest's efforts toward Indian salvation reached a spiritual apex on

New Year's Day 1888 when, in an elaborate ceremony before several hundred astonished and perplexed Lakotas, he signed with his own blood the transfer of his chieftainship of the Dakota Nation to the Sacred Heart of Jesus.[6] The following Christmas he renewed this extraordinary transaction:

> Preached (in Sioux) on Nativity, showing how our Lord preferred the gift of the hearts and little lambs of the poor, to the gold, etc. of the rich Magi. He was announced to the poor shepherds by *angels,* but to the Magi by a *star* only. We too are poor and have only our hearts and the lambs of the Sacred Heart (the children) to offer. We will first do as the shepherds did, and lastly will offer the gifts of the Kings—the last "royal chieftainship" of the Dakotas.
>
> Then we read and renewed the consecration to the Sacred Heart of last January, with the oaths of allegiance, and the transfer of the chieftainship from me to the Sacred Heart. Then I announced, formally, that the Sacred Heart of Jesus was now our "Royal Chief." In opening the sermon, I addressed the Indians as the "Nation of the Sacred Heart," and announced to them, as the angels did, a great joy, in the birth of Christ long ago at Bethlehem, and again today, on the altar, at mass.[7]

The priest's medical training was a wonderful fit with his missionary work. Measles, tuberculosis, smallpox, and other diseases were epidemic among the poorly nourished and ill-housed tribes, and the death rate was tragically high. Over the twenty-six months of his journals, Craft reports more than forty deaths, many of them infants and children.

He maintained an effective relationship with the agency physician, Dr. Ambler Caskie, often drawing medical supplies from Caskie's office. During camp and hospital visits, he would administer vaccinations; provide medicines such as tonics, phosphates, castor oil, laudanum, morphine, and brandy; dress wounds; and set occasional fractures. The medical treatments were supplemented with a full range of sacraments—baptism, penance, Holy Eucharist, marriage, and extreme unction. The baptisms, he feared, did not "take" as well as the vaccinations: "For instance, there's old Antelope, baptized 3 times, so he says. It certainly didn't take either time."[8] And to a male Indian who offered himself for baptism in return for citizen's clothes, he had this advice: "He may wait until he learns that God's grace makes better clothes for the soul, than the white man's cast off duds do for the body."[9]

Sometimes, as in the case of Ed Khağí-ska, the situation called for an array of sacraments. Mrs. McLaughlin sent word at 9:30 one December evening that Ed was dying and wanted to see a priest. Khągí-ska, it seems, had refused to marry the woman he lived with, and she, of course, wasn't the least bit interested in the Catholic Church. Now that he was near death, Ed was apparently having second thoughts about his predicament. Craft was suspicious, but he went anyway, "leaving our chance of success to . . . the Sacred Heart." He found the dying Indian well disposed toward conversion, but his live-in partner balked at the priest's presence. Mrs. McLaughlin took her next door for some brief instruction while Craft heard Ed's last confession. Khągí-ska was quite deaf, rendering a softly murmured, reverent confession unworkable. He promptly dismissed the remaining family members so that he and Ed could honor the secrecy of the confessional. When the extraordinary session ended, the family returned as Craft baptized Ed's mate, joined them in marriage, and completed the last rites. Four sacraments—baptism, penance, marriage, and extreme unction—were administered in less than two hours. He added a plenary indulgence for Ed, left a scapular and a picture of the Sacred Heart, and "got back in time to say the Rosary, at 11:30 P.M."[10]

Ed Khągí-ska died the next day. Not all his patients, however, were so receptive to his efforts.

Once, at Grand River, an old woman sent for me. I got there after a lively contest with a bucking horse, bad roads, and several execrable snow drifts. The old lady was very sick, but "yellowness" of the Government mule type squinted and glittered in her eye, and "Satan's mother-in-law" was stamped in big letters on every line of her wrinkled phiz. I had seen such imps before, but she was very low, and divine pity getting the better of disgust, I laid myself out to save her miserable soul.

Charitable Missionary. "My daughter, did you send for me?" Satan's Mother-in-law. "Yes." C.M. "Well, as you are very sick, I will instruct and baptize you and—" S.M. "Oh the devil! I know all about that. Won't have it. Onions. Onions." C.M.: "But my daughter, think of your soul first. God's grace—" S.M.: "I don't want any grace. I want onions, onions, onions." C.M.: "Alas daughter, I have no onions, but I will give you the grace of God, and—" S.M.: "Don't! I tell you I won't have it! *Onions!*"

No use. After gravely informing her that her son-in-law below was better able than I to satisfy those who preferred onions to grace, I departed, venting my disappointment in a good solid kick on the paunch of a worthless, vicious yellow cur that came to take leave. He left, "par levibus ventis, volu-crique simillima somno" [like the swift winds, and most like a fleeting dream], for the shelter of the nearest tipi, and I left to rustle something to eat, and to make brand-new resolutions concerning sick-calls.[11]

He could, however, be just as strict in the conduct of his missionary affairs with white parishioners. Describing a family of white settlers in the area, he wrote:

For unlimited *"cheek,"* I think that family bears away the palm. Mrs. Parkins wants me to say mass there, so they can all go to communion. For several rea-sons, I won't. They never come to mass here. Such favors are granted only to good Catholics who are capable of appreciation, and these people have mani-fested such a spirit of malignant enmity towards Sisters and priests, as to put them without the circle of those we consider good Catholics. It has been too long the custom here to consult the wishes and the convenience of such people, until they consider themselves entitled to our service, and treat us with con-tempt; imagining, perhaps, that if we don't make ourselves their slaves, a note to the Bishop will enlist him in their service, and bring us to our knees in short order. It is time to teach them their mistake, and give them a sharp reminder that they are not our masters.

Besides all this, their wicked desire to keep the Indians in their present state, that they may profit by their necessities, is enough to unfit them to receive any sacraments—unless their dispositions undergo a very great change, which, at present, don't seem at all likely. It is hard to forget their conduct, some years ago, in decoying an Indian girl into their house, locking her in, and sending for a depraved, diseased, white man, who could not get her otherwise; and closing their ears to her cries for help, while he ravished, ruined, and diseased her, caus-ing her death shortly after. Nothing can be too severe for such wretches; and, now that I know their evil dispositions, I shall not make it too easy for them to profane the sacraments. They must change towards God and His Church, before I change towards them.[12]

On another occasion, Craft recorded a distressing visit to a native youngster whose feet had frozen in the camps a year earlier. The feet be-came ulcerated, but the boy had worn his moccasins until the cankerous rot had glued them to his feet; beneath this crust the ulcers were eating into the bones. He cut the moccasins away in strips, but the bone had already become carious; amputation was the only option.

In addition to hearing the confessions of soldiers from Fort Yates, Craft also provided occasional medical counseling. One errant trooper who, with Craft's help, was trying to kick a morphine habit, made the mistake of asking the advice of the contract doctor from the fort. The doctor promptly had the soldier arrested, confined, and court-martialed. He eventually was acquitted, but in his journal the priest indicted the doctor, declaring him "a rascal [who] had . . . forfeited the confidence of everyone. A doctor who betrays professional secrets," he avowed, "is unfit to live."[13]

Sick calls also included visits to the agency jail, where he once visited Charles Rabbit. Charles had hemorrhaged from the lungs and also had tried to shoot himself, managing only to splinter his rib cage. Craft gave him cod liver oil and cough medicine and dressed the wound with soft cotton batting. Rabbit denied any attempt at suicide, claiming he had shot himself accidentally while picking up a Winchester rifle to shoot—of all things—a rabbit. "He certainly hit the wrong 'Rabbit,'" Craft observed.[14]

The next day, Father Craft saw Rabbit again to examine the wound: "Gave him more cotton. He is going to Hunhpati camp, so I won't venture to cut on it. An abscess has formed from the burrowing of matter under the shattered rib, some splinters came away, but more are there, and, probably, some pieces of cloth. An opening should be made in a depending part."[15]

A February 1889 journal entry provides an interesting contrast in the trappings of Indian medicine and Catholic preparation for death:

> I went to see Frances Ihawin in Waga's camp. I baptized her three years ago. She is now dying of consumption. It is a "devil's outfit" of the Red Fish type. The stepfather, Sinte-sna-mani, is "dead gone" in "devil worship" and "stone-throwing." The sick girl (age 13) laid on the ground, and near her were the stones for their incantations, and the medicine-drum with the horned demon painted on it. Before it were the wild sage, the tobacco board, and other things used in the incantations. Here, where in that part of the house set apart for sacred things, the orthodox Indian rules would require that all should be clean and orderly,—all was dirt, darkness, squalor, and disorder.
>
> The poor child was just conscious enough to receive the sacraments, and would soon be beyond the reach of evil. Always "simple"—almost idiotic, sick-

ness had left her but little reason. She probably never knew what sin was, and would soon be safe from knowing. I scarcely knew whether I could give her the last sacraments. I left it to the Sacred Heart of Jesus to dispose her. He is too anxious to save not to do all He can to aid my efforts. I asked her if she wished to receive the sacraments, and while waiting for her answer, explained them. She answered "Hau" [yes], the only word she had spoken for some time. I did not send the family out, but ordered them to stand back, and after putting on the stole, tried to get through with her confession.

Finding that she could not speak, I thought it best not to attempt to hear her confession, especially as she was not in a condition to remember anything. I repeated an act of contrition, and prayers to the Hearts of Jesus, Mary, and Joseph, and gave her conditional absolution. I then anointed her, gave her the scapular, gave the blessing for the sick, and the plenary indulgence, in art. mort. [*in articulo mortis;* at the point of death]. It was all I could do. An attempt to hear her confession would only have confused and disturbed her, and I was positive it would be useless.

I took every precaution, in case she should need absolution, but it is probable that she will go to heaven like a baptized infant. God has His own ways of lifting one to heaven from the greatest depths of misery. De profundis clamvi ad te Domine. [Out of the depths I cry to you, O Lord.]

Out of the depths of "devil dreaming," superstition, ignorance, savage degradation, misery and squalor, the miseries and danger of poor little Frances have cried out to the heart that could not refuse such pleading, though He will be deaf to the elaborate petitions of worldly Pharisees. The Heart of Jesus saves in strange and unsuspected ways.[16]

Frances recovered; another of his beloved relations was less fortunate. He stopped one time at Black Rabbit's camp to baptize his little sister "Chewing-Gum," whom he had instructed the previous Monday. She had died suddenly they said, though the appearance of the tent, and the smell of burnt sage, indicated that they had just carried her out for burial. He was devastated: "Poor dear little orphan sister. I hope the Baptisma Flaminis [baptism of fire] has given her the grace of which my stupid delay may have deprived her. That pale pinched face, lighting up with joy at the name of 'sister,' and hope and happiness at the thought of baptism and eternal life, will haunt me as long as I live. It will be a lesson for me, but it is a bitter one. I shall be well satisfied if the grief and pain are mine alone, and God will accept her desire of baptism."[17]

The priest also made resolute efforts to save the souls of the opposition. When old Red Fish was near death in 1889, Craft visited his camp to give him a last chance "for the glory of the Sacred Heart." Red Fish's wife refused to let him in the tent, but Craft brushed her aside, tore open the flap, and charged through the opening. He prayed for the old reprobate, who seemed to waver momentarily but then said conclusively that "he had many devils, and many crimes, and would not receive baptism." Four times the priest repeated his exhortations, and four times Red Fish balked. Unfazed by the old man's protestations, Craft sprinkled the tent and immediate surroundings liberally with holy water and, as he rode off, called to Red Fish to send word if he had a change of heart.[18]

Father Craft was no stranger to bizarre forms of penance and remorse practiced for centuries by priests and monks in pursuit of self-discipline and redemption. Prayer, fasting, and abstinence, always at the core of the ascetic ideal, were often supplemented with voluntary penances that would appear excessive, even repulsive, to modern sensibilities. Practices such as self-inflicted chastisement and the wearing of hair shirts and thorn belts were still occasionally engaged in during the late nineteenth century. While there is no evidence that Craft employed them, he was nevertheless sometimes moved to carry a penance to grotesque extremes—as he did once in response to the death of a young girl named Cunegunda:

Went at 7 A.M. to see Cunegunda. She had a hard night and is restless and delirious. Her father came again, I coaxed him away with an order for coffee and sugar, but let him in on the doctor's recommendation and his promise not to stay long. He staid too long again, and she had to tell him again to go. She sank rapidly after this. She was too weak for more opiates. I heard her confession and gave her a Plenary Indulgence. . . . I was about to give her brandy and water, and her pulse was imperceptible. She called to me "Be quick, Father, please be quick." I saw she was dying; after I lifted her higher on the pillows, and instead of giving the brandy, I called the sisters, put on the stole, and after repeating an act of contrition, and "Jesus, Mary, and Joseph help me" as a penance, I gave her the last absolution, and said the prayers for the dying. I sent for F[ather] Bede. He came before she died. She passed away quietly and happily at a quarter before 11 A.M.

I thought before she was too sick, of having her take her vows, as she has a vocation, but, fortunately, Sister Superior had already allowed her to do so yesterday, giving her the name of Sister Mary Aloysia, at her own request. I added "of the Sacred Heart." . . . I fast today for sister. To do some penance for her, and also to thank the Sacred Heart for His great mercy to her, I swallowed the matter she had coughed and vomited. It don't seem to nauseate me. I ought to be proud to do something for my sister, the bride of my Chief, the Sacred Heart of Jesus. So, sweet sister—the first "Lily of the Sacred Heart" the New Year gave Him—blooming in the midst of winters snow, far whiter, purer, and holier than snow or earthly lilies. Ven[erable] Sister Mary Aloysia of the Sacred Heart of Jesus, O.S.B. rest in peace in the eternal happiness you have gained, and pray for poor brother, still fighting hard and desperately for the Chief and his Church.[19]

A week later, the priest repeated this repugnant offering: "As a penance, to obtain from God the recovery of my sick sisters and cousins at the school, I swallowed the pus and mucous from the basin containing it." [20]

The medical treatments were not always of Indians, however. Once, when Craft experienced shortness of breath and an accelerated heartbeat, he visited Dr. Caskie: "After mass, I got Dr. Caskie to examine my heart's action. He can detect no enlargement, nor valvular trouble, but finds great rapidity, and functional derangement. Exposure, hardship, and continual anxiety and trouble for the past few years, keeping me under a severe mental strain, and deranging nervous functions—all combined have caused it. He gave me digitalis, and also pepsin, to correct the stomach, also much out of order, and a belladonna plaster to put over the heart." [21]

The medications were apparently effective, since Craft somehow avoided the diseases he both dealt with and defied; he still had thirty-two hard years of living ahead of him.

VIII

HUMOR AND WHIMSY

Bishop Marty once remarked that Father Craft was not flexible enough for a Jesuit vocation but was "good-natured" nonetheless.[1] In support of the bishop's observation, many entries in Craft's journals reflect the humor he often saw in the desperate circumstances that surrounded him. One example is this lyrical account of a local wedding that ends with a novel twist. The groom was William Pamplin, a white farmer who settled in an area near Selfridge, North Dakota, currently known as Pamplin Hills. His Indian bride was the widow of Barney Lannegan, a white man who had worked on the construction of Fort Yates in 1874–75. Agent James McLaughlin officiated at the ceremony; witnesses included Dr. Caskie and the agency's uniformed Indian police:

Mr. Pamplin will marry Mrs. Lanigan, a full-blood. Best thing he can do. "A broth of a boy was Johnny Lanigan," and his "widdy" seems to be a "raete and dacint craytur." "Long life to them," and may Mr. Pamplin never come to grief for disregarding the advice to "Beware of vidders." St. Paul says "The younger widows avoid," but as this one is "fair and forty," and therefore "no chicken," it's all right, no doubt. "Maidens, like moths, are ever caught by glare,"[2] and Pamplin does well not to tie up to a copper-colored maiden, who would be caught up by the glare of the first white-blanketed "ho-bu,"[3] whose skunk perfumed draperies, and "Itowapi kin le" [image bearing] melodies, would be wafted towards her on Dakota's gentle zephyrs. Besides, has Mr. Pamplin not been highly honored? Few men, living under our republican institutions, can attain to the high honor of being presented, with their brides, at court—even a police court. His services to the Government have, evidently, been appreciated very highly, for has the Government not watched solicitously over each changing phase of his romantic courtship, until it was brought to a happy conclusion under its protecting aegis?

Wandering with his inamorata past the habitations of the dead, over the classic hills of Išna-paha [Lone hill], many gentle breezes from Mini-šo-še's [Missouri River's] silver-locked waves brought the roses to their cheeks, and gently waved their flowing šinas [blankets or shawls]; while beneath their feet the earliest blossoms of spring time, waking from their slumbers, tried to rise from their snowy couch, and gently sighed. "Dear friends, accept our sympathetic congratulations; we too are white-robed 'Ho-bu's."

The blue-robed guardian of Dakota's peace, followed afar, but ever vigilant, lest malignant spirits, wandering from their burial-place, on deeds of evil bent, should venture to distract a tryst so fair. Softly approaching, bowing low, while in his hand his gold-bound cap of office gracefully swept the snowy plateau in lowly salutation, with gently modulated voice he softly whispered. "Brave knight—fair lady—I come an humble ambassador from the palace of Justice to the court of Cupid. Bravest of the brave—fairest of the fair, graciously deign to accompany me to the royal residence, where honors meet will be duly rendered to you to whom such honors are most justly due."

Gallantly he marshaled them; courteously, but pensively they followed. The knight escorted the lady to the palace of Justice, where rank on rank of blue-robed belted knights received them with martial honors and courteous salutation, and leaving the fair lady with her attendant damsels, he passed beneath the smiling moonbeam's gentle rays to his lonely couch, to dream sweet dreams of the morrow and the morrow's joys.

> Day dawned on Išna-paha's steep,
> On Mini-šo-še broad and deep.
> And pahin's [porcupine's] mountains lone,
> The snowy plains, the palace keep.
> The guarded cells where captives weep,
> In yellow lustre shone.

The golden sunbeams had scarcely smiled their morning salutation to the fair river, and lonely hill in robes of white and silver draped, when the gallant Sir

William presented himself at the palace of Justice, to kiss the snow-white hand of his lady, and to receive with her the high honors awaiting them.

In the royal hall, surrounded by his blue-robed belted knights, his courtiers, and his venerable gray-haired counselors, the King of Justice, throned in state received them. What pen could record the splendor of that reception. What minstrel played or poet sang of honors high like those conferred upon them. Suffice it to say, that Sir William and his lady fair saluted amid applause of ladies and of knights as King and Queen of Love and Beauty, were earnestly besought by the venerable gray-bearded Monarch, and his gray haired Chancellor, to grace the royal presence with their nuptials, and that they graciously consented. Modest and retiring as becomes a gallant knight, Sir William rode rapidly with his bride-elect to their residence, to avoid the proffered honors of a "shivaree" or "skimmelton," and prepared to solemnize his nuptials with a splendor unequaled in magnificence and pomp. Long may this worthy pair survive to bless our land with many worthy descendants, now that

> "The rosebud that graces our highlands,
> Is wreathed in a garland round William to twine,"
> and long may it be told in song and story, how—
> The Black Robe heard their plighted troth,
> And gave to them the nuptial oath.
> How bluff King James the curtain drew,
> While Caskie's hand the stocking threw.
> And wished that every married pair,
> Love like this Knight and lady fair.

The probability is that the gallant and amorous Sir William will, out of the goodness of his heart, wish happiness like his own to all misguided bachelors, and will contrive, too, that they come to it in the same way. That it is clearly a "put up job," there is none so blind who does not see. However, it serves him right, and may all those who, for the sake of corrupting the Indians, try to destroy the work of God's priests among them, come speedily and surely to the same trap, and be "double-dead immortal-cinched" in the same way.

Pamplin, fearing that the police and other Indians would expose his squaw-trading, took his stand with other cowards and enemies against me in the Sitting Bull affair, and now he is getting justly paid, by their exposing him. Had he then acted like a man, he would never have been compelled to marry such a worthless character, as there are others deeper in the affair than he, but now, since in consequence of his meanness "that has come to him which he feared," why, let him take it, and dandle it on his knee, with other many-sired children.[4]

The next day Craft told Pamplin that it was all a "put up job to trap him and save someone else." Pamplin wanted Father Craft to help him, but the priest declined. "Let him reap as he has sown," Craft wrote. "I can't fight the battle of those who serve under Satan's colors."[5]

The journals also served to vent the frustrations the missionary faced each day. Craft made several trips to Grand River seeking to baptize One Bull's child but was rejected each time. Finally One Bull brought the child in for baptism.

He wouldn't let me do it when I went to Grand River on purpose, but when I ceased to wish it, he asked for it, and when he found out that I didn't care to wear myself out seeking lost sheep that didn't want to be found, he packed up the lost sheep and brought it to me. Just so it is with all of them. Kindness has no effect; but neglect and contempt bring them to their senses. If they want "cold shoulder," and think they can live on it, they will be soon satisfied, for there is a large supply of it in this world. Charity and kindness are rare, and like pearls, should not be offered to such swine.[6]

Craft's fluency in the Sioux language also reveals some interesting Lakota expressions:

Sat down to smoke, after unsaddling Pinch—that rascal is tough as steel, came back fresh as a daisy, and golden with "yellowness." Ate supper, kicked off chaparejos and boots, lit a cigarette and philosophized. Thought of Žatela's and No Heart's camps, peace—rest—contentment, etc. Martin Catka came to ask about the hour for mass tomorrow. Very good—seems to have a soul, and, even to *know* it.

Saw a fair cousin of mine, who seems to prefer the serpent's den to the eagle's nest, and the white blanket of the "ho-bu" to the white robe of innocence I gave her in baptism. In fact, she won't prepare for confession and communion, goes much in bad company, and to night dances, and likes to be courted at night. Got mad, and disgusted, and began to feel tired. Thought of new expletives—something deep, long, bitter, loud, and filling and rasping to the throat, and soothing to a ruffled temper. "Gnaška cincapi!" [Frog children!] might, I think, be *broadened* and *deepened*. How would "Natapeha cincapi!" [Toad children!] fill the bill. "Excellent well in faith." Mem. Employ it for the future. Cigarette needs relighting. Just like an Indian. Won't go, if not watched. Lit it again, smoked, meditated on the sedative and curative effects of a consciousness of Indian conscientiousness, and the proneness of the reverse, to bring on a relapse of fatigue, soreness, crossness, etc—execrated, in most choice and elegant Sioux, the general yellowness of things in general. Went to bed and slept the sleep of the tired, vexed, and thoroughly bad tempered man—At least that's what I'm now going to do, so I may as well consider it done.[7]

Old Frank Holy Running must have had a sense of humor, too:

Woke up this morning, and the first object my eyes rested on, was old Frank Wakan-inyanka (or Ota-inyanka), an inveterate cooler, unmitigated humbug, and consummate hypocrite. He will tiptoe piously into the house, making the sign of the cross, his lips pursed up like a dried up potato, and his ugly phiz devoutly elongated; and after making a genuflection before the stove, he will recite in the "holy tone" the Lords prayer, in Dakota, and, scarcely pausing to take breath he will launch into the most outrageous coffee-cooling for all sorts of things, from a pipeful of tobacco to some food or money. He can't be got to his duties, won't go to mass when there is an Indian feast within smelling-distance, and lives in the worst devil-worshiping outfit that ever brought God's anger upon a tribe of pagans.[8]

On the other hand, Father Craft got along very well with Crazy Man, an avid teller of stories of "ye older times," who was always quick to flourish the scars on his leg where a bear bit him many years earlier. The cultural transition grudgingly taking place on Standing Rock Reservation took surprising and fascinating turns. One of the more subtle evolutions had to have been the day Craft observed Mad Bear, chief of the Yanktonai Sioux, purchasing green ribbons at the local store for his girls to wear in the school's St. Patrick's Day parade.[9]

External influences on Standing Rock came not only from the land near the Celtic Sea:

High-bear came to ask me to write a note for him. Read him passages from the Old Testament, describing Jewish perverseness, and its consequent punishment, and proved, much to his horror and astonishment, that it was identical with Indian perverseness, and would probably be punished in the same way.

He might profit by it, if it were not quite certain that its effects will be washed from his mind by the first drink of coffee or dog-soup; for an Indian's thoughts are all centered in his stomach, and his ideas may be truly said to be well digested; those that are evil being assimilated, and those that might lead to good being cast off with other excrementitious matter, for which he has no earthly use.

Cottonwood (Waga) also came, to ask about issue, boss-farmer, etc. He smiled even unto his collar-button, assured us that he was a just man, and knew no evil, and was a great friend to the "wašicun" [white man]—which must be true, as he kept the word "wašicun" under his tongue, and chewed and mouthed it, and dwelt upon it as long as possible, though, from the faces he made over it, it must have tasted very bitter. What a convincing proof of devoted attachment, when, for the sake of the "wašicun" he mouths so long and earnestly that "dear sacred name" in spite of its evident bitterness. Confound the dirty, cowardly hypocrite.

Mr. Wells skinned and prepared for mounting, a booted lynx, killed at Fort Rice bottom (poisoned). It must have died with a cramp in its stomach, or when trying to propitiate a much hated enemy who "had him down," for his grin strongly resembles the "fascinating smile" of Waga, when conversing with his "wašicun koda" [white man friend]. Sweet resemblance! Waga and a poisoned lynx! It's a fact, though.[10]

Beef issue day, in Craft's eyes, was an especially disheartening, pathetic scene on Standing Rock. Scrawny, underweight cattle, herded from Missouri for top prices, were released from pens as demoralized braves relived the glory of past buffalo hunts by running them down with muzzle loaders, cheese knives, and assorted bludgeons. The steers, with tongues cut out or half severed from their throats, long before they were dead or senseless, would rise and charge their tormentors until several better-aimed shots mercifully ended their misery.[11] The feasts that followed were often major distractions as the priest sought to bring the tribes to the table of the Lord:

Only about 30 came to 2nd mass. Žatela had a big "wakicaǵapi"[12] at "Bearghost's" and the smell of wasna,[13] beef, dog, and coffee, proved stronger than the allurements of grace, and led a big crowd by the nose. I talked about Holy Communion, and tried to feed their souls, but the hearts of my hearers had gone after their noses towards the "wakicaǵapi" and its steaming kettles, and as soon as mass was over they hastened whither their hearts and noses led them. Well, good appetite to them, and full stomachs—at least they came to mass, while others were guzzling.[14]

More than a touch of cynicism is revealed in this entry:

Went before breakfast to help Mr. Wells find his horse Daisy, who ran away last night trailing a 70 feet lariat, which, Mr. Wells fondly imagined, would not be stolen, because it was soaked in red paint, and could easily be identified. I maintained that, paint or no paint, the lariat would be taken. After sending Antony and Andrew Ireland to look for the horse, we found it with the field-glass, only a mile away. Of course, the lariat was gone—neatly untied from the short halter-rope. The halter and short rope were not taken, and therefore the thief must have some remains of conscience—a rare thing in this neighborhood. He must be one of our *best Indians,* and by searching among them, we may find the lariat.[15]

During the fall of 1889, the priest lamented the heavy work the Benedictine sisters faced in harvesting their corn crop. Two September entries describe the situation:

Went around to hire men to cut Sister's corn. It isn't right for the Sisters to do such work. Panian and the others thought many would come if I made a "bee" and got them some beer. Agreed. Went with Panian and notified them. . . . I saw Sr. Josephine and another Sister working at the corn, though I had told Rev. Sr. Hildegarde I would attend to it. I therefore went to work with them myself, and cut corn and carried and stacked to relieve the Sisters, all the afternoon. If it's good enough for the Brides of Jesus, it's good enough for me. If God don't punish these Zell [South Dakota] people for their treatment of their Sisters and priests, unless they soon repent and atone for it, I don't know who He will punish.[16]

A few men came to cut corn, about 8 A.M. Went to Panian's and to Jolitz' and ordered beer for them. They will drink it at Jolitz'. It will be cooler, and further from the convent. They finished it before night—thanks to the Sacred Heart, to whom I had recommended it. Paid $2.75 to Jolitz for the keg of beer.

The Sisters are now freed from a long, tedious, weary work, interfering with their spiritual duties. In a decent community they would never have to do such work, but here—without beer—no one will aid them. Those who helped today, have their reward in that beer keg. They deserve no other. Prohibition cranks asked me to attend their meeting tonight. Refused, without ceremony.[17]

The next day, Craft reported that the prohibition meeting the night before was a "fizzle."

Finally, there is this self-deprecating notation: "Today is the 5th anniversary of my ordination. He, he, he! Had I only known then what awaited me—I didn't—the fool's wit comes afterwards."[18]

IX

THE LAND BOOMERS

The discovery of gold and other mineral resources in the Black Hills attracted a large influx of white prospectors and settlers, and in 1888 Congress passed the Dawes Sioux bill, establishing a commission to negotiate the purchase of eleven million acres of Sioux land at a price of fifty cents an acre.

The Dawes bill commission was a complete failure. Its members included two of Craft's old nemeses, Captain Pratt and the Reverend Mr. Cleveland from Rosebud, and Judge John V. Wright of Tennessee. Major McLaughlin acted as a fourth commissioner by virtue of his position as agent.

McLaughlin maintained a neutral position because he felt the price was too low, and Father Craft did his best to stay out of the whole affair. However, as it became increasingly evident that the Indians were not going to sell, an exasperated Pratt wrote to Craft to enlist the support of the Standing Rock missionaries, admonishing that "*every true friend* of theirs should . . . use all honorable and fair means to induce the acceptance of the offer by the Indians."[1]

Pratt invited Craft to attend their councils with the tribes. Craft, though, went to Agent McLaughlin and declined the invitation. He explained that as priests and missionaries, their general orders were to never meddle in government business not connected with their work unless in special cases where they could do great good for the Indians, and this didn't appear to be one of them. Pratt, however, persisted. Acting through

McLaughlin, he demanded that the priest put his refusal of assistance in writing. Craft again declined, protesting that Pratt "has no right to seek our aid—much less demand a written answer, or other formality. If he misrepresents us, the law, and public opinion will protect us, as both are on our side."[2]

From afar, Craft watched through his telescope as the commission began to crumble. Old White Bull spoke, then John Grass, and finally Gall, who announced that this would be their last council. It was time for everyone to go home: "A big yell of approbation followed. Everyone repeated 'we'll go home now,' and yelled in various keys, and all stampeded. Major McLaughlin called them back, and told them he would give them bread before they left, and then they all scattered again. I thought I would have to get Mrs. McLaughlin out, in case the Indians should send a shower of old bones, sticks, etc. at the Commissioners, but they omitted this part of the usual proceedings of the regular stampede."[3]

The commission tarried for another week before traveling to the Cheyenne River and Pine Ridge agencies, where they were met with the same strong opposition to the treaty. In the summer of 1889, however, a new commission returned, led by Maj. Gen. George Crook. The other members of the commission were Charles Foster, past governor of Ohio, and Maj. William Warner of Missouri, commander of the Grand Army of the Republic. The government had increased its offer to $1.25 per acre, but with an artful proviso: land not sold during the first three years of the treaty would be reduced to seventy-five cents an acre, and to fifty cents after five years. The tribes were justly suspicious of these conditions, but this time they were dealing with more formidable government spokesmen. Crook, especially, was a man they had come to respect through past skirmishes. Perhaps of equal moment, though, McLaughlin and Craft gave their full support to the 1889 Sioux bill.

Craft, in fact, took an active part both in the arrangements for the negotiations and in the discussions themselves. In June he wrote to General Crook offering to help the Sioux commission. He registered the letter under the name of F. M. C. Basset, "so Post Masters won't give away my plans."[4] Basset, of course, was the name of his Mohawk paternal grandmother. Crook replied by telegram on 25 July; three days later, the two of them met at Fort Yates. On 31 July, after consulting Crook, Grass, and Mad Bear, Craft wired a lawyer in Bismarck asking if the government could open the reservation without the consent of the Indians. The lawyer, a fellow named Hanitch, replied that the government could take and sell the entire reservation without consulting the Indians. At a council on 1 August, Sitting Bull sent Crawler and a few of his followers to quarrel with Grass about his conduct of the negotiations. Grass, being counseled by Craft and aware of the lawyer's response, announced that he could do nothing and that Sitting Bull had better suggest something if he had any better ideas.[5]

Sitting Bull wandered day and night through the camps, a stentorian voice pleading for resistance to this latest assault by *wašíchus* (white men). Craft, however, aware that the tribes at Cheyenne River and Pine Ridge were already signing the agreement, told them they had been outflanked and that the best they could hope for was to hold off for better terms. "This is like a war council," he told them, "and they should give their views quietly as to fight, escape, or a surrender on good terms."[6]

Craft described the next day's council:

After Crook spoke, the tables were brought out. Grass said he had given his objections, and been clearly answered, and that Indians below were signing, and he also would sign if Crook and other Commissioners would make certain promises. They did so. Antelope and a few others tried to object, but were not listened to. I was sure that [Sitting] Bull or others would make some demonstration, and therefore I had St. Joseph's boys and those they controlled (about 200) ranged along inside the platform, and on the outer edge, so as to be ready, and instructed them not to sign until I gave the order. I kept my opinion back, and spoke of holding off for better terms.

[Sitting] Bull came outside with a mounted party, and just as Grass and Mad Bear rose to sign, they began shouting and running their horses in a circle. A stampede followed, to see what was the matter, but all returned. Grass and Mad Bear then signed, followed by a few other chiefs. [Sitting] Bull then came in, and wanted to speak, but no one would listen to him. He then rushed out calling on all to stampede and follow him. The stampede began. This is just what I wanted. If I could check and turn it in our favor, success was certain. I called to our boys to sign at once as [Sitting] Bull had made a bad break and disgraced the Agency. I went up to the table and touched the pen, and our boys at once began signing. I then went outside the platform and called to the Indians to halt and listen. They at once stopped. I then said what I had

[said] to our boys, and advised all to leave [Sitting] Bull and follow us, as the best thing they could do, and said that after such a break as [Sitting] Bull had made, we could not afford to wait for better terms, but must sign at once.

The Indians remained quiet, and the advance to the tables of St. Joseph's boys on and outside of the platform, had the appearance of a very large crowd anxious to sign, and gave the necessary counter-stampede I wanted, and encouraged many of [Sitting] Bull's party to leave him and sign. He did not return. The signing began at 5 P.M. and lasted till about 8 P.M. In that time 279 signed, and the opposition was completely broken. I sent for [Sitting] Bull to come in and sign, and make amends, but though he promised, he didn't come.[7]

Agent McLaughlin, in his autobiography, tells it all a little differently. The agent writes of a clandestine meeting with John Grass wherein he coached the chief on how to recant his previous opposition to the bill: He "fixed up the speech [Grass] was to make receding from his former position gracefully, thus to bring him the active support of the other chiefs and settle the matter."[8]

McLaughlin also described the hectic scene at the signing: "When the first four signatures were attached . . . Mrs. McLaughlin . . . reported that Sitting Bull and some of his followers were making a demonstration out in front and trouble was imminent. Lieutenant Bull Head was prepared for such an emergency, and rushing with his detachment of police to the front of the building, soon quelled the disturbance, by forcing Sitting Bull and his mounted squad to vacate the grounds."[9]

McLaughlin never referred to Craft in his account of the treaty signing (Craft's name failed to appear *anywhere* in McLaughlin's book), and neither Craft nor McLaughlin was mentioned in General Crook's account of the affair. Crook took full credit for stopping Sitting Bull and made this interesting, pertinent comment about John Grass: Grass, he wrote, "asked questions that showed he thoroughly understood the subject. His remarks had more sense in them than we heard from all the Indians since engaged on this duty."[10]

The world will never know whether it was Craft's counseling, McLaughlin's coaching, or Crook's leadership that brought the 1889 Sioux bill to a successful conclusion for the government, but this much is certain: with those three aligned against them, the Lakotas had no chance of keeping their lands.

X

FORT BERTHOLD

When Father Craft arrived on the Dakota reservations, the Catholic Church had been in the New World for hundreds of years and had yet to conclude that Native Americans were capable of understanding or achieving the sanctity of a religious profession. Many young girls found role models in the sisters who taught at the agency boarding school, but the Benedictines, steeped in centuries of monastic traditions with strong European ties, were at best noncommittal about the idea of Indian priests or nuns. Those on Standing Rock were sympathetic to Craft's efforts, and the nuns were certainly willing to accept an occasional postulant, but all of them, especially Father Stephan, maintained an expectation that "persons of the character and stamp of the Indians" would inevitably fail in their vocations.[1]

As a convert and priest of Indian blood, Craft risked his life and calling to foster religious vocations among the tribes. In addition to the students he sent to the various government and missionary boarding schools, he often recommended young girls to the Benedictine novitiates at Zell (present-day South Dakota) and Avoca, Minnesota. In 1885 Ellen Clark, a half-blood, became the first Sioux to enter the Benedictine order at Zell; she made her profession as Sister Gregory the next year.

This could be perilous work. Craft once entered a tribal camp to retrieve a youngster named Theodora who had expressed an interest in a vocation. The older men opposed the move, and the girl, though she wanted to go, was afraid and told Craft they intended to stab him. Craft laughed at them, but the girl refused to leave until he obtained the permission of Bull Head, the lieutenant of McLaughlin's Indian police force. As they sought out Bull Head, they encountered Sitting Bull. The chief was apparently looking for some way to make amends for bringing those earlier charges against the priest; he intervened immediately, telling the others not to stand in the way of Theodora's removal. Craft, though, refused to even recognize Sitting Bull, a tactic he often used to take a haughty Indian down a peg or two. He spoke through an interpreter, saying that until the chief had the decency to accept blame and ask for pardon publicly, he would not acknowledge his presence. He wanted to forgive him, and "in my heart, I really *do* forgive him; but my position demands a full public reparation, and I really have no right to let it go, and he ought to be man enough to do it."[2]

The insult to the priesthood apparently transcended the personal attack on Craft. Theodora's last name was Pi'íc'iyawį, and like several of Craft's postulants, she was very ill. When Sitting Bull approved her release from the camp, Craft paid Bull Head five dollars to arrange for a horse and wagon to transport her to the mission. The priest administered the last rites and covered Theodora with his raincoat to protect her from a cold, persistent rain. Bull Head, in turn, hired Šiná lúta to bring Theodora in. He took two days to do it, wearing Craft's raincoat all the way.

Theodora Pi'íc'iyawį, the first full-blood Sioux to make her perpetual vows, did so as Sister Mary Gertrude of the Sacred Heart, O.S.B., on 21 May 1889. As Father Craft began the ceremonies of investiture, a terrible windstorm arose, which ceased abruptly after her vows. The priest saw this as a sign of the vanquishment of Satan and the triumph of the Sacred Heart.[3] Theodora died of consumption on Friday, 14 June 1889, and was buried the next day.

Unable to count on temporal support for his efforts to encourage Indian vocations, the priest increasingly relied on spiritual support—the intercession of the souls of the departed. Twelve-year-old Cunegunda, a daughter of Black Bear, whose death inspired Craft's desperate sacrifice, was another who was enlisted in the cause.

Two of the priest's healthier candidates for the Benedictine sisterhood were Josephine Crowfeather and Annie Gaudreau. Josephine, whom he often called Josie, was the young lady who had come to his defense in the Sitting Bull affair. He paid their dowry to enter the novitiate, and as they boarded the train on 22 June 1888, he gave a parting blessing: "'Say to your sister, Thou hast obtained mercy.' God grant them final perseverance, and to me, through their prayers, the same, and eternal happiness with them in heaven."[4]

Early in August, Craft sponsored another half-blood, Emma Halsey. For a few days he was warmed by the thought of having successfully placed three postulants at the Benedictine novitiate. His euphoria vanished, however, when visiting sisters from Zell summoned him to St. Scholastica's. Nearing the school, he was tortured by a terrible presentiment that Josephine was with them.

His worst fears were realized. Josephine had written to the bishop and mother superior claiming she never really wanted to go the convent, but that Father Craft and Sister Gertrude had "fooled" her. She used the word *hnayan*, which they translated "to fool" rather than "to coax." They also reported that she was "afraid of Father Craft," when what she meant was that she was afraid he would be disappointed by her return. She was right about that. "If she is lost," he wrote, "there is no hope for me."[5]

The bishop instructed Sister Gertrude to return Josephine to her father, but Craft intervened again. It was the first sign of a major breach between Craft and his superiors. "I can never love or trust a Shepard who casts, and even drives, his sheep to the wolves. *That* one," he averred of Josephine, "I am determined to save, and will spare no effort to do it."[6]

He caught the next train to Chicago, where he met Bishop Marty and Father Stephan, who greeted him with the news that he was to be transferred from the bishop's jurisdiction to the Bureau of Catholic Indian Missions. In that capacity they wanted him to establish a mission among the Mandans, Gros Ventres, and Arikarees on Fort Berthold Reservation, about 150 miles northwest of Fort Yates. Stephan, director of the Bureau of Catholic Indian Missions, was to become his superior.

Craft refused absolutely. Until Josie was safe in her vocation, his work on Standing Rock remained unfinished. He presented his case on behalf of Josephine to a divided audience. Marty finally agreed that she could be a postulant at Fort Yates or Avoca, Minnesota, whichever she preferred; Stephan summarily dismissed the idea that any Indian could sustain a vocation. The bishop won out, though, and with that assurance, Craft guardedly accepted the new assignment.

Boarding the night train from Chicago at 11:30 on 8 September, he reached St. Paul the next afternoon and caught the 4:30 train to Bismarck, where he arrived at 8:00 on the morning of 9 September. He stayed at the hospital in Bismarck, celebrating mass at 6:30 the next morning. A day-long stage ride brought him to Winona, across the river from Fort Yates, at 6:00. He crossed the Missouri River and reached the agency about 8:00 in the evening. Josie was the first to greet him.

Major McLaughlin, who confirmed that he was to take Josephine and four other girls to St. Francis Xavier Academy at Avoca, Minnesota, met him too. Claudia Crowfeather, Josie's sister, also wanted to go; Craft obtained the agent's consent by offering to pay for her transportation. On Wednesday, 12 September, Father Craft recrossed the Missouri with a half-dozen postulants for the Benedictine novitiate. Thanks to the priest's intimidating manner, the trip was uneventful. However, he often had to remind inquisitive passengers that the girls must be treated with respect, and when they saw him "determined to punish insolent curiosity, they were quite civil."[7]

Arriving in Avoca on Saturday, 12 September, Craft spent the next several days ensuring that Josephine would be comfortable and safe in her new surroundings. He even took the girls sailing on a nearby lake. As he said mass on 24 September, the Feast of Our Lady of Mercy, he "seemed to hear—or rather feel—a voice speaking from the tabernacle the words of the text, 'Say to your sister, Thou hast obtained mercy.'"[8]

The priest then embarked on a postal crusade designed to bolster Josie's resolve to persevere in her vocation. He sent her a fifteen-decade rosary, touched by his own beads to make it a relic of European shrines, and ordered a copy of the *Blessed Ones of 1888,* which included a biography of Blessed Sister Josephine Mary of Saint Agnes, whose life and trials he felt resembled Josie's. Sister Josephine was the daughter of pious and humble peasants who lived in the small village of Beniganim, near Valencia, Spain. She entered the Discalced Augustinian order in 1644. Almost two centuries after her death in 1696, Pope Leo XIII had just formally beatified the heroic nature of a life devoted to God; a life known for its prophecies and spiritual insights.[9] Sister Josephine Mary of Saint Agnes stood at the threshold of sainthood:

I packed up and sent Josie's book, with letter referring to Bl. Sister Josephine Mary's call, and her answer to the Holy Infant, and suggesting that Josie, as she is called in the same way, should answer as her holy patron did, especially when Our Lord gives her the holy kiss of peace and love in Holy Communion, and also before the Blessed Sacrament.

—I wrote on the fly leaf.

> *The Sacred Heart of Jesus*
> Through his lieutenant
> Wanbli-cinca-aglahpaya[10]
> Sends this token of His holy love
> To her whom He has chosen
> First of the nation,
> *Josephine Mary of the Sacred Heart.*

And also crossed the names of Josie and her patron, as I do our initials, and wrote, in diamond form, on the cross, "The Heart of the Holy Child Jesus," "Calls you, sister, as He called her." "May He give you grace, sister," "To answer Him like her."[11]

With Josie safely sheltered at Avoca, Craft left for Fort Berthold to arrange a council meeting with the three tribes. These were a more docile people than the Standing Rock Sioux, more like those on Rosebud. Since the days of DeSmet they too had sought Catholic priests, and once again Francis M. Craft would be the first to answer their call.

Crow Heart, Sitting Bear, Bad Gun, and Good Bear spoke for the tribes as they selected a site for the mission on the Little Missouri Bottom. Craft drove a stake to mark the location, close to timber, with a service road to the river, a good well at the district farmer's house, and plenty of lignite coal in nearby hills.

The advance work done, he returned to Fort Yates for the winter months, using the time to promote his own plan for the mission at Fort Berthold. He wanted the assignment permanently, with two or three Benedictine sisters, and he wanted Josephine and the other Indian and mixed-blood novices to make their novitiate under his direction. He offered the bishop his own salary for the sisters' support; he would subsist on mass intentions.[12]

For the present, Bishop Marty preferred to staff the new mission with Belgian Benedictines, but if that proved impractical, he tentatively agreed to Craft's proposal. In April, however, Marty committed to the concept of Indian sisters; he adopted Annie and Cecilia Gaudreau as his personal financial responsibility and provided Craft with a Benedictine constitution and ceremonial to guide him in establishing rules and rites for the new congregation.[13] Of course only a bishop has canonical authority to formally invest nuns or priests, but given the dire circumstances, that technicality did not deter Father Craft, especially in those cases where death was imminent.

On Easter Sunday, Josephine Crowfeather made her profession as a Benedictine postulant. Craft shook hands with her and congratulated her before the congregation just as, two years before, she had supported him when no one else came forward: "Thanks be to the Sacred Heart of Jesus. May He grant her final perseverance in her holy vocation and to me grace to perfect my sacrifice for her, and may He establish firmly the religious vocations of *all* Indian and mixed-blood aspirants, and give them abundant grace, and final perseverance."[14]

The story was carried in Catholic newspapers throughout the Midwest and East. Typical was the account in the *Dakota Catholic,* which reported that the "ceremony was an impressive one, not only for the whites present, but also for the members of her tribe upon whom this event is likely to produce a marked religious effect."[15]

Tangible success such as that demonstrated by Josephine's religious profession at Avoca was a rare experience for Craft. His pious efforts were as likely to manifest themselves in strange and wondrous ways. In the case of this episode recorded that same summer, some might even say *miraculous* ways:

Last night I put out the candle, and laid down dressed, and went to sleep saying my beads. I woke suddenly; the room was lighted, and a Sister stood by the head of the bed. I recognized Rev. Sister Mary Christina, O.S.B.,[16] my sister, now dying at Zell. I spoke to her, and she answered me, and then knelt at the side of the bed and said in English "Brother, please wash my face." She seemed pale and worn, and her face seemed stained as if with paint or medicine. Something seemed to tell me to give her my blessing and I did so. I got a wet towel and washed her face. She seemed much better and happier, and rose, saying: "Thank you, brother, I feel so much better. I feel quite well. I must go now. Good bye."

She disappeared, and the room was dark again. I looked for my beads, and could not find them. This morning the towel was wet. If it was a dream it was a strange one. I seemed to wake and see her near me. When she disappeared, I seemed not to wake, but to be still awake, and looked for my beads. Perhaps she wants me to pray for her. I at once wrote for her an intention in the list of the League, and remembered her at mass today. May the S[acred] Heart aid her. . . .

. . . Sent love and best regards to my sister, Rev. Sister Mary Christina, O.S.B., and offered to take her purgatory for her. If she does not get the message on earth, she will know it and, I hope, avail herself of it when free from the body. . . .

Telegram from Rev. Sr. Hildegarde. My dear sister in the Sacred Heart, Rev. Sister Mary Christina, O.S.B. passed to eternal rest on August 20th at 11:30 A.M. on the Feast of St. Bernard, within the Octave of the Assumption, as she desired. R.I.P. . . .

Said mass for my sister, Rev. Sister Mary Christina, O.S.B. at 6:30 A.M. As she was to be buried yesterday, the mass was "in die depositionis."[17] I begged a mass from the other Fathers, so Sister had four masses today. . . .

. . . We returned, bringing back Mr. Wm. Halsey whom we met on the way. He was much edified by the novices at Zell. Their life was, he says, a new revelation to him. He says he never saw one die as holily and happily as Sister. In dying, our dead sister Rev. Sister Mary Gertrude of the Sacred Heart, O.S.B. (Theodora Pi'íc'iyawį) was with her, and Jesus seemed to come to her from the crucifix. . . .

I found my beads. Mr. Halsey says they are the same as those sister used when dying. The night I saw her, he was with her. . . . I wonder if Sister took my beads and returned them.[18]

These temporal and spiritual triumphs, however, had no effect on the Fort Berthold Indians. When Craft returned to the Little Missouri Bottom the next spring, he found his stake gone and the land sold—to the Congregationalists. Undaunted, he selected another site at a place called Elbowoods, struck another agreement with the tribes, and caught the train to St. Paul to meet with Father Stephan. At breakfast, Stephan berated him for having been expelled from Rosebud six years earlier, warned him that the Bureau could not afford to defend a priest if the Indian Department required his removal, and adamantly opposed the concept of Indian sisters. Craft gave him "a sharp setting down," and after reaching an uneasy truce they left together to select builders and lumber suppliers.[19]

XI

A SPECIAL ENVOY

Craft returned to Sacred Heart Mission at Elbowoods in the fall of 1889. The building neared completion, but he was concerned about the silence that had followed Stephan's attack in Chicago that past summer. He desperately needed supplies, and winter was setting in. There was a box of schoolbooks, but no money for fuel or stoves and no school furniture, and what building materials remained were in short supply. Coal would soon be frozen in the ground. In November the Bureau of Catholic Indian Missions told him that the benefactor of the mission, Katharine Drexel, would not provide equipment or operating costs. Moreover, she wanted the school to be named St. Edward's, after a member of the Drexel family.[1] Craft replied that they could name the school whatever they pleased, "but the mission of the Ree, Gros Ventre, and Mandan tribes, which I founded, I have named Sacred Heart Mission.[2]

Katharine Drexel, a wealthy Philadelphia heiress and philanthropist, had provided $12,000 toward the construction costs. Both Bishop Marty and Father Stephan relied heavily on her generous financial support. They first visited her in 1885, seeking money for St. Francis Mission on Rosebud Reservation, where Father Craft had been expelled only a year before. At the request of the two ecclesiastics, Katharine Drexel and her sisters, Elizabeth and Louise, traveled to Dakota Territory to learn firsthand the plight of the Sioux. During fall 1887 the three young women visited St. Francis Mission at Rosebud and Immaculate Conception Mission at Stephan (now in South Dakota and named after their host), before journeying on to St.

Paul, where they met Bishop John Ireland. The next year they returned to Indian Country, visiting other missions they had financed in Wisconsin and Minnesota.[3]

In May 1889 Katharine Drexel entered the novitiate of the Sisters of Mercy in Pittsburgh, Pennsylvania. It satisfied her immediate religious needs, but still she searched for a way to connect more directly with the country's struggling minorities in her personal ministry. Even as Craft was constructing St. Edward's School, Father Stephan and Miss Drexel began to lay the foundations for her own order of religious women, to be named the Sisters of the Blessed Sacrament. Early in 1891, Bishop Patrick J. Ryan of Philadelphia suggested that the words "for Indians and Colored People," be added to the title.[4]

Long before the official change of the name, though, rumors circulated concerning the proposed transfer of sisters from other orders into Katharine Drexel's community. Although it is clear from the start that the new congregation's purpose was to serve Indians and other minorities, there is no indication that it planned to recruit postulants from those groups. Stephan, of course, would have opposed such a move, and in fact the next attempt to establish an order of Native American sisters would not occur until the 1920s.[5]

Still, the news was more than enough to worry a besieged and paranoid priest at Fort Berthold. Craft immediately viewed the new order as a threat to his own plans. Miss Drexel had the money and Stephan had the administrative leverage. Together they were formidable competitors: "Indications lead me to fear that some mischief may be plotted against Sr. Josephine. I hear that F. Stephan and Miss Drexel intend to draw from other Orders to fill theirs, and such a thing would be ruinous to vocations, and I don't intend to allow it in my sister's case. Should there be a question of her leaving the O.S.B.—which God forbid—then my authority as her guardian and protector would be again in force. I hope there is no truth in the report."[6]

Craft received assurances from Bishop Marty that his wishes regarding Josie's vocation as a Benedictine would be respected. To confirm it he wrote to Mother Gertrude, enclosing a note for $200 at 12 percent annual interest for Sister Josephine's dowry.[7] Still worried about Stephan and Drexel, however, he wrote Father George L. Willard at the Bureau of Catholic Indian Missions, offering to help them secure candidates for their new order if they in turn would leave his alone.[8]

In November Craft advised Father George L. Willard that the construction of the school building was completed and that the workmen were about to leave. There was some painting to be finished, but the contractor wanted to put it off until spring.

The priest was dismayed by the seemingly wretched planning of his mission. Why would Miss Drexel contribute $12,000 to build a schoolhouse yet not be willing to pay for desks? Why hadn't Bishop Marty told him in the fall that operating costs would not be forthcoming? Why hadn't the Bureau already contracted with the Department of Indian Affairs for the education of students?

Craft's mission was suddenly entangled in a disastrous mix of church and state politics. A convergence of misfortunes doomed it as surely as the rising waters of the Garrison Dam would wash away its traces in the 1950s. Thomas J. Morgan, enthusiastically backed by Major McLaughlin and by Herbert Welsh of the Indian Rights Association, had just been appointed commissioner of Indian Affairs. Morgan, a staunch advocate of the separation of church and state, refused to extend contracts to any new church schools and called instead for severe cutbacks in existing ones. Father Stephan, desperately trying to salvage the best of a bad situation and wary of Craft's past record, flatly refused to support any mission that employed him.[9] Bishop Marty was sympathetic to Craft's plight but was no longer his superior. North and South Dakota had just reached statehood and, concurrently, the geography of the Catholic diocese was split as well. Bishop John Shanley, Marty's successor and Craft's new ordinary, was far too busy establishing a new diocese in Jamestown, North Dakota, to be concerned about a new mission at Fort Berthold. The contractor need not have hurried to finish painting the building. St. Edward's School would not open for another twenty-one years.

With no apparent prospects for financial support, Craft decided to generate his own funds for Sacred Heart Mission. He left Fort Berthold in mid-December 1889 and spent the next three months gathering material and Indian memorabilia for a series of lectures in the East. Both Bishop Marty and Bishop Shanley gave their blessings to his travels. He took a stage to Bismarck, stopping overnight at a hotel in Washburn, North Dakota. At dinner, he put a dime in the hand of an infant asleep in a cradle, "in honor of the Holy Infant." From Bismarck, the train took him through Jamestown, North Dakota, down to Yankton, South Dakota, with a stop at Zell, South Dakota, and a side trip to Avoca, Minnesota, to check on his postulants. Between Oakes and Redfield, South Dakota, an obstreperous scoundrel had the temerity to address him in obscene terms. Craft shut him up by threatening to throw him through the train window. Then it was on to Valentine, Nebraska, via Sioux Falls, and finally to Rosebud Reservation. He secured photographs of Spotted Tail and the slain chief's family; collected beadwork, moccasins, and other Native artifacts; and enjoyed several reunions with his adopted family members. He even encountered Spotted Tail's assassin, Crow Dog, and gave him a verbal "blasting for killing my father."[10] In Sioux Falls he corrected proofs for a Sioux prayer book and prepared several articles for publication in the eastern press.

Disillusioned by the lack of support his mission had received, he found solace in recently published attacks on Father Damien, the Leper of Molokai. Damien had devoted his life to the care of lepers in the Hawaiian Islands. After his death in 1889, malicious rumors of the heroic priest's alleged moral debasement were rampant in the anti-Catholic press. The charges against Damien were proved groundless and contrived, although he did have disagreements with his superiors and fellow priests, causing Craft to note: "I see the preachers are attacking the character of F[ather] Damien. 'Wonder not if the world hate you.' If we do our duty the world will attack us, and the attack will be in proportion to our merit before God."[11]

Bemoaning that his "one bitter regret was that I ever began this work,"[12] Craft was driven by a passionate determination that Josephine Crowfeather would prevail in her vocation. Once that victory was ensured, he vowed that his "work *must* be among the poor, and I will go where it will be undisturbed by church factions and worldly priests, and where it will soonest be happily ended. Africa seems the best field—if Lavigerie lives until I am ready to go.[13] He offers his priests 'nothing but martyrdom,' and I desire nothing else."[14]

Craft left Rosebud on 26 March 1890, traveling by train from Valentine, Nebraska, to Chicago, where he bought a ticket on the Wabash, Grand Trunk, and West Shore Railroad to Poughkeepsie, New York. He detrained, however, at Fultonville, New York, at 6:00 P.M. on 1 April. The next morning he hired a buggy and driver to take him to nearby Auriesville, site of the Shrine of Our Lady of Martyrs. He prayed for the vocations of Josephine and the others, taking red willow cuttings from bushes near the shrine of Kateri Tekakwitha.[15] Kateri (Catharine) was a seventeenth-century Mohawk Indian maiden revered for her lifelong pursuit of a religious vocation in the face of rejection by both family and church. Born in Auriesville in 1656, she fled as a young girl to the Jesuit community at Caughnawaga on the St. Lawrence River in Canada, seeking fulfillment of her dream. Like Father Stephan, the Jesuits were unprepared to accept the notion of Indian sisters.[16]

That evening Craft wrote each of his postulants a letter, enclosing a piece of the red willow. Later that month he received a response from Sister Mary Catharine, O.S.B., telling him she had made her sacred vows at Yankton, South Dakota, on 21 April. "Thanks be to the Sacred Heart of Jesus," he wrote. "Say to your sister, 'Thou hast obtained mercy.'"[17]

Josie—daughter of Joseph Crowfeather, sister of Francis Craft—had taken the name Catharine as a Benedictine religious. A bond had been forged across centuries, continents, and cultures, joining Blessed Sister Josephine Mary, a native of Beniganim, Spain; Blessed Kateri Tekakwitha, a Mohawk of New York and Canada;[18] and Sister Mary Catharine, O.S.B., a Lakota Sioux. Father Craft was the architect who brought it all together.

Boarding another train to Poughkeepsie, he spent a few days sharpening his lecture theme, then did the same in Brooklyn, where he also drafted articles for the *Poor Souls Advocate* and other publications. On 10 May he called on Bishop John Laughlin of Brooklyn, who treated him rudely and refused to let him solicit funds in his diocese. Father Stephan had gotten there before him.

Stung by this rejection, Craft visited Patrick Ford, the firebrand editor of the *Irish World,* a New York newspaper Ford had founded in 1870. Another Ford, Austin, was editor of the *New York Freeman's Journal and Catholic Register.* Through these two partisan channels, the priest presented his views on Indian acculturation, engaging in what would become a two-year battle of words with Commissioner Morgan.

The commissioner had commanded the Fourteenth United States Colored Infantry in the Civil War. He had been ordained a Baptist minister in 1869, and his résumé included considerable experience as an educator in the frontier West. His nomination, along with Methodist clergyman Daniel Dorchester, as superintendent of Indian schools was bitterly contested in Congress by Father Stephan and the Catholic press.[19] Stephan's attacks on Morgan were strident, inflammatory, and relentless. In the end they were also unsuccessful. Morgan, however, was unaware of just how strident, inflammatory, and relentless the rhetoric was about to get.

Craft had no choice. He charged into the very middle of the dispute, which left him with Stephan on one flank and Morgan on the other. His one hope was to penetrate beyond the reach of either, to the protection and understanding of average American citizens who, he felt, were sure to be appalled by the dirty politics, fraud, and graft so prevalent on the reservations.

He suggested to Bishop Marty that detectives be employed to visit all agencies, a recommendation that was quickly dismissed as just another symptom of Craft's advancing paranoia. To the priest, though, it was a straightforward military strategy: eliminate the enemy.

One of the first of Craft's articles to appear in the press was a self-interview published in the *Freeman's Journal*. In it the priest provided a brief account of the Indians' despair on the reservations and proposed that the federal government "do away with the Indian Department, with all its officials and useless expenses, and place the Indians under the care of the War Department."[20] He followed this with a protracted essay in the *Irish World* on the subject of Catholic missions in America, over the anonymous byline "A Catholic Indian Missionary." It was classic Craft, from his unique version of Indian history to the sketches of Spotted Tail, Sister Mary Catharine, and Bishop Marty that accompanied it. He wrote of the disappearance of almost an entire race and the repeopling of the continent by Europeans, referring by name to fifty-eight tribes from coast to coast:

These numerous tribes have almost entirely disappeared. In the territory claimed by the United States less than three hundred thousand now remain. What has become of them? Europeans, ignorant of the former and our later policy toward the Indians, very naturally suppose that, like the former barbarians of Europe, they still exist, no longer as savages, but as a civilized people, or have mingled with the white settlers of the country. We know too well that this is not the case. Though we might well desire to forget facts disgraceful to us, history, with cold, truthful, merciless justice, brings them before us, and makes us see that all "Indian Policy" has always been a policy of extermination, and it remains so today. Government civilization of the remnant of the tribes is merely an excuse for the existence of an Indian Department, with its officials and salaries, that politicians and not Indians may live.[21]

Reports on the relative success of Father Craft's lecture tour are mixed and puzzling. A journal entry on 21 April 1890 states that donations from a

Poughkeepsie, New York, audience totaled $62.68. Bishop Shanley wrote in January 1891 that Craft had "failed signally. During his eight month sojourn in and around the populous Eastern cities he succeeded in collecting $80.00 for missionary purposes."[22]

After the first four months of Craft's eastern tour, however, Father Stephan reported to Bishop Shanley, through Secretary Charles S. Lusk of the Bureau of Catholic Indian Missions, that Father Craft had collected as much as $7,000 or $8,000 for the mission and school at Fort Berthold, suggesting that it "would be well for you to look pretty closely into this matter.[23]

Stephan's allegation has a foreboding edge to it. Surely Craft's potential missionary bounty was severely restricted when the bishop of the Brooklyn diocese rejected his request to solicit funds—probably at the recommendation of Stephan himself. To amass $7,500 over a four-month period, assuming an average collection of $75, would have required that Craft conduct one hundred separate lectures—about one per day—at churches outside the populous Brooklyn area. Stephan's apparent attempt to undermine Craft's credibility with the bishop was matched by his reaction to the anonymous article in the *Irish World*. Easily recognizing it as Craft's work, Stephan wrote to Ford's editor asking him to refrain from giving the subject any further publicity until he (Stephan) had a chance to "throw such additional light on the subject as will, perhaps, induce him [Ford] to change his views."[24]

With his access to the press temporarily stymied, Craft collaborated with James R. O'Beirne to prohibit exploitative display of Indians in Wild West shows. A brigadier general who had won a Medal of Honor in the Civil War, O'Beirne, with powerful political and military connections, was in charge of the United States Department of Immigration's New York office. When two despondent Sioux arrived at the Barge office after a transoceanic trip from Dr. W. F. Carver's Wild West show in Germany, with no money and no clothes except those on their backs, Craft and O'Beirne arranged for their transport back to Pine Ridge Agency. Their protests to the Interior Department eventually ended the outrageous practice of exhibiting Indians.[25]

Father Stephan then called Craft to Washington DC in yet another attempt to diminish the priest's growing popularity with the eastern establishment. Desperate to get him out of the public eye, he proposed that the priest start another mission, this one among the Navaho Indians in New

Mexico and Arizona. Craft responded predictably. On letterhead of the Bureau of Catholic Indian Missions, he set out his own conditions. First, "the safety of the Indian Sisters must be assured." He knew that would end it right there, but he continued: Second, "my position must be so fixed that I cannot be crowded out by incoming [Protestant] missionaries." Third, "my methods in Indian work must be thoroughly understood and approved by recognized Church authorities, the same as in the case of De Nobili." Fourth, he insisted on "such an official position as will command the respect and silence the opposition of those who respect nothing but dignities." Fifth, "Church authorities must not be induced by the enemies of Christianity and civilization to do anything against me or my work, either by omission or commission." If these conditions were met, he guaranteed the success of the mission "within three years after I have mastered the language—which will take about six months. If [these conditions are] not done, let who will take the mission, for *I will not.*"[26]

But Craft also had an unstated reason for rejecting Stephan's gambit. He was already on another mission, initiated by General O'Beirne. For his trip to the capital, the general had provided Craft with a letter of introduction to Secretary of War Redfield Proctor, suggesting that the priest be sent "on a quasi-official . . . confidential mission, under the secret service of the War Department" to quiet a resurgence of Indian unrest on the Dakota reservations.[27]

Early in December 1890, Craft met with Secretary Proctor and Secretary of Interior John W. Noble.[28] The subject of these discussions was the "Messiah craze," the Ghost Dance that caused tumultuous and frenzied reactions among the Plains tribes. Panic-stricken settlers across the Dakotas called for federal troops to quiet the Indians as thousands of them danced to a staccato rhythm reminiscent of Frosted's drumbeat two years before.

After these audiences with senior government officials, Craft returned to Pine Ridge Agency, arriving at Holy Rosary Mission on 10 December 1890. Most of the dancers were on Pine Ridge Reservation, in an almost inaccessible part of the Cuny Table plateau called the Stronghold, deep in the Badlands northwest of the agency. Sporadic dances were occurring throughout the Sioux reservations, however. Craft first saw the dance performed in the Rosebud Indian camp on the evening of 14 December. "He found it to be all right, quite catholic and even edifying."[29]

In desperation, the Sioux, along with many other tribes, had turned to Wovoka's new religion, which promised the final triumph of traditional

Indian ways over the ravages of the white man's civilization. The Ghost Dance was its outward sign, a celebration of its covenant, a petition to Wakhą́ Thą́ka for its fulfillment. The trances and visions of the participants have been compared to the agony of Joan of Arc and to events described in both the Old and New Testaments as well as the Koran, and the dancers have been likened to Quakers, Shakers, and Kentucky revivalists.[30] Father Craft's observation is not at all surprising.

Federal troops had been dispatched in November, and among their concerns was whether Sitting Bull, from his cabin on Grand River, would support the dancers or, worse yet, go to Pine Ridge himself. Agent McLaughlin, jealous of his own authority on Standing Rock, ordered his police to arrest the chief on the morning of 15 December. Sitting Bull, Lt. Bull Head, and several others died in the bloody clash that followed.

Reports of the death of the most notorious and publicized Indian in history had a huge effect on people back East. General O'Beirne wrote to Craft on 17 December expressing concern that the killing of Sitting Bull would lead to a "genuine, full-fledged Indian War." He asked the priest to send written accounts, "about a column for each letter, sending the correspondence . . . in such way they will not know it along the stations of the mail route, and closed with sealing wax; or, if you think better, put them under cover to me to be forwarded to the Herald."[31]

On 20 December Father Craft, now functioning as a missionary, a sub rosa news correspondent, and a quasi-government peace envoy, sent off a dispatch that not only blamed McLaughlin for Sitting Bull's death but included the following statement published in the *Freeman's Journal:*

> Just as the tree can be traced from its smallest branches to its root, just so all this Indian trouble can be traced through all its phases to its true cause, *starvation, abject misery, and despair,* the cause of which is the outrageous conduct of the Indian Department for many years, culminating in the later blunders and cruelties of the present Commissioner Morgan. You can see now how the prophecies of the FREEMAN'S JOURNAL have been verified. If the army had charge this never could have happened, and if it could be kept now in charge, the Indians will have some hope of life and civilization.[32]

By the time this article appeared in the New York press on 3 January 1891, it was subordinate to the *Freeman's Journal's* erroneous lead story on that day: the obituary of Father Craft.

XII

WOUNDED KNEE

After the death of Sitting Bull, several hundred skittish Standing Rock Hunkpapas fled toward Cheyenne River Reservation. Concerned that they might join the dancers in the Stronghold, Agent James McLaughlin's envoys managed to coax most of them back to Standing Rock. About a hundred continued south, intending to join up with Big Foot, chief of the Miniconjous, who was on his way to Pine Ridge Agency with a band of some 350 men, women, and children.

On Sunday, 28 December, Craft learned that Big Foot's band had been intercepted and was camped on Wounded Knee Creek, where Col. James W. Forsyth, commander of the famous Seventh Cavalry, planned to disarm them. Gen. John R. Brooke, directing the operation from Pine Ridge Agency, was well aware of the favorable influence any Black Robe would have over restless Indians. Earlier that month he had sent Father John Jutz, the Jesuit missionary at Holy Rosary Mission, to negotiate with Two Strike and others in the Stronghold. Jutz brought the Sicangu chief back to the agency for a council with Brooke, and by mid-December almost a thousand of his people had come in peaceably. Brooke hoped Father Craft could be similarly persuasive in the disarming of Big Foot's band.

In company with Colonel Forsyth, some soldiers, and a few civilian spectators, Craft arrived at Wounded Knee near midnight on 28 December. In the morning he circulated among the Indians as Forsyth explained the procedure for disarming. The colonel had assembled the male Indians on an expanse of ground between the military camp and the Indian camp.

The Indian camp formed a loose crescent on the south, with the military tents in tight formation opposite them. On the east flank, Forsyth stationed a troop of mounted cavalry; between the Indians and their camp he put B and K troops, dismounted. Across the rear of the Indian camp was a line of dismounted troops, behind them a row of Taylor's Indian scouts, and beyond them another rank of mounted cavalry. Cemetery Hill, two hundred yards to the west, afforded a commanding view of the whole scene; there, following standard deployment procedures, he placed a battery of four Hotchkiss guns. More mounted troops on either side of the battery closed off the perimeter. Forsyth's total command numbered approximately 500 men, armed with single-shot Remington rifles; some had Colt revolvers.

These were close quarters for such an assemblage—maybe one hundred yards across, a little less between the two camps. Boxed in this arena were about 120 Indian men; 230 of their women and children remained in camp.

This was the setting for what today is almost universally considered a massacre; reckless and outrageous slaughter of unarmed Indian men, women, and children by vengeful white troops of the Seventh Cavalry. What happened there has been so revised, rewritten, and distorted in the retelling that recent accounts suggest Big Foot's Miniconjous stood helpless and bewildered as they were given the last rites by an unnamed Black Robe. These latest versions imply that the command to fire was withheld until after the priest had administered this symbolic version of extreme unction, the last sacrament of the Catholic Church, to the assembled Indians.

Father Craft, always his own best defense, provided detailed eyewitness accounts of the battle. One such report was in a deposition submitted to the federal commission charged with investigating the tragic event.[1] Others were in letters to James E. Kelly, an artist friend who converted Craft's verbal descriptions into sketches.[2]

Father Craft first put to rest any thought that Big Foot's band of Indians was simply a displaced group of peaceable innocents. "[These] . . . Indians with whom I was speaking were the worst element of their Agency, whose camp had for years been the rendezvous of all the worst characters on the Sioux Reservation," he wrote.

About 8:30 in the morning, Colonel Forsyth spoke through an interpreter, "kindly and pleasantly," according to the priest, as he explained the necessity of the Indians' surrendering their guns. Big Foot and others denied there were any weapons, saying all their guns had been burned up. Forsyth, though, reminded them that only the day before every man had been seen to have at least one firearm. The Indians were then directed to return to their camp, a few at a time, to retrieve any weapons. Again they denied having any. Forsyth then sent troopers into the Indian camp to search for and collect any guns, but they returned with very few.

A medicine man began praying and singing, circling around the Indians, preparing them for death and invoking sacred protection from the white man's bullets. At the same time, a soldier noticed guns under the Indians' blankets. The Indians were then directed to come forward, one by one, to open their blankets and lay down their arms.

Fifteen or twenty guns had been collected when a trooper cried out, "Look out, look at that" as he caught a glimpse of rifles hidden beneath the Indians' robes. Craft tried to reassure them, but few listened to him. Nervous laughter broke out from both sides. Forsyth lightheartedly tried to beguile the Indians as he asked them again to come forward one by one and surrender the guns, "saying he would not take them by force if he had to wait ten years."

Craft circulated among the Indians, passing out cigarettes to calm them. Suddenly several threw aside their blankets, raised their guns, and leveled them at the lines of B and K troops. Most had twelve-shot Winchester repeating rifles. The priest ran along the Indians' lines, urging them to stop. Lt. W. W. Robinson Jr. also rode up from behind the Indians to talk to them. There was still a chance to avoid bloodshed as the Indians laughed and began to lower their rifles, when a deaf brave named Black Fox, unable to comprehend all that was happening, fired off a round.

"The next second," wrote Craft, "the Indians . . . poured volley after volley into the lines of B and K Troops, their fire also mowing down like grass the crowd of their own women and children who stood looking on behind the soldiers. . . . The soldiers did not fire until they were actually compelled to, and after the Indians had fired many shots."

A major reason for the military's delayed response was that their ill-conceived formation had placed their comrades in their line of fire. If Wounded Knee was a massacre, it surely did not begin with that intent in mind.

The Indians broke into small parties, charging back and forth, firing as they ran, desperately trying to breach the ranks of soldiers that surrounded them. Some broke through toward the south, and as they passed the Indian camp many of the women and children ran out with them. The Hotchkiss battery opened up on them as they crossed the agency road. It was impossible, said Craft, for the Hotchkiss artillerymen to distinguish between males, who were still firing backward as they ran, and the women and children who joined them. Others sought the protection of a ravine, from which they continued their lethal assault. In reply, the battery raked the ravine with explosive shells, almost one per second.

Scouts called to the women and children to lie down, but few obeyed, and the soldiers sought to move them from harm's way to the cavalry camp. "Many soldiers were shot down doing this," wrote Craft. As the battle ended, a few Indians who had reached the Indian camp resumed firing. An interpreter who went to stop them was fired on, prompting another artillery barrage, but by then most of the women and children had already left or had been removed from the camp.

The clattering enfilade filled the air with swirling clouds of noxious smoke as Father Craft exhorted several Indians to lie flat. One grabbed his long winter overcoat, causing the priest to literally drag the man around with him. A mortally wounded soldier named James E. Kelley staggered into them, blood pumping from his wounds. Craft gave the young man absolution as his hands slipped from the priest's shoulders. Exploding shrapnel and shot knocked them to the ground. As the Indian tried to help Craft to his feet, adversaries from both sides misread the scene as an assault. Soldiers assumed that Indian had killed Kelley and was attacking Craft, and that is exactly what the Indians thought too. Craft pushed the Indian behind him, shielding him from soldiers who raised their rifles to fire, as another Indian named Tantanyan Kuetpi (Aimed at him)[3] ran by, plunging a long, broad-bladed knife into the priest's back. It entered under his right shoulder blade near the spine and passed through his lungs to the upper part of his breast. Almost immediately, a metal fragment hit near the same laceration. He felt more shock than pain, later saying that there was less bleeding than he would expect from such a wound, and that he

could scarcely distinguish what pierced the body from what merely grazed and tore the clothes. . . . If the soldiers had been the bloodthirsty, excited savages they have been falsely described, I never could have managed to save that Indian, as I must admit his helping me to rise just then and just as he did, made it look very much as if he had killed Kelly and then grappled me—at

least it must have seemed so to that party of soldiers, who just came up return-
ing from another part of the field, and had not seen the beginning of the affair.
They all behaved well through the fight, and would not have lost half as many
as they did if they had tried to kill instead of trying to save the Indians—even
the fighting men.[4]

There has been an effort to charge the soldiers with cruelty and slaughter,
but it is a vile slander. They worked hard to stop the fight, and to save lives.
After the battle, some of them had little Indian babies wrapped in their coats,
carrying them off the field. The poor little ones crowed and laughed at their
blue-coated "mothers," and the soldiers broke down and cried like babies, and
cursed everything and everybody that caused the war—in fact everything except the Indians.[5]

The first news from the field at Wounded Knee reported that Craft had
not survived: "Father Craft Killed," proclaimed the headline of the *New
York Freeman's Journal* of Saturday, 3 January 1891. "The Great Indian Mis-
sionary Shot through the Lungs While Fulfilling His Mission of Peace."
"A Noble Martyr." "One of the Horrible Results of Morgan's Inane Indian
Policy."

Bishop Shanley capitalized on Father Craft's wounds to dramatize the
need for funding the mission's activities. Father Stephan, however, was far
less enthusiastic about the notoriety attendant on Craft's wounding. The
priest had already been too much of a headache for Stephan and the har-
ried Bureau of Catholic Indian Missions. The Wounded Knee affair would
surely place Craft, whom he already considered a loose cannon, at center
stage. A letter to Bishop Shanley on 23 January offered only the following
terse comment: "Father Craft was stabbed below the shoulder blade by
an Indian from his old parish of Rosebud. He went with the military and
then went over to the Indians to talk with them to surrender their guns.
It seems that the Indians believed him to be with their enemies and hence
the hatred and while he supported the wounded Indian, the Indian drew
his knife and stabbed him in the back."[6]

The debate since the carnage at Wounded Knee Creek has left unre-
solved the turmoil and controversy that marked the event at the time. The
army described it as an "affair" but soon settled on a "battle," which their
opponents claimed was, more accurately, a "massacre." Eighteen Congressional Medals of Honor granted for valor displayed there are now viewed
in some quarters as little more than a military cover-up for the slaughter

FIGURE 13. Father Craft recovering after Wounded Knee, 1891. He wears a missionary crucifix and the medal of the Sons of the Revolution. Northwest Photo Company. Denver Public Library, Western History Collection.

of innocent Indians. Today there is an ongoing movement to have these awards posthumously rescinded. Maj. Gen. Nelson A. Miles, commander of the Division of the Missouri, brought charges against Colonel Forsyth for allowing the killing of noncombatants and for deploying his troops in such a manner as to enable them to fire on each other. A military court of inquiry exonerated Forsyth and his troops. History, however, has not been so kind.

Craft's statements, for all their conflict with today's popular consensus, generally conform with contemporary accounts. Some of his editorial comments seem far afield, but his description of the attempted disarming and the movements of the Indians can all be reconciled with other eyewitness reports. Troops on the east and west flanks withheld their fire for several minutes, as did the Hotchkiss guns, until the Indians who had crossed back into the camp began firing from there as well; even so, several soldiers died in the crossfire of their own bullets.[7] Today's scholarship, however, emphatically disagrees with the priest's conclusion that the Indians were responsible for the death of their own women and children. For the rest of his life Craft never varied from his position, always defending the military as public sentiment turned increasingly against it.

Soon after the battle, a burial detail interred 146 Indians in a single mass grave on Cemetery Hill near Wounded Knee Creek: 84 men, 44 women, and 18 children. As much as he defended the actions of the military, the priest's fundamental empathy and compassion for the Indians led him to a proposition that deeply confounded his Jesuit associates. From his hospital bed at Pine Ridge, Craft made plans to join the Indian dead: "I wrote a letter to the commanding officer here, to be given to him in case of my death, asking and authorizing him to take charge of the body and have it buried in the trench with the Indian dead at Wounded Knee. I had to leave it to him because Father Jutz declared he wouldn't officiate if I arranged it so, and seemed quite put out because I preferred the Indian to the white dead."[8]

It was not to be. This Black Robe, an observer noted, was too tough to die just then: "Father Craft must have had . . . his full share of vitality. The wound which he received on that occasion would undoubtedly have killed some men. He was laid up but a short time, and if he stopped smoking cigarettes for two days because of that little cut, I have no record of it."[9]

BITTER AFTERMATH

Father Craft's prognosis remained guarded as Commissioner Morgan, rankled by the priest's comments in the eastern press, fired off a letter to the recovering missionary. Referring to Craft's charge that the "outrageous conduct of the Indian Department" was at the root of Indian misery, Morgan challenged him to "at once publicly justify this serious charge, by citation of specific facts, or . . . withdraw it.[1]

Morgan fueled the polemics with a news release dredging up the seven-year-old discredited charges that caused Craft's expulsion from Rosebud. Craft had it reprinted in the *Freeman's Journal,* along with a detailed response that concluded:

> The removal of missionaries from their work to satisfy the malice and quiet the guilty fears of a corrupt political ring would be one more reason why that ring should cease to exist. We are in free America and not in enslaved China, and it is time that the Indian Department should be made to feel it. It should be taught that it cannot exile American citizens. If "persons whose presence among the Indians is detrimental to the public service" should be removed, we have certainly had evidence enough to convince us that the Indian Department had better go without further delay.[2]

The "corrupt political ring" Craft referred to was also called the "Indian Ring," a largely mythical group suspected of gross embezzlement of Indian funds and supplies. He sought the support of the Bureau of Catholic Indian Missions in his dispute with Commissioner Morgan but was emphatically repudiated by its director. Father Stephan not only refused to support Craft's charges against Morgan but disavowed any connection with the priest, stating that Craft was "not now and never has been an agent of the Bureau. . . . I will neither take it upon myself to substantiate Father Craft's charges against Morgan nor take any notice of his letters."[3]

Stephan conveniently ignored the fact that he and Bishop Marty had transferred Craft to the Bureau in mid-1888, that the priest had built St. Edward's School for it, and that he had just authorized Craft to tour the Dakota missions "and report back to me the standing of said schools."[4]

Even as he was being abandoned by those who should have been his allies, Craft seemed always in the middle of the conflicting forces that swirled around the "Indian question." In both its simple and its complex forms, this question was "What do we do with the Indians?" General O'Beirne, supported by a segment of liberal eastern reformers and the War Department, nominated Craft for a military chaplaincy, prompting a howl of protest by anti-Catholic groups represented by the National League for the Protection of American Institutions. The *New York Sun* reported that Secretary of War Redfield Proctor "seemed very favorable toward the proposition."[5] This, of course, only intensified opposition from anti-Catholic sources. The Reverend James M. King, general secretary of the National League for the Protection of American Institutions, argued against the nomination, stating that Craft was "a disturber of the peace and a breeder of disloyalty to the United States Government. The Indian Bureau can furnish you with abundant evidence of the unfitness of 'Father Craft' for a Chaplaincy in the Army."[6]

Commissioner Morgan concluded that Craft was "considered a very weak if not an unbalanced man mentally,"[7] and for the first several months of 1891 news accounts across the country were filled with charges and countercharges about the controversial priest. According to eastern publisher Eugene T. McAuliffe, Craft's letters and other articles supporting or opposing his positions appeared in leading newspapers in Boston, Chicago, New Orleans, New York, Philadelphia, Washington, and other cities.[8]

A letter to the editor of the *Daily Inter-Ocean* exemplifies the venom directed toward Craft:

The Indian War is over in this part of the country, and the army of soldiers, newspaper men, priests, cranks, and Indian, too, are going East to fight it all over again in Washington. Your paper is very much liked here and among the soldiers, for it has told the truth on both sides of the Indian question, and there are two sides to it. Now, I wish you would say something on one subject that no one seems to think much about, and that is the work of the Catholic priests.

I have a ranch in this country, and go a good deal among them, and have been at Pine Ridge a good many times this winter, and know that the Catholic priests are worse enemies to the Government than old Sitting Bull was. I have read what the Jesuit priests are in foreign countries, and these here are the same breed. Father Jutz, who has charge of the Holy Rosary Catholic Mission, is a German, who can hardly talk English yet. He isn't a plain Catholic priest, but a Jesuit, one of the kind who believes it is right to lie or do anything else if it will help his Church. He doesn't believe in the Government or anything else, except to increase the power and influence of his Church. . . .

Father Craft is another priest who is doing lots of harm. He was at the battle of Wounded Knee, and an Indian stuck a knife into his back when he was running for some place to hide in. He has told a lot of wonderful stories about his adventures there, but he tells a different story to every person. I was up at Finley's Hotel one day,[9] and heard a lot of the reporters laughing about him. They had each interviewed him, and he had told a different yarn to each, and they were comparing notes. They said he was "the daisiest liar" they had struck yet. . . .

The priests tell the Indians that they must obey the church's orders first; that the priests are higher than the agent of the great father; that if they steal or lie or do anything else wrong, if they will give the priest a quarter, or some buckskin, or something of that kind, the priest can forgive them and it is all right. The priests will fight any agent that is not a Catholic, and make all the trouble they can among the Indians for them. The confessional teaches the Indian to lie and steal. The priests hate the Government, and we who live out here have good reason to believe that they put up the Indians to make war so as to get the commissioners and every one else into trouble, and then say that the Catholics are the only ones who have any influence and are the only friends of the Indian. . . .

. . . some one wants to watch these priests. They have no business here. This war has hurt all of our settlers, and we don't want any more. If they are going to put the agencies into the hands of the army officers we wish they would shut up all these Catholic schools and run these crafty, treacherous, black gowned enemies of the Government out, too.

A Frontiersman.[10]

Craft had this diatribe reprinted in the *Freeman's Journal,* responding as only he could:

A letter of that kind, low, ignorant, and abusive in form, and evidently false in matter, with the misleading comments of a man capable of accepting and then grossly abusing the hospitality of Rev. Father Jutz, was sure to be treated with the contempt it deserved by all Americans. . . . The statements of Bailey and the "Frontiersman" deserve no more notice than they have already had.[11] Rev. Father Jutz has already exposed them, and army officers and press representatives, writing from the places to which they refer, have so clearly and truly stated all the facts which they have misrepresented as to make it evident that the spirit that prompted them must have been the "evil genius of the Agencies," so often described by the FREEMAN'S JOURNAL, and that the same spirit animated those who lately uttered the disgusting slanders against the army before the Department in Washington. . . .

The readers of your journal are just and honorable men, living in an enlightened and civilized community, where the laws of honor and decency are respected, and slander treated with merited contempt. They cannot, therefore, realize the disgusting annoyances and misrepresentations to which life in a low and lawless community subjects those who, laboring to save an oppressed and degraded people, have to battle for their material and moral elevation against the opposition of those who do not scruple to attain vile ends by viler means. They can readily understand, from the matter and manner of the late attack on missionaries, that the mental vision of one low slanderer, diseased and colored by his own moral infirmities, would naturally give, in his eyes, the same unnatural color to the holiest motives and actions of others; but they may not so readily see, unless informed, that in and near the Indian country there are very many such instances of mental and moral degradation, and the calumny and slander are not confined to a few only, but are in reality the vices of many, and are regarded on Indian reservations as essential parts of the methods employed to annoy and remove those whose presence is displeasing to the enemies of Indian civilization.

This fact has been recognized and clearly stated by every intelligent person who has investigated the subject. Mr. J. B. Harrison, agent of the Indian Rights Association, writes as follows of the slanderers I have mentioned, their greed for the spoils of the poor Indians, and their system of attack upon all who excite their jealousy, or oppose and expose their villainies:

"Moral assassination, or the destruction of reputation and character, is often resorted to on Indian reservations as a means of obtaining the dismissal of a teacher or other Government employé whose place is coveted by some person who naturally employs the vilest and most dishonorable means for the attainment of any object, simply because such means are to him most familiar and congenial. I have often been told in towns near Indian reservations, that for ten dollars one could obtain ten affidavits accusing any man or woman of any crime whatever, and I have no reason to doubt the truth of the assertion. No degree of excellence, or purity, or elevation of character, affords the least security or protection against the foulest accusations, and the rule that virtue and goodness are sure to triumph in the end, has some exceptions in the Indian service. After careful observation and study of the psychology of many Indian reservations, especially that of the white people on and near them, I am obliged to conclude that in all cases of charges of wrong-doing or impropriety of any kind against any person in the Indian service, the presumption is in the accused person's favor."

. . . It is easy for one to face a storm of clean lead and steel, on an honorable field of battle, when he sees before him the tempting prize of death for his people in the line of duty, and the certainty of eternal peace and rest; but the case is far different when the line of duty leads through a hail, not of clean lead, but of foul slander and abuse, the poisoned missiles of unscrupulous enemies that, without killing, rend and torture cruelly; when those to be defended are all helpless, and some treacherous; when there is little hope of victory or even of death, but the prospect of a blackened reputation, and a dishonorable exile. This is the position of every Indian missionary who dares to do his duty, under the present system of the Indian Agencies.[12]

The anonymous "Frontiersman" and other anti-Catholic factions successfully defeated the movement to secure a military chaplaincy for the contentious priest. It was little more than a trial balloon anyway, floated by General O'Beirne; there is no evidence that Craft actively sought the position.

In April, angered and exasperated by Father Stephan's withdrawal of support, Craft resigned from the Bureau of Catholic Indian Missions.[13]

Ironically, on 2 July Commissioner Morgan also severed relations with Father Stephan. He honored the reduced funding provided in previously approved contracts but dealt directly with the schools involved, deliberately bypassing the Washington office of the Bureau.[14] It was the death knell of the contract school system. By the end of the century, all direct government funding to denominational Indian schools would be phased out. The more immediate problem for Father Craft, however, was his vacant school building at Sacred Heart Mission.

XIV

THE ORIGINS
OF THE INDIAN SISTERHOOD

In the midst of the furor of events associated with Wounded Knee, Craft's novices at Avoca, Minnesota, expressed their hopes for his recovery. Their prayers, they professed, "spared your life. We hope with all our hearts that you will get perfectly well very soon for we are indeed anxious to see our good Father Craft, who has done so much for us poor Indians. We hope you will come soon, for we are waiting patiently to see you."[1]

The letter was signed by Susie Bordeaux, Claudia Crowfeather, Jane Moccasin, Mary Blackeyes, Nellie Dubray, Alice White Deer, and Ede Ms [sic]. As Craft's and Morgan's verbal volleys subsided, the priest turned his attention to these Native American candidates who, with Josephine Crowfeather, Annie Gaudreau, Annie Pleets and Ellen Clark, formed the nucleus of his Indian sisterhood.

For several years, dating back to Ellen Clark's profession as a Benedictine sister in 1886, Craft had prayed and pondered over the possibility of establishing a community of Indian sisters. Journal entries in January and February 1889 record his first musings on the subject, and circumstances after Wounded Knee impelled him to implement his plan.

Agent McLaughlin, however, used Craft's absence from Standing Rock to actively undermine the priest's strategy to staff the Fort Berthold mission with Indian Benedictine sisters. He wrote to Herbert Welsh, a prominent reformer with the Indian Rights Association who also served on the United States Board of Indian Commissioners, characterizing Craft as "possessing very poor judgement—wild and erratic . . . that he meant well but had an unbalanced mind. A phrenological examination of Father Craft would disclose 'imagination' strongly developed and anything he may think possible is liable to become so fixed in his mind that he will announce it as real with an earnestness that would impress those not well acquainted with him as actual facts. . . . You are at liberty to use this at any time as my opinion of Father Craft."[2]

Concurrently, McLaughlin wrote to the sister in charge of the convent at Avoca, seeking return of all of Craft's postulants.[3] The girls protested, stating that they would "not go back to Standing Rock because if we do we know the people there will keep us and will not let us be Sisters."[4] Bishop Marty intervened, and by mid-July all of Craft's postulants were at the convent at Yankton, South Dakota, about three hundred miles southeast of Standing Rock.[5]

In November Bishop Shanley authorized Father Craft to take Sister Mary Catharine and postulants Claudia Crowfeather, Jane Moccasin, Alice White Deer, Nellie Dubray, and Susie Bordeaux from the convent at Yankton to Sacred Heart Mission at Fort Berthold.[6] In Craft's mail at the agency, though, there was another letter from Commissioner Morgan, again threatening his removal over the statements he had published the previous winter. Craft referred Morgan's letter to a St. Paul attorney and sent a copy to Patrick Ford, asking him to intervene with Secretary of Interior John W. Noble.[7]

Secretary Noble put a quietus on Morgan, temporarily neutralizing McLaughlin's and Stephan's attempts to frustrate Craft's plans. His arriving at the empty St. Edward's school building at the start of another Dakota winter, with no heat, no supplies, and a half-dozen displaced and totally dependent young Indian women, seems to support McLaughlin's opinion of the priest's mental state. Craft, however, showed astounding resilience in intensely stressful circumstances. He converted the building into a convent and boarding school and set about establishing the first house of Indian Benedictine sisters. Mother Mary Catharine, appointed by Craft as mother superior of the community, wrote to Sister Gertrude McDermott on 10 December, announcing that the five postulants had received the holy habit of the Indian Congregation of the Order of St. Benedict on the Feast of the Immaculate Conception. Her sister Claudia, dying of consumption, took her vows with the religious name Sister Mary Theresa, O.S.B., on 6 December.[8] She died on 13 December. Craft had warned her of the risks and hardships the community faced, "but she insisted on coming with us, preferring to die in labor for God and her people than to live without it."[9] He wrote further: "These Indian Sisters have passed through trials that would have shaken most vocations, and their perseverance proves that our Indian race is capable of all the good and the spiritual advantages that race prejudice has so long refused them. I would have gladly have kept them longer where they would not have had so much to suffer, but I had no place but this where they would be safe from the annoyance of those who insist on holding and verifying the absurd theory that Indians cannot be priests or Sisters."[10]

Commissioner Morgan continued to monitor Craft's activities, and in the spring of 1892 Agent John S. Murphy at Fort Berthold Reservation reported that the school had ten "boarders" and ten "day pupils."[11] As he recruited students for the school, Craft also sought to meet the educational needs of his sisterhood, calling on his friend Kelly to supply books for the sisters' "Scholasticate." He asked for the "best in the line of sacred and profane history, geography, grammar, arithmetic, algebra, geometry, music, composition, etc. etc.—chemistry, and English philosophy might also be needed—and you might also be able to judge what they would cost. I would need, at present, six or eight of each."[12]

The Benedictine sisters at Avoca, Fort Yates, and Yankton had apparently provided a sound educational foundation for Craft to build on. In observance of Saint Patrick's Day 1892, Craft's sisters sent a letter of gratitude to Patrick Ford, who had been instrumental in persuading Secretary Noble to call off Commissioner Morgan's assault. Ford, editor of the *Irish World,* reproduced the letter in facsimile in the 2 April 1892 issue. Composed in the fine hand of Mother Mary Catharine (Josephine Crowfeather), the letter was spread across three full-length center columns of the New York paper and depicted the coat-of-arms of the sisterhood beneath a bower of shamrocks. In December Josephine conveyed the sisters' Christmas greetings beneath an arbor of flowers. She had learned her lessons well.

The July and August 1892 issues of the *Poor Souls' Advocate,* a monthly periodical published by a group of priests in Evansville, Indiana, carried an extended article titled "Indian Vocations" over the byline of Sister Mary Liguori Sound of the Flying Lance (Alice White Deer). In a letter to Father Herman J. Heuser, theology professor at Overbrook Seminary in Philadelphia, Craft described it as "the first literary effort of an Indian Sister, and 'the other side' as the Indian sees it."[13] The essay posited the prejudice and false assumptions directed toward Indian vocations, told the story of the establishment of Craft's community at Fort Berthold, and ended with a plaintive cry for help:

After four centuries of missionary labor among the Indians; after many thousand Indian virgins passed away to obtain from the Church in heaven what the Church on earth seemed to deny them, there is at last an Indian community among the Indians. What the Mohawk Catharine [Tekakwitha] and her friend Theresa[14] and their pious Indian maidens dreamed of and sighed for two centuries ago on the banks of the St. Lawrence, the Dakota Catharine [Crowfeather] and her sister Theresa [Claudia Crowfeather] and their companions have realized on the banks of the Missouri. The tribal brother and relative of the Mohawk Catharine, and the adopted brother of the Dakota Catharine, aided by the prayers of the Lily of the Mohawk, came from the battlefield, with wounds still bleeding, as from the dead, to unite the dead hopes of the past with the living realities of the present, and to aid his sister of the nineteenth century to realize the plans of his sister of the seventeenth. Who will say that Catharine Thekakwitha [*sic*] does not, with her community in heaven, aid that other Catharine Ptesanwanyakapi [They see a white buffalo] and her community on earth.

But why was it so long delayed? Why was it even now so hard to accomplish? The doctrines of our Church have not changed. Why then should its practice not be the same as in apostolic times? The apostles would not refuse baptism to those who had received the Holy Spirit as well as they, and why should their successors refuse a place in the sanctuary or cloister to those who, though of different speech and color, have been equally favored with divine vocations? Will they still say against fact and reason, that we are incapable of doing what we have actually done? If we have fought our way against such tremendous odds as the forces of the missionary body must have been, to the place to which God called us, how much more easily could we have attained it, had those odds been in our favor. It may be that none will hear us. It may be that race prejudice is stronger than charity. It may be that we shall be driven or starved from what we have gained. We do not pretend to greater perfection or strength than white people possess, or that we can succeed without the helps without which they could not hope to succeed. If God has wonderfully aided us so far, it is not just to ask him to work a perpetual miracle. We ask only to be recognized as Catholics, and as sharers in the spiritual wealth of our Mother, the Catholic Church. We ask Americans to permit Americans to labor for the welfare of our own American people, and we ask Catholics to aid us and permit us to aid them in promoting the salvation of souls, and the glory of God, our Father, and the Church our Mother.

Sister Mary Liguori
(Sound of the Flying Lance)[15]

Others wanted to join his community, but Father Craft could not afford their transportation costs, nor could he support them if they came. He anguished knowing that he could not trust their care to other convents in the West.[16] To his credit, though, he did not eschew forewarning his postulants of the difficulties they faced in pursuing a vocation with his besieged congregation:

Another Indian girl, anxious to suffer for vocations' sake, will soon be here. I have told her all she must expect, but she "don't scare," and wonders why I take so much pains to warn her, when I "ought to know that God is more powerful than our enemies." Indian faith is pretty solid. I wish I had more of it. Perhaps only full bloods can have it in its fullness. The fact is Indians are logical. "God has said it: therefore it is so," they say, and they can't understand why the white man won't see it in the same light. If it "be done to them according to their faith," they will come through safely, though prospects are now rather "shadowy" to say the least.[17]

In August, Commissioner Morgan wired Agent Murphy seeking word on Craft's current status. Murphy advised that the priest had "five or six Sioux Indian Sisters . . . living in the building erected . . . in 1889," and that they boarded "fourteen . . . Indian children."[18]

Although forsaken by Father Stephan, Bishop Shanley had not yet fully abandoned the struggling little group on the western fringe of his diocese. When Katharine Drexel proposed a potential candidate for Craft's community, however, the bishop stopped short of a spirited endorsement of it:

We have a community of Indian Nuns at the Fort Berthold Mission, that is, there is one nun with five novices. How it is going to turn out, God knows. I was there about three weeks ago to examine the state of affairs. I found the Indian Sisters happy, obedient, pious—but unspeakably poor; living on salt-pork and bread. It is Bethlehem. The Sioux girls can do that uncomplainingly, for they have been used to such life from babyhood. In my opinion it would be too hard a life for anyone else. I believe that our Indian community, if it is to succeed, must recruit itself from Dakota tribes, and therefore I could not advise your young friend to come out here.

I have some hopes of starting a good school at Berthold next summer. The Indian community will come to Fargo and support itself by needlework. Some other teaching order will surely be found to take charge of the School.

I will be in the East in January and will talk the matter over with you. You were so kind as to give me, through Fr. Stephan, six hundred dollars, in April '91, for the support of the missionary at Berthold. I was able to add four hundred to that, so that one thousand dollars has started a convent, and kept six Sisters and a priest one year and a half.[19]

Bishop Shanley's letter typifies the uncertain reaction of the Catholic clergy and hierarchy to Father Craft's valiant venture in Dakota. At best, they viewed it as an "experiment."[20] Others, like Father Stephan, actively opposed the priest's endeavor and refused to fund any part of it at all. And Commissioner Morgan, of course, still had a vendetta to pursue.

None of this could stem the enthusiasm of Father Craft and his sisters as they strove to establish the first Indian convent in the West. Not long after Bishop Shanley visited them in October 1892, the sisters wrote to Father Jerome Hunt, O.S.B., at Devils Lake, who had the letter published in *Die Katholischen Missionen:*

There is now a convent of Indian Sisters in the very place in which not so many years ago, the Mandan and Sioux so often met in bloody battle and the sisters whose prayers and hymns silenced the war-cry of the hostile tribes are the children of those same wild warriors; they are the same little girls whom you saw some years ago dressed in the colors, and feathers which distinguish their tribe. Today you would scarcely recognize the little Ptesanwanyakapiwin in our Reverend Mother M. Catharine; or the little Tasagyesnawin in our tall prioress, Mother M. Liguori; nor would you suspect that the grave of our first prioress, Mother M. Teresa contains the remains of the little Cangles-Kawin whom you knew so well in her youth. From the beginning of our foundation, difficulties of all kinds confronted us; God has conquered them all. . . . We had not the means to establish a convent; but God helped us. Through the efforts of Father Craft and Bishop Shanley, He induced our friends in the East to furnish the necessary means. All were surprised that our undertaking was succeeding. We ourselves were not surprised at all; for in as much as God has given us a vocation He has promised us His aid and He will be true to His promises if we do our duty. Our good Bishop Shanley visited us last October. He was greatly pleased with our community and remarked that we were really the only genuinely American congregation and that we could be assured that through us God would accomplish a great work among our people. On December 8 our novices pronounced their vows and we chose the officers of our community.[21]

Other events in the West during these formative years, however, signaled the combined indifference and hostility that would confront Father Craft's plans for an Indian sisterhood. Even as he transported his Indian sisters to Fort Berthold, the first Catholic Indian Congress assembled early in July 1891 on Standing Rock Indian Reservation, only 150 miles away. Two thousand Indian converts and catechists from reservations throughout the West gathered with missionaries and hierarchy to celebrate their catholicity. The *Irish World* vividly described the next year's congress at Cheyenne River Agency: "Under the awning in the centre sat Bishop Marty, accompanied by Fathers Jerome, Perrig, Digmann, Bernard, Francis, Fintan, and Bede. Around them were seated the chiefs and the representatives of the various Indian societies, and in four or five rows around the great outer circle were fully two thousand Indians seated flat upon the ground."[22]

Familiar names, John Grass and William Halsey, led the Standing Rock delegation. Following several days of religious ceremony, Christian oration, processions, and feasting, the convention adjourned to meet again on 4 July 1893. The congress was held every Fourth of July weekend for decades. Neither Father Craft nor his Indian sisters were invited, nor would they ever be.

XV

THE DEATH OF
SACRED WHITE BUFFALO

Having laid precarious foundations for his community of Indian sisters, Craft concentrated his energies on obtaining ecclesiastical approbation for his congregation. Bishop Marty and Bishop Shanley had been reluctantly ensnared in his project, caught by the priest's tenacious pursuit of his cause. To succeed finally, he needed the support of the American Catholic hierarchy, which in turn might sustain further efforts to obtain approval from Rome. If he went through normal channels, this procedure would take decades.

About this same time, Pope Leo XIII was encouraging improved relations between the American Catholic bishops and the Holy See. For many years during the great European migration to the United States, nationalism had divided the American Catholic Church, creating pockets of feuding ethnic groups that increasingly lacked unity of purpose. To consolidate the bishops through a single channel, the pontiff named Monsignor Francesco Satolli as the first apostolic delegate to the United States. He arrived in New York in October 1892. The conservative wing of the American Catholic hierarchy was wary of the papal delegate, fearing the position would serve only to inflame the rabid anti-Catholic fervor that warned of a menacing foreign influence in the affairs of the Catholic Church in America. The principal United States Catholic leader who supported the apostolic delegate's appointment was Archbishop John Ireland of St. Paul, whose purview included the dioceses of Sioux Falls and Jamestown in the Dakotas.[1] Ireland, together with Cardinal James Gibbons of Baltimore and Denis J. O'Connell, rector of the American College in Rome, had carefully contrived the introduction of the apostolic delegation's office to coincide with the opening of the World's Columbian Exposition in Chicago. Satolli's visit was purportedly to exhibit papal artifacts at the fair; even Gibbons was apparently unaware that the new office was to become a permanent feature in American Catholic relations with the Vatican.[2]

Father Craft asked Bishop Ireland to obtain a papal blessing on his sisterhood from Monsignor Satolli, but the prelate demurred, suggesting through his secretary that "it would be better for Mother Catharine to make the application herself for the Apostolic Benediction."[3] Mother Mary Catharine was too ill to communicate, so Craft corresponded through Mother Mary Liguori Sound of the Flying Lance (Alice White Deer), finally obtaining the papal blessing from Monsignor Satolli.[4] He reviewed it all in a letter to his friend James Kelly:

> Rev. Mother Catharine is still very weak. Her health has been badly shattered by hardship and anxiety, and I don't know what the result will be. It would be cruel to lose her now, when our success seems certain. While it was still possible that Satolli's opponents might succeed in forcing the Pope to recall him, I wrote to Archb. Ireland to offer Msgr. Satolli the best wishes and the allegiance of the Indian Sisters, and the only American priest on the missions, and to ask for Mother Catharine, through Satolli, the blessing of the Holy Father, as she has deserved well of the Church for her heroic perseverance under great trials, and for giving to the Church its first Indian Congregation.
>
> As we put ourselves on record for Leo [Pope Leo XIII], Satolli, Ireland, and progress, during the crisis of their affairs, I hope they will be found on the side of the Indian Sisters if their aid is ever needed. It seems to me that we are safe while Satolli remains. We are willing to starve quietly, if the Church will allow Indians the same rights it grants to other races, and Satolli can't very well refuse us that much. . . .
>
> What became of Austin Ford? I never hear from him or the Freeman's Journal. . . . Please give my best regards to all our friends . . . and hoping to hear from you often.[5]

Craft had a premonition that his eastern friends were quietly rejecting him. The metaphorical desert he experienced with the Jesuits at West Park in 1879 was materializing again in the frigid Dakota winter of 1893. In the meantime, others on the agency, frustrated by the Catholics' long-term failure to establish a legitimate mission school, unwittingly eroded the shaky foundation on which the little community was based. Chief Sitting Bear's son, Frank Wells, complained to Bishop Shanley, "We would like to have a Priest like they have at Standing Rock. He instrucks his Indians. The Priest here do nothing, only gets mad, sometimes."[6]

Craft may have been oblivious to this opposing groundswell, but if he had knowledge of it, he probably ignored it. He was going over the bishop's head anyway, and he wrote next to the acknowledged leader of the American hierarchy: Cardinal Gibbons, head of the Archdiocese of Baltimore. Like Ireland, Gibbons was also a strong supporter of Catholic "Americanism."[7]

> The kind interest you take in the progress of our Indians, and in every Catholic American effort to show the truth and harmony of the progressive principles of our Church and country, assures me that you will be pleased to see, by the enclosed letter of the Indian Sisters, how much our aboriginal Americans can do, even in the first generation, if rightly directed, for Catholic and American progress.
>
> If the spiritual as well as the temporal progress of our Indians has hitherto been delayed, and if, even yet, there are attempts to destroy the proofs of Indian capability of progress, it must be evident that the fault is not with Indians, Church or Government, but rather with the race-prejudice and conservatism of a comparatively few minds, too narrow to be truly Catholic or American.
>
> The progressive spirit of the Indian Sisters and their success in overcoming, so far, the opposition of race-prejudice and conservatism, should convince us that the same hope, instruction, chance, and incentive to progressive effort thought necessary for the white race, would produce the same results with Indians.[8]

On 6 April Agent John S. Murphy, under threat of replacement by another political appointee, wrote to solicit Bishop Shanley's support. In his letter he mentioned the sentiments of Frank Wells, stating: "Procrastination and indecision in the missionary work on [Fort Berthold] reservation have had a baleful effect. These Indians are sorely in need of an active healthy priest—one who thinks more of the glory of God and the salvation of souls than of amply [ample] plaudits and newspaper notoriety. I say this without any particular disparagement to Fr. Craft who is physically unable to cope with the work to be done here. Fr. Craft is a poor man."[9]

Although Craft's grassroots support was becoming increasingly sparse at Fort Berthold, he had reason to believe more fertile ground lay back East. Cardinal Gibbons had responded to his recent letter, recognizing "the great good which has been already accomplished by our devoted Sisters, in behalf of the Indians, as well as by our noble missionary priests, quorum magna pars fuisti [of whom you have been a great part]. . . . The life of self denial led by yourself and your colleagues is an impulse to us all."[10]

Mother Mary Catharine's consumptive condition deteriorated during March and April. Twice during that period she repeated her vows at Craft's direction, each time in anticipation of her death.[11] She was twenty-six years old.

On Sunday, 30 April, a contingent of Indians and headmen came to express their respects and to pray for her recovery. Early in the morning of 2 May she asked her sisters to dress her in full religious habit and bring her to the chapel of Sacred Heart Mission. Their voices raised in singing the English version of "Holy God We Praise Thy Name," a cordon of Sioux nuns laid their foundress on a pallet before the altar of the Lord. Craft described the event to Kelly:

> It was a scene not to be forgotten, and never witnessed before, except perhaps at the death of St. Benedict.[12] The Indian Brides of Christ, whom she had led from the camp to the convent, their dark tear-stained faces, their voices quivering with grief, singing the triumphant music of the Church. . . . The dying champion of her Church and race, who had bravely taken up the conflict that others feared, against the race-prejudice and conservatism of four centuries, seeming to grow stronger and happier as death came nearer; and the Sacred Heart waiting before her on the altar to receive the gallant spirit that had fought for Him so well, and wrested victory even from death.[13]

The priest celebrated mass and distributed Holy Eucharist, first to the moribund Mother Catharine and then to her companions, then exposed the host for an hour of worship in a Benediction of the Blessed Sacrament: "Pressing her crucifix to her lips, and fixing her eyes upon the Tabernacle . . . her Lord came for her, blessed her and her Sisters, and took her with

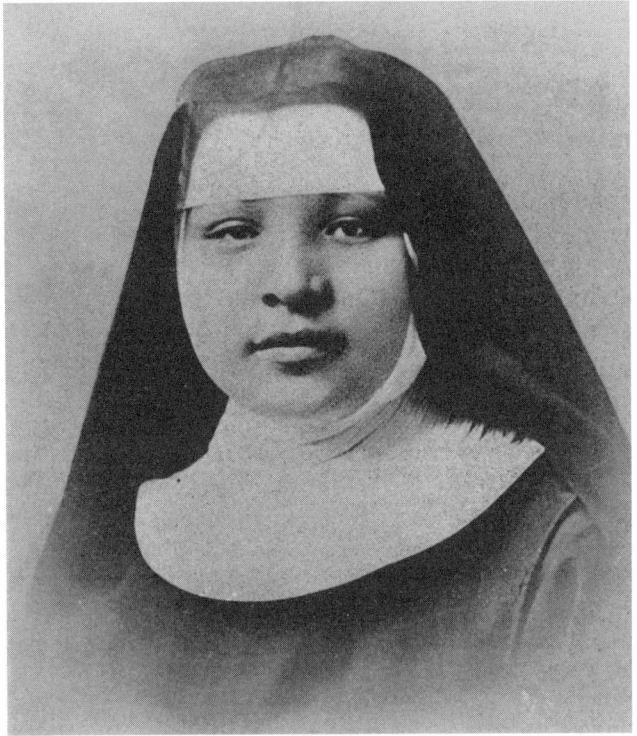

FIGURE 14. Mother Mary Catharine Sacred White Buffalo (Josephine Crowfeather), about 1892. Photographer unknown. Marquette University Archives.

Him, she was gone while the smoke of the incense still floated about the altar.[14]

One of the first persons Father Craft notified of Mother Catharine's demise was Cardinal Gibbons, who responded: "I read with interest your touching account of the edifying death of your Sister, Rev. Mother M. Catharine, which was a fitting sequel to a life consecrated to God and to her fellow creatures. I pray and trust that she has already received the reward promised to those who have illustrated in their daily lives the highest maxims of the Gospel."[15]

Determined that his sisterhood would outlive the death of its foundress, Craft asked the artist and sculptor James Kelly to produce a life-size statue of her. He provided Kelly with photographs of her taken in life and de-

tailed facial measurements taken in death. In sketches and additional descriptions of the death scene, he conveyed exquisite detail in a series of
extensive letters:

> The face had not lost *all* its former sweet and gentle expression, but it had
> an air of majesty and dignity, and calm intelligence, and stern resolution. It
> showed a high spirit, great energy, deep thought, and indomitable will; and ex-
> pressed the habit of "counsel, conflict, conquest, and command." The features
> were very much thinner than in the photo; the eyes very bright and penetrat-
> ing, and seemed larger; the nose, prominent, high, and aquiline, was thinner,
> and seemed higher and more prominent, at least they seemed so, but not as
> much as one would expect from an Indian face, as the Dakota face does not
> differ as greatly from the white American.[16]

Other letters gave the dimensions of the chapel and altar, described
the ciborium he used for exposition of the host, the beaded moccasins
she wore, the broad gold "Mother General's ring" inscribed "with IHS
on the centre," and the habit she had made from the torn cassock he
had worn at the Battle of Wounded Knee.[17] He had grandiose plans for
Mother Catharine's sculptured image. One copy was to be a gift for Monsignor Satolli and another for Pope Leo XIII, with the original to reside
in Congress's Statuary Hall in Washington DC.[18] Kelly's dramatic sketch
of Mother Mary Catharine's death appeared in papers throughout the
country; however, although photos of it exist, the statue itself has never
been found. Mother Catharine was buried next to her sister Claudia (Sister Mary Theresa Crowfeather) in the Catholic cemetery at Elbowoods,
North Dakota. As the waters of Lake Sakakawea rose behind the Garrison
Dam in the 1950s, their graves were moved to Queen of Peace Cemetery at
Raub, North Dakota, indicated by plain markers that incorrectly identify
them only as "Grey Nuns."[19]

After Mother Mary Catharine's death, Craft decided to give up the des-
ignation "Benedictine" and changed the name of the order from "Congregation of Indian Sisters of the Order of St. Benedict" to simply the
"Congregation of American Sisters." The new name, he said, was foreseen
by Mother Catharine as "more distinctly American" and was also dictated
"by an article of their Constitution requiring the immediate change of
anything that shall at any time be found an obstacle to progress."[20]

Against staggering odds, Craft had managed to keep his community together for more than two years. He eventually gained the confidence of the agent and the Fort Berthold tribes, and by late 1893 even the Standing Rock bands were contributing to the support of the Catholic Indians at Sacred Heart Mission.[21]

XVI

ILLUSIONS OF SUCCESS

The year 1894 provided a brief respite, enabling Father Craft to focus on developing the skills of his congregation. Daniel M. Browning, a circuit judge from Illinois, had replaced Craft's nemesis, Thomas J. Morgan, as United States commissioner of Indian affairs. In this quiet interlude, Father Craft transformed his Indian sisters in ways that seem impossible considering the overwhelming obstacles he faced. Under his tutelage, they refined their English literacy, acquired a basic understanding of science and history, and developed nursing skills far beyond the scope of Native medicine. If the sisters' true progress was only a fraction of that described by Craft, it was remarkable by any standards. Meriting the increasing esteem of the local tribes, Craft's congregation of sisters, unlike most Catholic religious communities of the day, was not walled off in a self-supporting convent or abbey but lived and did their work directly among the people. And they did so not with heavy German accents or thick Irish brogues, but in the vernacular of those they served. Even so, occasional eastern visitors would often be astonished to discover that these dedicated young women, so properly attired in religious dress the equal of a Philadelphia convent's, were the daughters of Sioux families from blighted camps on Devils Lake, Rosebud, and Standing Rock. For years the entire thrust of the government's solution to the "Indian Problem" had been to assimilate Indians into the developing Euro-American culture; cut their hair, teach them the English language, give them a trade or skill, turn Native Americans into Euro-Americans. Father Craft was doing exactly that, and doing it with more success than a dozen Captain Pratts at Carlisle, Genoa, or Hampton. To top it off, this was an *American* work! He was mystified by the inexplicable failure of his superiors to recognize his accomplishments. It almost compelled him to present his sisters as more white than Indian.

Without federal or religious support, however, Craft's efforts to establish a school at St. Edward's soon proved impractical. Undaunted, he not only restructured the operation into a medical clinic but arranged for a Bureau of Indian Affairs subsidy that paid fifty cents a day for each patient.[1] Though the amount was small, it was an important recognition of the Indian sisters by federal authorities.

During the year, he added two full-blood Sioux and a half-blood Chippewa as postulants, bringing his community to eight sisters. In September he brought the group to St. Paul, supposedly to visit other schools and hospitals. More likely, though, it was to impress Archbishop Ireland, with whom they stayed. In his account of the visit, Craft wrote that the sisters favorably impressed their counterparts and "fairly captured" a conference of Indian school teachers.[2] Ireland's reaction, however, was clearly less than favorable. "Father," probed the archbishop, "do you not think you have eight sisters too many?" Craft replied: "If that is the case, you have one priest too many!"[3]

If there was an argument, it was probably brief. Craft's inclination would have been to simply ignore the bishop's negative reaction and forge ahead with his plans. Things were going so well that by spring 1895 even a recently promoted Monsignor Stephan was moved to reestablish lines of communication. Craft responded, using the opportunity to further promote his cause. His project was not only *American*, it was uniquely *Catholic*. Protestants in this situation, he reasoned, would encourage, trumpet, and capitalize on their success. He was more than willing to give the church all the credit if it would simply recognize and accept the accomplishment.[4]

Monsignor Stephan, however, did not reply. So a month later, Craft took up his pen once more to plead for support from the Bureau of Catholic Indian Missions. Bishop Shanley had told him to count on $600 a year from his diocese, but that was back in 1893, and since then he had received only $200. He was already $800 in arrears and in trouble with his creditors.[5] Stephan filed Craft's letters with terse notations: "Answered 24 July 1895, will answer more fully later on," and "Urges that financial aid be furnished his mission."[6] No funds materialized, though.

Still Craft pressed on. Three more novices took their initial vows on

18 August (all of them converts from the local Protestant mission), raising the strength of the order to eleven sisters. He also persuaded the Fort Berthold Indian agent to write to Cardinal Gibbons supporting his efforts.[7] In December five of the sisters made their perpetual vows before a congregation of Indians who filled the large double hall of St. Edward's School. "We are making great preparations for Christmas," Craft effused, "and expect to have a grand time, even better than last year."[8]

By 1896 the agent at Fort Berthold offered positive comments on Craft's mission: "The Sisters are efficient in their care of the sick, either at their homes or when brought to the mission, and their kindly ministrations have a beneficent influence." According to the same report, Craft claimed that his mission had 552 communicants over seven years of age; nearly half of the entire population of the Three Tribes on Fort Berthold Reservation was Catholic.[9]

Monsignor Stephan too was reluctantly acknowledging that Craft just might be succeeding in his mission as he requested photographs of the sisters. Craft eventually sent him a photo showing some of the sisters ministering to a patient, with medicines and medical equipment apparent in the background.[10]

Father Craft's determination to accumulate the very latest in medical equipment is revealed in a letter he wrote to Kelly in April 1896:

> Speaking of photos, if you get any news of improvements in Prof. Roentgen's discoveries, in X rays, or hear that they are generally using instruments of the kind, especially those improved by Edison, or can find out where and at what price they can be obtained, please let me know. Perhaps houses that deal in electrical goods may know something about them. I heard that Edison had perfected an instrument by which the surgeon could look directly upon the bones, or foreign substances within the body, while his hands would be free to use instruments or set fractures. If such a thing is ever on the market, like other instruments, I will try to get it for the Sisters' Hospital. I would like, especially, to find out what force of electricity would be required to use such instruments. If they are getting into general use, the hospitals would perhaps know of them.[11]

Word of the discovery of X rays in November 1895 by Wilhelm Conrad Röntgen in Würzburg, Germany, spread rapidly throughout the world. The equipment Röntgen used in his fortuitous discovery was readily avail-

FIGURE 15. The Native American order and its founder and chaplain, about 1897. The child is unidentified. Photographer unknown. Marquette University Archives.

able in college laboratories. By early February 1896 X rays were in clinical use in the United States, and by June of that year they were used to pinpoint the location of bullets and other foreign objects in the human body. Although several decades would pass before rural electrification reached the Dakota reservations, Craft's inquiry to Kelly was not as farfetched or quixotic as it first appears. Some of the earliest X-ray equipment was powered from storage batteries that could have been charged by steam engines or windmills. Moreover, Father Craft knew that Kelly was a friend of Thomas Edison and so was likely to know about the subject.

By September of that year, things were going so well that the sisters had stationery printed with the heading "Convent of American Sisters, Elbow Woods, N.D."[12] It was on this letterhead that Craft legally established his community of sisters, filing articles of incorporation with the state of North Dakota. The official certificate of incorporation from the secretary of state was received on 20 September 1896.[13] The sisters were now incorporated under state law, with the legal title "Congregation of American Sisters."[14] He also designed an official seal for the organization and opened a checking account in the order's name at the Red River Valley National Bank.[15] To shield themselves with the protection of citizenship and prevent their forcible return to the camps, the Indian sisters formally renounced "all Indian or tribal right, claim, help, or connection."[16]

Over six incredibly difficult years, he had established a convent of a dozen Indian sisters who had received what he considered the approbation of the Holy See. Of equal moment, the sisters were legally protected citizens of the United States whose legitimacy was accepted by Native Americans, the state and federal governments, and the liberal establishment in the East. Even Monsignor Stephan seemed to be softening in his resistance.

Tragically, each illusory measure of success further sealed the fate of Craft's sisterhood. Magnified beyond reality, these superficial trappings of progress served only to increase the sisters' utter dependency on their founder. They were so much a product of his will that survival without him was impossible.

XVII

A MALICIOUS ASSAULT

Early in 1897, Sacred Heart Convent served as the motherhouse of the Congregation of American Sisters as well as a functioning hospital with space for twenty-eight patients.[1] The priest continued to promote his sisterhood in the press, with articles appearing in the *Puritan,* a newly published journal for women, and the *Irish World.* The latter piece was accompanied by a sketch of Mother Mary Catharine Sacred White Buffalo's successor, Alice White Deer, who had taken the name Mother Mary Liguori Sound of the Flying Lance. In these articles, Craft asserted his belief that the symbolism and mysticism of the Native culture was "more in sympathy with the Roman Catholic Church than with any other Christian body."[2] He was certain that the spirit of the heroic, sacrificial life of Mother Mary Catharine Sacred White Buffalo sustained and nurtured the congregation she had founded, which only now was beginning to flourish in the midst of grim desperation.

However, the corrupt climate that abetted the "moral assassination" so prevalent on most Indian reservations proved even more malevolent and depraved on Fort Berthold than it had been on Standing Rock or Rosebud. John S. Murphy, a former Indian agent at Fort Berthold who had previously been fired by the Department of Indian Affairs, had stayed in the area, plotting ways to reclaim his job. In a brazen attempt to drag down his replacement along with Craft's sisters, he initiated scandalous rumors of sexual liaisons between them and the agent's staff, including the district farmer, carpenter, blacksmith, chief clerk, and school superintendent. After these outrageously destructive allegations that Murphy, a Catholic himself, brought before Bishop Shanley, Agent F. Glenn Mattoon wired the United States commissioner of Indian Affairs. He had already suspended the agency personnel purportedly involved and asked that the commissioner send an inspector immediately.[3] For his trouble, the commissioner requested Mattoon's resignation by return wire, "to take place when your successor is appointed."[4]

Craft was reluctant to believe that the bishop would lend support to former agent Murphy's allegations or allow himself to be used in such a manner. Still, he had his doubts and would not have been surprised to find "everything Catholic . . . in some way in it." He had little confidence in "men of the Church, wherever there is a question of race—especially the Indian race."[5] "In the case of a white congregation," he declared, "the situation would not be at all serious, but it is far different with those whose destruction would be a relief to the Church . . . and we know that the human side of the Church is very *human,* and not always *humane.*"[6]

Agent Mattoon wired his resignation on 16 April, which was acknowledged by Secretary of Interior Cornelius N. Bliss the next day.[7] Once again, Craft sought the support of Monsignor Stephan, pleading that "an attempt to injure [the sisters] in this way will be charged upon the Church and the Department, and will raise issues that neither would care to have raised. It is the foulest and vilest piece of rascality on record. We demand a fair investigation, and have informed our friends. . . . The attack . . . is evidently intended . . . as a weapon to attack others, and to raise a foul scandal.[8]

If his religious superiors were not directly involved in the original plot, they were, Craft believed, Machiavellian enough to stand aside and let it destroy his sisterhood. Bishop Shanley expressed immediate support for the fired agent Murphy, Archbishop Ireland wrote "that he is far away, and does not thoroughly understand the case, and therefore can do nothing," and Monsignor Stephan excused himself until after the "Secretary of Interior [appoints] an Inspector to investigate the whole business."[9]

Disheartened and disillusioned, Father Craft sought the aid of his eastern allies in defense of the sisters. He implored James Kelly to summon influential friends to come to his aid. "If I were a Mason," he wrote, "the Masons would help. . . . If the Sisters must be destroyed, I must go first. . . . I wouldn't like to close my career fighting the Church in defense of those for whose safety it should be more zealous than I, but, if some help don't come along pretty soon, it is likely to end that way, as honor, charity, justice, and conscience will leave no other course open to me."[10]

Father Craft's Congregation of American Sisters, literally his world, his life's work, was collapsing around him. Several of the Native women in his community, presumably "those of the stamp and character of the Indian," as mockingly described years earlier by Monsignor Stephan, returned to their camps. Who could blame them? The priest's mission on Fort Berthold had endured more than six years with the Church seemingly grudging every step it took. Now, in its moment of crisis, Stephan and the rest of the Catholic hierarchy were opting out, taking a walk.

Four of Craft's sisters persevered, a fairly large proportion in these circumstances. Alice White Deer, Mother Catharine's replacement as prioress of the order, was an early casualty who withdrew into an unknown past. Susie Bordeaux, whose name in religion was Mother Mary Anthony, became the new prioress. She was a granddaughter of Spotted Tail and grandniece of Red Cloud.[11] Ellen Clark (Sister Mary Gertrude), who led the way to the Benedictines on Standing Rock in 1885, stayed on. She had ten years invested in her vocation and apparently nowhere else to go. Annie Pleets (Sister Mary Bridget), who had made her profession with Mother Catharine, remained steadfast, as did Josephine Two Bears, who had professed as Sister Mary Joseph.

Early in May, Craft advised Monsignor Stephan that he and the sisters had "had enough of the Indian service." Along with their reputations, they had lost whatever remnants of confidence or hope they may have had for eventual acceptance. "As long as the attitude of the Church, and the interests and methods of reservations are what they are, the work of the Sisters, no matter how useful, would be extremely painful, their position dangerous, and their future doubtful."[12]

Only a few weeks later, Stephan wrote to Bishop Shanley:

I regret to have to inform you that very grave charges have been filed against the Indian Sisters of Fort Berthold with the Secretary of the Interior. The condition of affairs there is so serious that the good name of our Indian schools, and of the Sisters in general is at stake. Unless the evil is speedily rectified, an open scandal may be the result, and plenty of material furnished to our enemies, the A.P.A.'s [American Protective Association].

I would therefore respectfully suggest that you investigate this matter, and bring about a better state of affairs, and thus safeguard our interests among the Indians.[13]

Craft determined to take the remaining four back east, where they might serve among other minorities or the poor. He left Fort Berthold during the summer of 1897 to visit other reservation sites at Oak Creek, Standing Rock, and Cheyenne River. On 30 September he completed a letter to Father Daniel Hudson that was begun at Oak Creek. Craft was now just as trapped as his remaining sisters:

> No, I can't abandon the work—in fact, I *dare* not, or I would then be compelled . . . to abandon missions, priesthood, Church, and all. The Sisters represent the whole case of Catholicity among the Indians. . . . If they are to sink now, it will be because the Church is determined to crush them. . . . I really believe that, were it not for race and national prejudice, financial interests, the fear of having theories exploded, and of being . . . compelled to work a little harder for, and a little nearer to the Indian, *all* the Catholic missionaries would welcome the Indian Sisters as a blessing . . . there is no hope in the Church. We wait for God to act. Our enemies say "Where is now their God." *They* ought to know, as they are theologians, and know whether their God and ours is the Christ who said much about shepherds and sheep, and died on Calvary for *His* sheep. Their words and deeds would seem to show that they think He is *not* the same. We shall see.[14]

A note from the Benedictine missionary Fintan Wiederkehr, O.S.B., to his abbot described the wretched state of Craft and the sisters as they left Fort Berthold: "F. Craft and his Sisters, in coming here, were driven by sheer necessity. During this past winter in Fort Berthold they often had only rats and ravens to eat."[15]

When the priest and his four nuns reached Cheyenne River Agency, Bishop Thomas O'Gorman of Sioux Falls (Bishop Marty's successor),[16] refused to grant faculties to Craft and sent word through Father Fintan that Craft was unwelcome in his diocese:

> A diocese may be likened to a reservation. Fr. Craft and his Sisters have wandered from the reservation where they belong. I, as the agent, that is to say the Bishop, of the reservation known in ecclesiastical language as the Diocese of

Sioux Falls comprising the State of So. Dak. have ordered and do again order Fr. Craft and his Sisters to leave my reservation or diocese and go back to that where they belong. . . .

How can I know, unless duly informed by the Bishop under whom they formerly lived, that Fr. Craft is a priest in good standing, or that the ladies with him are "Sisters" in the true meaning of that word. It is only a Bishop can make women Sisters. A priest may put the habit on them, but that does not make them "Religious"; no more than a layman is made a priest by putting on the vestments of a priest. The quality of "Sisters" can come to women only from the Bishop or Pope. I have never been informed by Bishop or Pope that they had given this quality to the ladies who accompany Fr. Craft.

But even if they were "Sisters" in the regular and [full sense] that gives them no right to be brought by Fr. Craft into my reservation without my permission. Let them go back to North Dakota whence they ran away. I have so ordered them. If they do not, they are disobedient to authority. Father Craft has no faculties in my diocese.[17]

With Bishop O'Gorman's approval,[18] Indian agent Peter Couchman went to Craft's residence to persuade the sisters to return to their homes. Shortly before the agent arrived on a frigid March morning, Craft and the four sisters crossed the Missouri River on the ice, escaping beyond the eastern boundary of the reservation and beyond the jurisdiction of the agent.[19]

From Standing Rock Reservation, Father Martin Kenel, O.S.B., kept his abbot posted regarding Craft's movements, advising him that "Father Craft and his vagabond Sisters have done great harm, and almost ruined Fr. Fintan's Mission at Cheyenne. . . . None of the Bishops want Fr. Craft but he defies them all and acts like a crazy man."[20]

Father Fintan tried again to convince the sisters that they must obey the properly constituted bishop of Sioux Falls if they wished to remain Catholic nuns in the service of the Indians. He prepared his own speech on the subject:

Bishop O'Gorman told me orally that he is willing to take your community and send you for a short while to a novitiate and then send the whole Com[munity], as Sisters in the regular and full sense of that word, to the Indians again, to work among them. The Sisterhood is an ecclesiastical instit[ution] and therefore it must come under ecclesiastical authority and jurisdiction and there is no exception to this rule and the Pope does not give special dispensations in regard to the mentioned rule.

If you desire to be Cath[olic] Sisters and remain within this diocese you have to put yourself under the jurisdiction of the ordinary of the Diocese, Bp. O'Gorman. The Church and the Bishops and priests are not against you and Indian vocations.[21]

As the sisters contemplated Father Wiederkehr's plea, Agent Couchman served Craft with his notice of expulsion from Cheyenne River Agency.[22] Undaunted by these attacks from both religious and secular fronts, Craft pulled out his Sons of the Revolution stationery[23] and wrote to Secretary Bliss. If he was the raving madman the consensus indicated, he was nevertheless as rational as ever when he took up the pen:

> I received today . . . the enclosed letter from Maj. Peter Couchman, Agent at Cheyenne Agency, S.D. Although it was evident from your letter to me, that the matter was attended to and you would not permit us to be further annoyed, the Sisters and I remained away from the reservation for the sake of peace, and did not intend to return there until another Agent would take charge. We have therefore given Maj. Couchman no cause for this action. If an Agent, influenced by one religious organization, could obtain from the Department authority to remove another religious organization from the reservation, without a fair hearing, you can easily understand how far this could be carried. The wrong might, in the end, be righted, but it would take time, and, in the meantime, the organization attacked would be ruined and its members scattered. . . .
>
> Will you kindly take action in the matter and inform me of results.[24]

Craft saw only one peaceful and honorable way out of his quandary. Archbishop Ireland would have to use his influence to get Stephan and the others to change their course,

> to abandon mean and useless subterfuges and dark-lantern methods of persecution, and to deal with us honorably and openly, as true bishops and pastors of souls. . . . Here we are, the only American Order of Sisters, and the only ones to take up the progressive views of Leo XIII, the representatives of the theory that Rome in America is American, laboring to bring honor to the Church by showing what it can do for the Indians, and working among the poor of

Christ in poverty and suffering; and for this we are about to be cast out of the Church. We have been prudent and careful, and have given no cause for this, and have made appeals to Orders, bishops, Archbishops, and Delegates, that should have touched their hearts, if Christian zeal, faith, honor, chivalry, or charity existed therein, but without avail.[25]

Despite his protests and the logic of his appeals, the secretary of interior affirmed the decision to exclude Craft from Cheyenne River Reservation. Consequently the priest wrote again to Secretary Bliss, requesting the "reasons for this action, in full, so I can rightly understand it. I am sure that you do not intend to act without hearing both sides of the case, or to leave me completely in the dark, and, consequently, unable to get a fair hearing and make a proper defense."[26]

The next month, he tried a last diplomatic gambit on Bishop O'Gorman by drafting a letter for a friend, Louis Black Tomahawk:

I am a prominent member of the Seven Nations of the Dakotas, and one of their chief counselors, and the one most active in securing their adherence to the Catholic faith. I was connected with the seven councils that went to different Agencies to establish Catholic Societies. Our work for the Catholic faith has been very successful, and the Societies increase rapidly. Many other Indians wish to become Catholics.

An Order of Indian Sisters came to our Agency (Cheyenne). The German priests have made every effort to break them up, and deceived the Agent to get him to help destroy them. The Indians all know this, and understand the base means used to effect it. They are all very indignant and, if their Sisters are persecuted and their Order destroyed, the Indians will no longer adhere to the Catholic Church, and the Societies will break up. . . .

There are many Catholic churches among the Dakotas, where there is no priest, and where the Indians alone have prayers for themselves. It is seldom that a priest goes there. When we are sick and dying, no priest comes to us. We die without the sacraments, and our people bury us.

Now our Sisters come to us, and they have with them as their priest the one who for seventeen years never refused to go through cold and storms to attend the dying Indians, and who stood with them and was wounded with them in war, when all others left them. Now we hope that they will do something for us, and now the German priests try to take our last hope from us, and they say that you are doing this. . . .

Our Sisters have been Sisters a long time, and have had an Order for ten years. If you try to break them up just because the Germans ask you to do it, you will ruin us all, and will gain nothing. We have lost many of our Sisters now, and it is time for you to think before the Church loses us and all our Sisters, if you will do us this great wrong. I hope you will answer me at once.[27]

Craft wrote a second letter for Black Tomahawk to send to Monsignor Sebastiano Martinelli, the apostolic delegate who replaced Satolli. It was basically the same as the one to Bishop O'Gorman and met with the same response. None. The crushing blow, however, came in June from Thomas Ryan, acting secretary for the Department of Interior:

Replying to your letter of the 28th ultimo, asking for the reasons for Department order excluding you from the Cheyenne River Indian Reservation, and stating that you understand that order to apply only to the reservation named, you are informed that the order of exclusion is adhered to, and the same is hereby extended to all other Indian reservations. This is enclosed in letter to agents at Standing Rock, Rosebud, Pine Ridge, Ft. Berthold, Crow Creek, and Lower Brule, with letter saying "All Indian Agents in the section where this man is located should be informed of this order, and instructed to act accordingly.[28]

Craft remained in Pierre, South Dakota, as he planned his next maneuver. The rumormongers, though, still hounded him; this time from James E. Jenkins, the agent of the Sisseton Indian Agency, more than two hundred miles away:

I am informed that one Craft, an ex-priest, is living with four Indian girls in the house of an Indian named Blackhawk, about ½ mile from the ferry landing on the west bank of the river, near Pierre. One of these girls is, or was, known as Sister Gregory, "O.S.B." Her real name is Ellen Nora Clifford, and she is an Allottee of this reservation (a daughter of Mrs. Mary Clifford).[29] The girl is very anxious to come home and her mother, who has only recently heard the sort of man Craft is, would very much like to get her daughter out from under his influence. . . .

If this man Craft is living in open adultery with these girls would it not be well to have warrants sworn out for his arrest? Certainly he should not be allowed to continue his relations with these other girls.[30]

XVIII

A STRATEGIC RETREAT

Characteristically, as he came under attack by the United States Department of Interior, Father Craft sought refuge in the War Department. When the battleship *Maine* exploded and sank at anchor in Havana, Cuba, on 15 February 1898, Craft knew that America's entry into the Cuban insurrection against Spain would require massive movement of troops eastward and that the nursing skills of the remaining four sisters could well be their ticket out of the reservations. He telegraphed the War Department, offering their services in the nation's war effort. In addition to volunteering to serve wherever needed — "Cuba, Puerto Rico, Manila, or any of the camps in the United States," Father Craft dropped the names of Senator Redfield Proctor, Maj. Gen. John M. Schofield, Gen. Nelson A. Miles, and Brig. Gen. John R. Brooke, and officers and surgeons at Pine Ridge Agency during the Indian War of 1890–91 "who remember my services with the army at that time."[1] The *Irish World* reported that Father Craft had volunteered his services along with five members of the Congregation of American Sisters.[2] Captain William M. Fisk wrote to him on 27 April 1898 advising that "it would give me great pleasure to have you and the Sisters in my Company."[3]

Soon after the war broke out, Congress authorized United States Army recruitment of a thousand civilian nurses to care for the wounded and other troops stricken by typhoid and yellow fever. Through the influence of General O'Beirne,[4] Anita Newcomb McGee, acting assistant surgeon of the Surgeon General's Office, confirmed on 8 October 1898 that Craft and his sisters would be offered contracts to serve as nurses "at Jackson-ville, Florida or Lexington, Kentucky."[5] Each would be paid thirty dollars a month.

Probably before Agent Jenkins's scandalous allegations reached Chey-enne River or Washington, Father Craft and the sisters were already en route east and south. They served first at Camp Cuba Libre in Jackson-ville, Florida, arriving on 21 October, where for the next six weeks they worked in military hospitals, nursing the sick in wards for the treatment of infectious diseases.[6]

The sisters' experience with care of infectious diseases prompted their transfer directly to Cuba. Included in the thousand women recruited for army nursing service at the time were many minorities who were "selected by reason of having had [yellow fever]"[7] or who were otherwise considered immune to the disease. After transferring to Camp Onward in Savannah, Georgia, in early December, they sailed for Cuba on 18 December, arriving at Havana's Camp Columbia on 22 December.

Evidently no longer reluctant to correspond with the now very distant priest, Archbishop Ireland wrote again to Craft, saying that he was pleased to hear from him "and to know that you, and your good sisters from Dakota, are doing such great work for our sick soldiers. . . . Please give my compliments to the sisters and tell them that I rejoice very much at their success."[8] Craft's reputation preceded him, however, as the usual forces actively sought to frustrate his achievements. The 15 March 1889 New York Times reported: "Sisters Must Quit Cuba: The Pope's Representative Ex-pels Five Sisters of the American Order of the Sacred Heart"

The headline referred to Archbishop Placide L. Chapelle, who in Octo-ber 1898 had been named apostolic delegate to Cuba, Puerto Rico, and the Philippines. Chapelle had recently been reassigned as bishop of New Orleans, Louisiana, from the same position in Santa Fe, New Mexico, and was well acquainted with Monsignor Stephan of the Bureau of Catholic Indian Missions, as well as the papal delegate to the United States, Mon-signor Sebastiano Martinelli. The New York Times's account cites Father Craft as saying: "Archbishop Chapelle orders us to go away from here on account of the old hatred against the (Indian) sisters" and quotes General O'Beirne's explanation:

> Father Craft's reference to the "old hatred against the Indian Sisters" means just this, Gen. O'Beirne said. The order is purely American, and was established

on the Dakota border, about six years ago. Those who are in favor of the European idea in the management of orders and church affairs were antagonized, and Father Craft met with much opposition. . . .

I cannot account for the present move. It looks like a victory for the opponents of Americanism, and, coming at this particular time, it will be painful news to those who believed that the Vatican was in full sympathy with real Americanism.[9]

Craft provided more details of the situation in a letter to O'Beirne:

The first thing Chapelle did was to inform everyone that I was "not in good standing in the Church," "not recognized," "expelled from Indian country," etc. etc. and that the Indian Sisters were "squaws," "not an approved order," and "their establishment not authorized by the Church but the disapproved work of that very able and very dangerous man, Father Craft." Then he undertook to expel us from Cuba, and was enraged when the Bishop of Havana refused to aid him. Then he and his Washington allies set secular agents and corrupt rascals here at work to undermine and destroy us, and did not hesitate even to use the A.P.A. [American Protective Association] element, always ready to aid in destroying anything good in the Church.[10]

Archbishop Chapelle's order against Father Craft presumably stopped short of excommunication but certainly revoked the priest's faculties to preach or hear confessions in the Diocese of Havana. Even as they reeled from this latest blow from rivals within the Catholic Church, Craft's "squaws" were winning awards and recognition from government authorities:

The Sisters have borne the climate here as well as the natives, but have been much fatigued by their long service in military hospitals. They have gained honor and fame here, and among the many hundred patients who passed through their hands there were but two deaths—both cases of incurable tuberculosis. The Surgeon General wrote to them to praise and thank them, and the "Order of Spanish-American War Nurses" adopt them as members, and will soon send them their badges. They are the only Sisters who came with the Army to Cuba, and remained. . . .

So we win laurels and get along well. But as there is to be no more war, I heartily wish we were home. If the Secretary of the Interior would revoke his order excluding me from the Indian Country, we would gladly return. I don't like to keep the Sisters too long under the tension and strain that is a necessary accompaniment of the work here. As long as the Government has recognized the merit of our work, it cannot consistently exile us at the request of those who have merited nothing, and were in sympathy with the enemy. But influence is more mighty than merit. When Congressman Fitzgerald praised us in Congress, and said we would "live forever in the hearts of American soldiers,"[11] he might have asked if we deserved exile from the Indian Country—but he didn't.[12]

He wrote to Kelly again the following month, still determined to publicize what he considered the great success of his sisterhood:

Since I wrote you last, I was thinking that, as our Sisters are now members of the "Order of Spanish-American War Nurses," and have made quite a record in Cuba, it might be well if that bust of Mother Catharine, when finished, could be placed in Washington, either in Statuary Hall, or in some other public place. I think people in Washington would like to have it there, and it would not arouse opposition as the Marquette Statue did. In fact, the only opposition, if any, would come from such people as Msgr. Stephan, and would even be useful in showing up their animus. I thought I would suggest it, and you can think if it would be possible and advisable.[13]

After the brief war concluded, Craft opened an orphanage at Pinar del Rio in May 1899, staffed by his four sisters. Mother Mary Anthony (Susie Bordeaux) died on 15 October 1899; Craft officiated at the funeral and provided details for General O'Beirne:

Rev. Mother Mary Anthony, C.A.S., Assistant General of the Congregation of American Sisters, and member of the Order of Spanish-American War Nurses, died before the altar in the chapel on Sunday Oct. 15th. On Tuesday, Oct. 17th she was buried in the military cemetery with military honors, by the officers and soldiers of the 1st Infantry and 7th Cavalry. The firing party, bugler, and pall bearers, were soldiers of the 1st Infantry. The body, covered by the flag, was carried on the escort wagon, preceded by the firing party, and bugler and chaplain, escorted by the pall bearers, and followed by the Sisters, the orphans, and soldiers of the Infantry and Cavalry, and veterans who had served in the armies of Europe. I read the burial service, the same as for a soldier, the firing party fired three volleys over the grave, and the bugler sounded the "taps." "The soldier's last good night."

This is the first time in the history of our Army that a Sister was buried by the Army with the honors of war, and it will be of interest to the Army that the first Sister so buried, was a granddaughter of Chief Spotted Tail, and a grand-niece of Chief Red Cloud. She was much beloved by the soldiers whom she had nursed back to health at the sacrifice of her own life, and American soldiers mingled their tears and prayers with those of Cubans and Spaniards who loved her for her care of their orphans and sick. Byron's lines on Gen. Hoche might well apply to her.

> Brief, brave and glorious was her young career,
> Her mourners were two hosts, her friends and foes,
> And fitly may the soldier lingering here,
> Pray for her gallant spirit's bright repose.[14]

May God send me such a death, and grant me the "volley and taps," the "eighth sacrament of the Catholic soldier."[15]

The loss of Mother Mary Anthony from tuberculosis complicated by pneumonia stressed Craft's hapless little band to the breaking point. With the sisters already expelled from the island by the Vatican's representative, their nursing contracts annulled and transportation costs denied by federal authorities, Craft sought desperately for a way out. He appealed the initial denial of transportation costs and formally requested internment of Mother Mary Anthony's body at Arlington National Cemetery. During Christmas week he finally received approval for transportation to Fort Pierre, South Dakota, but "civilians dying abroad could not be disinterred and transported to the United States for interment at public expense."[16] Mother Mary Anthony's remains presumably still rest in grave 22, City Cemetery, Pinar del Rio, Cuba.[17]

Sister Mary Bridget (Annie Pleets) and Sister Mary Gertrude (Ellen Clark) broke with Father Craft early in December. In a letter to Father Fintan Wiederkehr, the Benedictine missionary at Cheyenne River, Sister Bridget advised:

> I had to take off the habit [because] I could not go back there. Sister Gregory and myself left him [Craft] and . . . he has sent us out without a cent among

Cuban families in this wild strange country. So you see that Father Craft always said he is the only one that protected us Indian Sisters. You see the truth now. He has only Sister Joseph now. I want to ask . . . your advise, what to do. *I know* dear Rev. Father it is against my vocation to give up sisterhood, but to get rid off [*sic*] Father Craft I had to, and I am *very very* unhappy now. In the mornings when I get up I thought I would find my habit but to my great sorrow I found dresses by my bed. If it would be possible, Father dear, will you help me, and send me some money so I could come home. I would be very glad if you would send me some money, for I want to come home, because I am getting sick and very unhappy. I want to be a sister again so I want to come home soon. My desire is the religious life, that's all, and no other. Please write soon, let me know if you will help me. The priests are all very funny here. You cannot go and ask their advise. They are very different from the priests in the United States.

No more Mother Bridget now but Annie B. Pleets.[18]

If there was a response from Father Fintan, it was probably too late. In the interim, Craft had successfully arranged transportation;[19] the two former nuns had arrived in New York City aboard the troopship *Sedgwick* on 8 January 1900. A train ride via St. Paul took them to their homes in the Dakotas. Neither of them returned to religious life. Annie Pleets married Joe Dubray, had three children, and used her medical experience in the practice of midwifery on Standing Rock Reservation. When she died in 1948, her long fifteen-decade rosary was among her treasured possessions. Ellen Clark returned to the reservation on Cheyenne River, married Joe Hodgkiss, and also had three children. When Joe died, she married a man named Crowfeather. Widowed a second time, she married Frank Philbrick in 1937.[20]

During the first part of 1900, Craft and Mother Joseph sought approval for their orphanage as well as assignment to a parish in Havana. In June the military governor of Cuba advised Craft that there was no objection to his maintaining an orphan asylum in Pinar del Rio, provided he agreed to efficiently maintain it, funded wholly from private contributions.[21] These short-lived objectives, though, were soon overshadowed by the possibility of another military campaign, which Craft explored with General O'Beirne:

I just sent you a cable message, asking if you could get me a chaplaincy to go with the 1st Infantry to China. . . .

If I can go with the 1st Infantry, I can at once turn the Asylum over to the Alcalde, and leave Mother Joseph with friends in New York, where I can have her taken care of, and then I will be free for the "strenuous life. . . ."

I would really like to see one more campaign before my "taps" are sounded.[22]

When O'Beirne was unable to obtain a chaplaincy for Craft, the priest finally recognized that he had exhausted all his options. Despite incredible perseverance against pervasive and widespread opposition, continuation of his Indian sisterhood was hopeless. His dream of a Native American religious congregation had ended. The conclusion of a letter to O'Beirne reveals his anguish over its ultimate disintegration:

I think, dear friend, that since the poor Indian girls came to me, nearly twelve years ago, to ask to be Sisters, I have maintained a long hard fight, against tremendous odds, to save them. We have proved what they could do, with the same care white Sisters get, and it is also clear that they can never get that necessary care. Now, when it is plain that it is useless to force upon the Church a thing it does not want and has so many means of opposing, surely prudence requires that we end it as honorably as possible. We have wrested victory from defeat on many a hard-fought field, to the day when rifles and bugle sang the requiem over the last of a warrior race and historic family. Now the hand of death closes upon the last of our shattered column, and, while we do not surrender, we must retire to save further slaughter.[23]

Several months later the full bitterness of a dozen years of rejection welled up in a letter to General O'Beirne:

Since I wrote you last, I have had several talks with Bishop Sbaretti,[24] and have drawn from him facts that fully verify what I told you of the unscrupulous character of the clique of German missionaries, Western bishops, and the Stephan and Martinelli combination at Washington—their unChristian purposes, and their unchangeably hostile attitude towards me. Sbaretti is of that party, depends upon them, and acts with them. It seems that I have been marked out for "squelching," for the reason that I took up literally the teachings of the Church as to the necessity for hard labor, self-sacrifice, and honesty of purpose, and chiefly because, in doing so, I took up the cause of the Indian Sisters.

Sbaretti had been promising to give me the first vacant parish, but it became plain to all that he was not sincere. Then a parish priest near here wished to leave, and asked the Bishop to give the parish to some one else, if he could find anyone to take it. Father Menendez asked the Bishop to give it to me, and asked me to apply for it, and I did so. Then the Bishop "showed the cloven hoof" plainly. He pretended not to know me, and required proof of my ordination, record, faculties, etc. I told him plainly, as did others, that this was as bad as asking the same of Ireland or Gibbons, as I was known all over the United States and Cuba, and also in Europe. However, I gave him the proofs he asked.

Then he wanted me to show that my conduct had always been correct, etc. I told him that this was insulting, but showed him that I could make my standing clearer than he could make his own. Finding that he could get nothing against me, he came out openly and said that he knew there was nothing against me personally, and that all the trouble I had ever had with Church people, or rather all their objections to me, came from my defense of the Indian Sisters, whom they did not wish to exist in the Church, or even on its records, as Sisters, now that all but one are gone, and then he said that they never were Sisters, and never were recognized by the Church as such, and told me that I would be required to admit this. He also wished to call their conduct and character in question.

I replied that I had documentary proof of the standing of the Sisters, and of their good conduct and character, and that any churchman, from the Pope down who dared say anything against them, would be at once publicly branded as liars, and slanderers of helpless women, as soon as I could get my evidence into the press. I also said that I thought I had about enough of such dirty work, and that I would not accept any parish he had, and would aid him no further. I also told him of some documents in my possession that seemed to show that the Church and its prelates were nearly as bad as his statements made them appear, and that I would investigate further. He seemed alarmed, and wanted to explain, and said he would see what he could do about the parish, and would write to me. I saw him next day and told him that he might as well state plainly what he intended to do, as I was getting tired and disgusted.

He said he would give me the parish if I would wind up the whole affair of the Indian Sisters by sending Mother Joseph, the only one left, back to the United States. He did not want her to remain in Cuba at all, even in a family

FIGURE 16. Father Craft and four members of the Congregation of American Sisters at Pinar del Rio, Cuba, about 1899. Left to right: Annie Pleets (Sister Mary Bridget), Ellen Clark (Sister Mary Gertrude), Father Craft, Josephine Two Bears (Sister Mary Joseph), and Susie Bordeaux (Mother Mary Anthony). Photographer unknown. Marquette University Archives.

or home of any kind, and did not even want me to spend the time to take her as far as New York, and get her a home there. He wanted me to send her alone, without any care for her safety or comfort. I drew him on far enough to get all this out of him, and to show further that he wanted to please his clique of friends in Washington by giving the last blow to the last of the Sisters. I then told him that such a proceeding would be called brutal by all civilized or semi-civilized people, that I would talk with Mother Joseph and other friends, and write what we thought of it. . . .

He is a very close friend of Msgr. Stephan. Those in Washington are as bad as he is, and you can easily see that, unless I turn rascal, there is nothing for me in the Catholic Church. I find that we can't even get transportation back from Cuba. I asked at the Quartermaster's office about it, and was shown an Order providing that no transportation be issued after contracts are annulled.

The Adjutant General, Scott, tried to make a special case of it, and pointed out to Gen. Wood[25] that the Order was issued long after our contracts were annulled, but Wood maintained that we could get no transportation. It looks very much as if we are stranded here in Cuba.

It is not very pleasant to reflect that the prelates of the Church have followed us up even here, with vindictive malice, and all to please such people as the brutal, ignorant, German monks, and that gray bearded personification of malice, imprudence, spite, and senile dementia, Stephan.

I am now barred from the Indian reservations, from the Army, from parochial work, and from everything that the Church can influence, and all because I have preferred hard work and self-sacrifice, to ease and honors. The only way in which I can remain on good terms with my persecutors, is to humiliate myself before base-born foreign scoundrels, and promise to be all kinds of subservient scoundrel at their bidding. As I cannot do this, I suppose I cannot remain in the Church.

The theories taught by the Catholic Church are beautiful, but evidently are not intended to be practiced. You see what a priest gets for trying it. Prelates, perhaps, dare not condemn him openly, and point out wherein he is wrong, but they will pursue him secretly, get Departments and officials against him, and move heaven and earth to destroy him. If I can ever get away from here, and get to New York, I shall have much material for the press.

We have yellow fever here, and I have finally been able to visit the patients in the military hospital. I have been up there three times today. Of course, I am risking life for nothing, as far as Church and Army are concerned, as neither will ever thank me for it.[26]

XIX

WAS FATHER CRAFT INSANE?

The question needs to be asked. Agent James McLaughlin at Standing Rock was among the first to assess Craft's sanity, advising Herbert Welsh of the Indian Rights Association that the priest's imagination was developed to the point where not only did fiction become his reality but he was entirely capable of convincing others of its legitimacy.[1] Commissioner Thomas J. Morgan, a prominent target of Craft's verbal assaults, wrote that the priest was "considered a very weak if not an unbalanced man mentally."[2] And in a letter to Mother Katharine Drexel, Bishop John Shanley also raised the specter of Craft's derangement: "Father Wilhelm's remarks about Father Craft are somewhat misleading. Poor Father Craft labored very faithfully for many years at Fort Berthold—up to two years ago—when his mind became diseased. The lonely life at that mission is enough to drive anyone crazy."[3]

Father Wilhelm was Joseph B. Wilhelm, an alcoholic priest who succeeded Father Craft at Fort Berthold. Often in trouble himself in previous missionary assignments at Dickinson, Glen Ullin, and Devils Lake, he lasted less than years before he was removed again at the request of the agent at Fort Berthold.[4] Unfortunately, neither Father Wilhelm's comments regarding Craft nor his letter to Mother Drexel have survived. In his reminiscences, Bishop Shanley expressed conflicting views concerning the morals charges laid against the priest as he fled from the Dakotas: "He is a freak, but—I believe he is moral."[5]

Craft's suspected mental instability was hinted at more than a few times in reports and news accounts from Wounded Knee. Frank Wells, Chief Sitting Bear's son, wrote that about the only thing Craft did was "get mad, sometimes."[6] Father Jerome Hunt, O.S.B., asked rhetorically: "Is the man crazy?"[7] And Agent John S. Murphy wrote that the Fort Berthold Indians were "sorely in need of an active healthy priest—one who thinks more of the glory of God and the salvation of souls than of . . . plaudits and newspaper notoriety," describing Father Craft as "a poor man . . . physically unable to cope with the work to be done."[8] Father Martin Kenel, O.S.B., advised Abbot Frowin Conrad, O.S.B., in 1898: "None of the Bishops wants Fr. Craft but he defies them all and acts like a crazy man."[9] Father Joseph A. Stephan thought Craft was dangerous and unstable if not insane, and there were, to be sure, enough reports and allegations to give weight to such claims.

Although very little is actually known about Father Craft, stories persist that he endangered the health of his Indian sisters—perhaps even contributed to the death of Mother Mary Catharine—by forbidding them to eat meat. The charge, however, fails in the face of Bishop Shanley's report that their diet was "salt-pork and bread,"[10] and in Father Fintan Wiederkehr's even less appealing account that they ate rats and ravens during their last winter at Fort Berthold.[11] Some accounts hold that the sisters fished to supplement their diets; others claim they angled without hooks in ponds without fish. Cats and rabbits may also have been a part of their meager sustenance.[12] Craft himself appears to have taken a rather practical approach to survival in the harsh Dakota environs—"Eat when you can, fast when you must"[13]—which may explain the provenance of many of these yarns.

There are stories that conjure up images of a cloaked and shadowy Craft brandishing a revolver, intimidating and terrorizing any sister who would dare to leave his congregation. But these undocumented tales need to be tested against his own writings and actions. Much of what we now know about Craft seems incredible enough without embellishing it with unsupported legends.

Was it a madman who, on Christmas Day 1888, transferred his chieftainship of the Dakota Nation to the Sacred Heart of Jesus? When Spotted Tail's band made Craft an honorary chief in 1883, it was unquestionably a nominal gesture of friendship, perhaps a bit more significant than the Indian names so liberally bestowed on whites, but not a symbol of great moment. However, as the chieftainship became central to the priest's acculturation, true to McLaughlin's assessment, he expanded the concept to include the whole of the Sioux Nation. Consistent with his own penchant for high theater and fully aware of the Indians' awe of ritual, in an elaborate ceremony on 1 January 1888, he consecrated the tribes to the Sacred Heart of Jesus.

Scholars date Catholic devotion to the Sacred Heart to the Middle Ages and before. It has endured as a special form of religious exercise concentrating on the human, spiritual, and divine love represented by the physical heart of Jesus, second person of the Blessed Trinity. Pope Clement XIII granted the observance approbation as a liturgical feast in 1765; Pius IX extended the observation to the universal church in 1856, and Leo XIII enhanced its importance during the second half of the nineteenth century.

Related to this celebration was the Apostleship of Prayer, a spiritual association of Catholics offering daily prayers, works, joys, and sufferings to the Sacred Heart in the form of daily mass, communion, and recitation of the rosary. It was begun in France in 1844 by Francis X. Gautrelet, S.J.; Father Henri Ramière, S.J., is credited with making it a world movement in 1861. Father Craft was especially dedicated to the observance, often sending money and prayerful intentions to the *Messenger of the Sacred Heart,* the monthly organ of the Apostleship. He was a strong believer in the power of the devotion, and throughout his journals he wrote of his being a soldier, a "lieutenant," in the service of God through the Sacred Heart of Jesus.

The religious significance of the consecration of Indian tribes to the care of the Sacred Heart is undiminished by Craft's theatrics. Indeed, his dramatic dedication of the Sioux Nation to the Sacred Heart of Jesus predated Pope Leo XIII's *Annum Sacrum* by ten years.[14] This encyclical consecrated the entire human race to the Sacred Heart. Father Craft's aim was sure; it was his delivery that set him apart.

Also separating him from his contemporaries was an aberrant penchant for penitential sacrifice that defies any modern-day understanding. We blench at the thought of Craft's swallowing the phlegm of the dying Indian girl named Cunegunda or consuming the foul contents of the schoolchildren's emesis basin. Yet a few weeks later, when he writes of resolutely "kissing little brothers' and sisters' sore eyes," some with "ulcerated and broken corneas," we can perhaps identify with the tradition of kissing an injury to make it well.

Father Craft was hundreds of years behind his time in some respects and a century ahead in others. His medical training may have given him some assurance that his digestive system was stronger than the contaminated cuspidors, or perhaps he was influenced by the publicity given at the time to Louis Pasteur's experiments with vaccines. But it was his boundless faith and commitment to sacrifice that impelled him to such desperate acts and provided the impetus to persevere against plainly insurmountable odds.

The notoriety given to James Edward Kelly's dramatic sketch of Mother Mary Catharine's death still raises questions about Craft's motives. Why move a dying woman from her sickbed to a makeshift couch in church? Was this just another of his cross publicity attempts? The priest certainly had an eye for news, and he was always eager to publicize his Indian sisterhood. But in this case the publicity was secondary to his main purpose, which was the health and salvation of his dearest sister. Years earlier, Father Bede Marty, O.S.B., had told Craft that he feared ridicule if they administered the last sacraments before death was imminent. Father Craft explained that the purpose of the sacrament was to heal the sick as well as to save the soul. In 1991, some hundred years later, the Catholic Church clarified the sacrament of extreme unction to encompass the healing of the sick, incorporating a ceremony for the seriously ill that takes place in church. And centuries ago Saint Benedict—certainly a sane man—asked his monks to carry him before the altar to die.

Several years after Mother Catharine's death, though, the Benedictine missionary at Cheyenne River Agency reported that not all of Craft's thoughts at the scene of her demise were pious and noble: "When his first Mother Prioress general Katherine Sacred White Buffalo was dying they carried her in the chapel and Fr. Craft gave her the blessing with the most holy Sacrament. In that solemn moment[—]in that awful and sacred moment when a soul of those poor Sisters was about to leave her body to appear before the tribunal of God, in that moment Fr. Craft says, that he would have plunged a deadly blade in Bishop Shanley's heart had he been there, because he was the murderer of that Sister; since he did not provide for them."[15]

Read in the light of Agent McLaughlin's observations to Herbert Welsh, the series of letters to James E. Kelly, Gen. James R. O'Beirne, and Daniel E. Hudson, C.S.C.,[16] reflect an advancing paranoia that tormented Father Craft. His immense pride would not allow him to even consider that *he* might be the target of the opposition from Stephan, Martin Marty, Shanley, and the others. Father Stephan arguably withdrew his support owing to Craft's reckless attacks on Commissioner Morgan and evidently persuaded Bishop Marty and Bishop Shanley to do the same. Father Craft, however, construed any failure to support him as a prejudicial attack on the Indian sisters. Believing himself too well liked to be the problem, he felt that any criticism of him had to be a cruel subterfuge to undermine the sisters. He even let himself believe idle rumors (or spread them himself) that he was in line to replace Bishop Marty if he would only abandon their cause.[17] On the one hand, Father Craft's paranoia was such that he equated the mere expression of doubt with some sort of dark conspiracy on the part of the skeptics to prove themselves right. On the other hand, near the turn of the century conspiratorial alliances were clearly in fashion throughout the Catholic hierarchy—in Rome, Cuba, America, Washington, and the Dakotas.

The Benedictine missionaries may well have expressed doubt over the viability of Indian vocations at the time. It was a legitimate subject of discussion in the religious press of the day. Father Craft himself had written an anonymous article promoting Indian vocations in the June 1897 issue of *Catholic World Magazine*.[18] A Jesuit missionary from Fort Belknap presented the opposing view in the September issue.[19]

For the first four hundred years of white European exploration and development of the New World, there were very few *white* American vocations, let alone *Native* American ones. In Craft's day, probably not more than 10 percent of the Catholic clergy in the United States was American born. On the frontier, where German and Swiss missionaries also served the pastoral needs of white settlers, the number was even smaller. With the exception of the Benedictine sisters who had supported the development of Josephine, Claudia, Annie, and others who formed Craft's congregation, there were few seminaries or novitiates available to educate Indian candidates for the priesthood or sisterhood.

For their part the Benedictines, immersed in centuries of conservative Catholicism, could hardly have been expected to openly receive a people they believed were not yet released from barbarism. Father Craft, however, as a progressive convert to the faith, felt no more bound by Benedictine tradition and culture than he had by the Jesuit pursuit of perfection twenty years earlier. The fragmented Indian tribes, some of which numbered only in the hundreds or, at most, a few thousand, could not have provided more than a minimal number of legitimate vocations. They comprised myriad cultures and customs, often were bitter enemies to each other, and spoke languages as different from one another as German is from Italian. Moreover, the unique dynamic that combined a close-knit Indian family unit with an equally important extended family of siblings, aunts, uncles, and cousins would discourage all but a very few from abandoning the solace of the tribe.

Understanding the tragic conflict between Father Craft and the American Catholic hierarchy over what should have been a noble and benevolent cause—the assimilation of the American Indian into religious orders—requires an awareness of a parallel movement that developed at a time of great upheaval in Catholic missionary annals. At its genesis was Mother Katharine Drexel, recently elevated to sainthood by Pope John Paul II,[20] and some princes of the Catholic Church who are unlikely to attain quite that level of perfection.

Katharine Drexel was the second of three daughters born to Francis A. Drexel, a successful investment banker with headquarters in Philadelphia and interests throughout the world. The Drexels were devout Catholics and benefactors of many charities through their great wealth; they instilled in their daughters a deep love of God and a strong willingness to share that wealth with those less fortunate. Father James O'Connor, pastor of St. Dominic's Church near the Drexels' summer home, soon became the primary spiritual adviser to the family, especially the Drexel children. Elizabeth had been born in 1855, Katharine on 26 November 1858, and Louise in 1863. When Father O'Connor was named bishop of Omaha, Nebraska, in 1876, Katharine corresponded regularly with him regarding her interest in a religious vocation.

In 1884, on the recommendation of Bishop O'Connor and Bishop Marty, Archbishop James Gibbons of Baltimore named Father Stephan director of the Bureau of Catholic Indian Missions.[21] It was the same year that Katharine and her father attended the installation of Patrick J. Ryan as archbishop of the Diocese of Philadelphia, and a bond was soon established between the Drexel family and the new archbishop. Father Craft, reinstated to Indian Country following the Rosebud conspiracy, began his ministry that same year on Standing Rock Reservation.

Francis A. Drexel died on 15 February 1885 (his wife had died two years earlier) leaving a $15.5 million estate, the largest of record to that date in Philadelphia. After 10 percent of the estate was distributed to specified charities, the remaining 90 percent was placed in a trust with the income to be shared equally by his three unmarried daughters. If they married, their spouses would not share in the inheritance, but any children they had would automatically become heirs to the estate. Any principal remaining after the death of the three sisters and their children would revert to the original charities listed in the will. Bishop O'Connor and Bishop Ryan were fully aware of these terms. They were also well aware that should Katharine Drexel enter an existing order of nuns, control of her inheritance would transfer to that congregation.

A few months after her father's death, at the suggestion of Bishop O'Connor, who had "told us of your many kindnesses," Father Stephan and Bishop Marty visited the three Drexel sisters.[22] Through O'Connor's influence, Katharine had developed a keen interest in the plight of Native and black Americans and had become increasingly engaged in supporting wide-ranging efforts to improve their conditions. Stephan and Marty asked Miss Drexel to help build more schools on the reservations.[23] By the end of that year, a $15,000 contribution from the Drexel sisters built St. Francis Mission and school on Rosebud Agency. Donations for Holy Rosary Mission on Pine Ridge and a new school serving Crow Creek Reservation soon followed.[24]

Bishop O'Connor and Father Stephan often corresponded with Miss Drexel, O'Connor providing spiritual counseling and Stephan offering updates on the status of schools and missions being constructed through her generosity. The bishop opposed Katharine's often-expressed desire to enter a contemplative order of sisters, citing the severe cultural dislocation a wealthy young socialite would encounter entering a cloistered existence. He urged her instead to take an annual vow of chastity, to continue her charitable work in society, and to "think, pray, wait, and all will turn out for your peace and happiness."[25]

When Ellen Clark became the first half-blood Benedictine religious at Zell, South Dakota, in 1886, the Drexel sisters were visiting vocational schools in Europe, seeking ideas to incorporate into similar institutions in America. In February 1887 they were received in audience by Pope Leo XIII. Katharine told the pontiff of her desire to devote her life in the service of God, "and after she had directed to him an appeal for laborers among the Indians in America—an entreaty inspired in her by Bishop O'Connor, Bishop Marty and Father Stephan—he suggested that maybe she should become a missionary herself."[26]

At the invitation of Bishop O'Connor, the adventurous Drexel sisters embarked in the fall of 1887 on a tour of St. Francis Mission at Rosebud (named in honor of their father), Holy Rosary on Pine Ridge Agency, and Immaculate Conception Mission at Stephan, South Dakota (a town bordering Crow Creek Reservation named for Father Stephan). It was their second trip to the frontier West. In September 1884 they had joined their father on a business trip by private railroad car to Yellowstone National Park and Portland, Oregon.

In August 1885 Bishop O'Connor had concluded that "your vocation is not to enter a religious order . . . though God does not will you to a religious order, He has, I am persuaded, a special mission for you in the world. He wishes you, in my opinion, to be in the world, but not of it, and to labor there for your own salvation and the salvation of others, just as you are now doing."[27] Two years later, his opinion remained unchanged:

> The question you will bear in mind is, not which of the two states—the religious or the secular—is the better. That was settled long ago. But in which you can give more glory to God, be of more service to your neighbor, and acquire more merit for yourself.
>
> Nor can there be any question as to whether or not you are called to be the bride of Christ. This you can be in the world as in religion, and that such is your vocation, I have had, for long no doubt.[28]

And a year later, in May 1888, Bishop O'Connor added: "I take all the responsibility for having 'kept you out of a convent' till now. . . . I am persuaded that God wishes you to be where you are at present."[29] The following summer, Father Craft delivered Josephine Crowfeather, Annie Pleets, and Emma Halsey to the convent at Zell, where they joined Ellen Clark in their journey as the first Indian Benedictine religious.

On 6 September 1888 Bishop Marty consented to Craft's transfer to the Bureau of Catholic Indian Missions. Father Stephan assigned him the job of building a new school at Fort Berthold, financed by a $12,000 gift from Katharine Drexel. Marty also agreed that Craft's postulants could go to the convent at Avoca, Minnesota, a more hospitable location than Zell, where Josephine had suffered a bad case of the blues. As Craft arrived at Avoca with Josephine, her sister Claudia, and four other Indian girls, the three Drexel sisters joined Bishop O'Connor and Father Stephan on a tour of missions in northern Michigan and Minnesota. When they returned,

Bishop O'Connor finally relented in his opposition to Katharine Drexel's vocation as a sister. Moreover, she insisted: "I want a missionary order for Indians and Colored people."[30] Within a month, Father Craft wrote in his journal: "I have an idea that God may intend that I or someone should found a congregation of Indian Sisters."[31]

On 12 February 1889, Katharine asked Bishop O'Connor if "it would not be well to organize a Bureau for Colored and Indian Missions?" The bishop replied: "You have decided to become a religious. The next thing for you to determine is, whether you shall establish a new order of the Indian and Colored people or, leaving your income for their benefit, enter an order already established, which will take more or less interest in these races. . . . The more I have thought of your case the more convinced I become that God has called you to establish an order for the objects above mentioned. The need for it is patent to everybody."[32]

Katharine expressed "reasons for not wishing, or rather for questioning whether I should found an order for Indian and Colored," stating her preference for a contemplative order. She was concerned that she lacked the stamina and virtue required for a missionary life and felt that an established order would be more efficient and timely. Additionally, she maintained that work among the Indians and blacks could be done by *all* orders, and her income could finance a bureau of Catholic missions that could administer the effort. But "if it be His Will for me to found an Order I shall do it."[33]

The bishop responded:

I was never so quietly sure of any vocation, not even of my own, as I am about yours. If you do not establish the order in question, you will allow to pass an opportunity of doing immense service to the Church, which may not occur again. Your objections are simply scruples. . . . We must have an order, and a strong order devoted exclusively to it, and, even then, I fear, it will be little more than half done. . . . An order established for the Negroes and the Indian will make a much more direct and *economical* use of your money than an Indian Bureau could. . . . The question is not, will you be all that you should be, but does God will that you be His instrument. . . .

I regard it as settled that you are to establish a new order, and I shall go to Philadelphia merely to arrange details. The Church has spoken to you through me, her unworthy organ, and you must hear her or take the consequences.[34]

A month later, O'Connor visited Archbishop Ireland in St. Paul, whose "face brightened up as I spoke . . . said he, 'it is just the thing we needed. It is a great, indispensable work. Miss Drexel is just the person to do it, and if she does not undertake it, it will remain undone.' . . . I am sure there is not a bishop in the country who . . . would take a different view of it."[35]

Concurring, Bishop Marty recommended that Katharine Drexel locate the motherhouse of her new order in Sioux Falls, South Dakota. Father Stephan could build the convent and chapel in which Katharine would take her vows at the end of her novitiate, and he hoped to start an adjoining Benedictine community of priests and brothers, "a missionary college with a large farm attached to it and its Theological Department at least connected with the seminary of this diocese."[36] Perhaps not entirely in conflict with these plans, Marty, just two days later, provided Father Craft with a Benedictine constitution and ceremonial. He also agreed to the priest's plan to move his novitiate to Fort Berthold and assumed financial responsibility for Annie and Cecilia Gaudreau.[37]

On 7 May 1889, Katharine Drexel entered the novitiate of the Sisters of Mercy at Pittsburgh, Pennsylvania, under the spiritual direction of Bishop O'Connor and Archbishop Ryan. She still had reservations about founding a new order of sisters: "Are you *sure* it is God's will for me to establish a new order when there are so many orders fitted for the purpose, which by adding a vow, made by each sister to devote herself to Indians and Colored, could effect the same good?"[38] Bishop O'Connor emphatically dismissed her anxiety: "I cannot consider, and I beg you not to consider for a moment, the proposed foundation an open question. I gave this matter all the deliberation in my power, and I have never for one instant doubted that the conclusion reached was in accord with the Divine Will. The prelates and heads of religious orders to whom I have spoken on the subject agree with me, some of them enthusiastically. If you expect an angel to be sent to enlighten you in regard to this matter, you may be looking for a little too much."[39]

In St. Paul in early July Craft met Father Stephan, who berated him for his Rosebud experience and adamantly objected to the concept of Indian sisters.[40] In a letter to Stephan's assistant, Craft wrote: "It is never right to condemn a whole class, as Stephan does, because of the faults of some."[41] Bishop O'Connor, in the meantime, suggested to Katharine Drexel that "it would . . . only be prudent to begin now, to lay aside, say, fifty thousand dollars a year as a fund for its [the new order's] support."[42]

In October, as Craft recorded that the sisters at the convent near Avoca, Minnesota, were discouraging vocations among Indian girls,[43] Katharine Drexel still expressed concern over a new order of nuns, especially its financing:

> It makes little difference whether there be a *new* order for Indians and Colored; but it seems to me it makes the greatest difference to have this order start out more wealthy than all the others. . . . Imagine an efficient Bureau and several holy men and intelligent men like Father Stephan whose business it would be to see to all the missions . . . into one grand whole just as the United States is a union of many states. If such an organization were established it would seem to me impossible that the missions would have to *fear* the closing down of the contracts with the Government or the obliterating of their rights, nor that the *Orders* engaged in the missionary work would leave the Indians and Colored and engage in labors amongst the white community.[44]

In November, Archbishop Ryan of Philadelphia presided at the ceremonial reception of Katharine Drexel as a novice at St. Mary's Convent in Pittsburgh. The bishops of Pittsburgh, Helena, Montana, and Boise, Idaho, were there; Bishop O'Connor was ill and unable to attend. Concerned by rumors that candidates would be drawn from other orders to fill hers, Craft offered his aid in securing postulants for their new order if they would leave his alone.[45] Evidently no one had explained to Craft that the intent of Katharine Drexel's new order was to work *for* or *among* Indians and colored people, not to provide a venue for service *by* Indians and colored people. The question of who first had the idea is irrelevant from many standpoints. What was crucial was *who supported* the cause.

The creation of the Diocese of Jamestown, North Dakota, in September 1889 largely removed Bishop Marty from Craft's world. Bishop Shanley continued to support the priest's effort as an "experiment," and when Father Stephan withdrew all support of Craft's mission early in 1890, Shanley authorized Craft's fund-raising trip to the East.[46] Bishop Marty gave his blessing to the trip, which was also supported by Father George L. Willard, Stephan's assistant at the Bureau of Catholic Indian Missions.[47]

Craft's fund-raising campaign, however, was undermined by Stephan, who also attempted to stifle his access to the Catholic press.[48] With the death of Bishop O'Connor in May of that year, the mantle of spiritual adviser to Katharine Drexel transferred to Archbishop Ryan of Philadelphia, who became her "father in God" for the next two decades.[49] Ryan's first correspondence with Katharine after Bishop O'Connor's demise advised her that "he [Bishop O'Connor] should be regarded in the future as the founder of your future order."[50] In July, arrangements had been made for Leo XIII's apostolic blessing on Sister Mary Katharine Drexel and her companions, who were to form the nucleus of the new congregation of sisters.

Early in December 1890, Father Craft rejected Stephan's proposal to send him among the Navaho Indians in New Mexico and Arizona, and fast-moving events thereafter put the beleaguered priest in the thick of the action at Wounded Knee. In January 1891 Stephan denied that Craft was ever an agent of the Bureau of Catholic Indian Missions.[51] Three weeks later, on 12 February, Stephan and Bishop Marty witnessed Katharine Drexel's religious profession as the foundress of the Sisters of the Blessed Sacrament. Archbishop Ryan, who administered her final vows, added the words "for Indians and Colored People" to the official title of Katharine's order.[52] Under his direction, Miss Drexel promised "poverty, chastity, and obedience, and to devote my life to the service of the Indians and the colored race and the prosecution until death of the duties of the Order of the Blessed Sacrament according to its approved rule and constitution under authority and in the presence of my Lord in God, the Most Reverend Archbishop of Philadelphia."[53]

In April 1891 Sister Katharine donated $600 "through Father Stephan" for the "support of the missionary at [Fort] Berthold." Bishop Shanley added "$400 to that, so that one thousand dollars has started a convent, and kept six Sisters and a priest [Father Craft] one year and a half."[54] With the assent of Bishop Shanley, Craft had brought Josephine and Claudia Crowfeather, Jane Moccasin, Alice White Deer, Nellie Dubray, and Susie Bordeaux to the unopened school at Fort Berthold in November 1891. Sister Gregory (Ellen Clark) and Sister Bridget (Annie Pleets) joined them there about the same time.

On 8 December, the Feast of the Immaculate Conception, six or eight young Indian women in Elbowoods, North Dakota, received the "Holy Habit" in "the first house of Indian Benedictine Sisters ever established."[55]

And by the end of that same month in Pittsburgh, Pennsylvania, there were twenty-eight novitiates in Katharine Drexel's convent.

During 1892, Father Craft made several attempts to find a safer refuge for his Dakota community:

> I think the only safety for the Sisters will be to take them East. If I can get any Eastern bishop to let us come to his diocese, I would gladly take the worst place in it. . . . I cannot and will not abandon the Sisters.[56]
>
> Could you not . . . find out through the Paulist Fathers, Gen. O'Beirne, and others of our friends, if I could get Archbishop [Michael A.] Corrigan [of New York], or Bishop [Charles] McDonnell [of Brooklyn], or some other Eastern Bishop, to let us come to his diocese. . . . It would be a good idea if I could establish my Indian community somewhere near the settlements of the New York Indians, and try to convert them. The interest taken in the shrine [of Katharine Tekakwitha] at Auriesville would seem to show that the people of New York would be in favor of a work like ours.[57]

Although desperately interested in getting the sisters east, Craft nevertheless avoided interfering with Katharine Drexel's efforts. He wrote again to Father Herman J. Heuser in July:

> Neither I nor my Sisters wish to ask assistance from Mother Katharine Drexel. She has been very kind to all the Missions, but naturally would not understand our position, and would act, as she usually does, upon the advice of B. Marty and F. Stephan, both of whom would like to get the community out of my hands, and force it into any position that would ensure its failure or destroy its usefulness. . . . Neither would we wish to be connected with the Sisters of the Most Blessed Sacrament, or any others. Our community must exist alone . . . to prove that Indians are capable of all that has been denied them.[58]

Katharine Drexel, however, was not averse to referring a potential candidate for Craft's order. In the fall of that year she enquired on behalf of a young woman interested in joining the priest's community; Bishop Shanley replied:

> We have a community of Indian Nuns at the Fort Berthold Mission, that is, there is one nun with five novices. How it is going to turn out, God knows.

I was there about three weeks ago to examine the state of affairs. I found the Indian Sisters happy, obedient, pious—but unspeakably poor; living on salt-pork and bread. It is Bethlehem. The Sioux girls can do that uncomplainingly, for they have been used to such life from babyhood. In my opinion it would be too hard a life for anyone else. I believe that our Indian community, if it is to succeed, must recruit itself from Dakota tribes, and therefore I could not advise your young friend to come out here.[59]

The young candidate was Georgiana Burton, a Seneca Indian who in 1893 became the first Native American admitted to the Sisters of the Blessed Sacrament. Mother Katharine was, in these earlier years, reluctant to accept candidates who might otherwise enter existing minority sister-hoods, such as the Oblate Sisters of Providence or the Sisters of the Holy Family.[60] Still, the acceptance of a member of the Seneca tribe in 1893 raises the question why none of Craft's sisters, even the Benedictine Sister Mary Gertrude (Ellen Clark), never made the transition to Mother Drexel's community. Georgiana Burton became the Sisters of the Blessed Sacrament's first Sister Mary Elizabeth on 26 September 1895; she died at St. Francis de Sales Convent, Powhatan, Virginia, on 2 June 1909.[61]

Cardinal Gibbons of Baltimore was the highest-ranking American prelate to visit Katharine Drexel during the formation of her community; Placide L. Chapelle, archbishop of Santa Fe, New Mexico, followed in 1893 to persuade her to assign the new order to St. Catherine's Indian School in his diocese. In 1893 Cardinal Gibbons wrote to Craft: "The life of self denial led by yourself and your colleagues is an impulse to us all."[62] In 1899 Archbishop Chapelle, then the pope's delegate to Cuba, expelled Craft and his sisters from the island.[63]

During 1895 Craft made a major effort to convince Stephan to help him bring the sisters east: "If I and the Sisters could serve the Church as well elsewhere, even in work for the whites or negroes, we would not be foolish enough to refuse an offer of a wider field and better returns. . . . Just make us an offer of a wider and more fruitful field and see if I am too attached to this one to accept it."[64]

And a month later: "If you had the Sisters in Washington to take care of the Bureau residence, or to publish an official organ of the Bureau, or to help in any other way, they would be a "drawing card," and even here could in many ways aid the Bureau."[65]

Stephan weakened a bit as 1896 began, asking Craft for photos of his congregation and promising "to send us the first financial aid you could get. I hope you won't forget it."[66] But when Bishop Marty died in May 1896, Craft had nowhere to run when the slanderous rumors and allegations destroyed his Indian sisterhood early that next year.

In the end, he had failed miserably. Only one of his Indian sisters remained. Banished again from Indian Country, he was unable to recruit replacements for his congregation. Ostracized by the church and persona non grata to the military, he was an intensely proud American stranded on foreign soil. How did it all happen? What was the crack in Craft's personality that thwarted a decade of herculean effort? For an answer, we need only consider the supreme arrogance so often exuded in his journals and letters. Audaciously, he attempted to *compel* God to come to the aid of the impoverished savages for whom he labored and sacrificed. He railed against government bureaucracies and policies that, he contended, encouraged corruption and degradation of the Indians. And he fought tenaciously against what he perceived as the myopic reluctance of his superiors to accept Indian vocations.

Katharine Drexel's Sisters of the Blessed Sacrament, however, soon became a successful and enduring legacy to a saintly life consecrated to the service of God for the well-being of Native Americans, blacks, and other minorities. When Mother Drexel passed to her reward in 1955 at age ninety-six, the Drexel estate had distributed a total of $39,800,000, substantially all of it to these noble causes. Today over 250 Sisters of the Blessed Sacrament run eighteen elementary schools, two secondary schools, and thirty religious and social service centers, as well as Xavier University in New Orleans. Operating in Arizona, California, Florida, Georgia, Illinois, Louisiana, New Mexico, New Jersey, New York, Pennsylvania, and Texas, these institutions have given hope and opportunity to generations of American minorities.

Was Father Craft insane? Or was he just crazy to think he could force an order of Indian nuns on a Catholic hierarchy in full pursuit of a timely and pragmatic alternative with its financial resources already in place? We may never know the answer. The record is inconclusive. The Jesuit community has only minimal records of Craft's educational curriculum; there are no personnel files on him in Jesuit archives for the Missouri Province, New York–Canada Mission, Maryland Province, or at Georgetown University. The documentation of recorded opinion on the priest's mental competence is, unfortunately, limited to what is presented here. Those most qualified to help us cannot do so. Father Stephan's records are widely dispersed and cunningly incomplete. One of Stephan's letters to Craft concerning the Dawes commission in July 1888 cautiously ended: "Please regard this letter as confidential, and, after perusal, destroy it."[67] Bishop Martin Marty's personal papers were also destroyed—some by an over-zealous housekeeper, the rest by Thomas O'Gorman, who in 1896 replaced him as bishop of Sioux Falls. O'Gorman, a professor of church history at the Catholic University of America and a lifelong friend of Bishop John Ireland of St. Paul, was elevated to the position by Archbishop Francesco Satolli, the first apostolic delegate to the United States. It was the same Bishop O'Gorman who collaborated with temporal authorities to have Craft arrested at Cheyenne River Reservation. The bishop is reported to have been "interrupted by a priest . . . as O'Gorman was methodically sorting his predecessor's letters and other documents and destroying most of them in a blazing fireplace. Despite the fact that he was recognized as an historian of some stature, the bishop seemingly made precipitous judgements regarding Marty's papers—especially those relating to person-nel problems—and did away with them on the basis that it would be better for all concerned to 'let sleeping dogs lie.'"[68]

Finally, Archbishop Ireland himself gave instructions at his death that left all his personal papers in ashes. So those inclined to judge Father Craft insane will need to reconcile their conclusion with the next eighteen years of his life. If he was not insane, he was certainly a visionary like those who throughout history have been feared, maligned, persecuted, and de-nounced as lunatics. He had a vision of establishing a religious congre-gation for Indian women and pursued it relentlessly for more than a de-cade. But no one in the American Catholic hierarchy had the vision to sustain it or the courage to condemn it. Even in defeat, he had fashioned a retreat that so gave the illusion of victory that his Indian nuns were praised in the halls of Congress. Critics then and now are quick to claim that Father Craft's congregation of Indian sisters was never legitimately established, that it had no canonical origin or approbation. The Catholic Church moves slowly. A decade is a blink of an eye. Bishops were certainly involved in the origins and initial support of Craft's effort to establish an order of Indian sisters. Even without final papal approbation, it still de-served a better ending.

The human side of the church, though, was *very* human. It too had failed to reach its full potential. Craft's arrogance and swaggering hubris,

Stephan's prejudice and treachery, Shanley's lack of resolve, Ireland's and Gibbons's duplicity—all shared culpability for the demise of the sisterhood. Consistent with the dismal history of Indian and white relations, the real victims as the tragedy unfolded at the turn of the century were the Indian sisters and their tribes.

A poem that prefaced Father Craft's journals provides a clue to his final reaction to his dilemma:

†

Thoughts in the saddle
On the general beauty and rectitude of things as they
ought to be, and as we would like to have them,
and
The general yellowness and utter undesirability and misery
of things as they are, and as we don't like to have them,
by
An Indian Missionary

	[Translation]
Tolle, lege, et si vere	Take, read, and if you think
Scripsi putas, miserere	I have truly written, have mercy
Sacerdoti misero.	On a wretched priest.
Bonum semen seminavit,	He sowed good seed,
Suo sanguine origavit,	He watered it with his blood,
Pro hoc gente barbaro.	For this barbarous nation.
Si non crescit terram crede	If it does not grow, consider
Aridam et malam esse.	The land arid and evil,
Et datam diabolo.[69]	And given to the devil.

Father Craft could expend extraordinary energy, suffer unspeakable hardship, and then just say "To hell with it! N'importe." After almost twenty grueling years he simply turned, and using a cane to steady his erect military bearing, walked offstage.

XX

HOMECOMING

Early in 1901, Craft and his last remaining sister sailed for America.[1] Mother Joseph (Josephine Two Bears) returned to her home in the Dakotas, married Joachim Hairychin in 1903, and died giving birth to twins in March 1909.[2]

As Father Craft retreated to his family's homestead in Milford, Pennsylvania, Monsignor Stephan, approaching eighty years of age, returned from an extended visit to Europe, where he had attempted to recover his failing health. Unable to resume the demanding travels and responsibilities of his position at the Bureau of Catholic Indian Missions, he moved to St. Elizabeth's Convent in Cornwell Heights, Pennsylvania, the motherhouse of Katharine Drexel's Sisters of the Blessed Sacrament for Indians and Colored People.[3] Craft and Stephan were now separated by little more than a hundred miles, but with the Indian sisters destroyed, the monsignor no longer had a reason to blacklist the priest. Either that or his deteriorating health had sapped his animus to pursue his long-standing feud. Stephan died that September and was buried in the convent cemetery. "May the God he served be his exceeding great reward," was inscribed on his tombstone.[4]

No longer under attack from his own quarter, Craft initially considered joining the Paulist Fathers, who at the time had a somewhat rebellious reputation themselves. The Paulists had been founded by Isaac Thomas Hecker, an American-born convert to Catholicism who had entered the Redemptorist order in the mid-1840s. With a few other American-born

Redemptorists, George Deshon, Augustine F. Hewitt, and Francis A. Baker—converts all—Hecker found himself in a European-dominated organization dedicated primarily to the service of German immigrants. He and his colleagues had been conducting missions among non-Catholics in the East and soon concluded that the Catholic Church in the United States needed a greater American identity. Success among American non-Catholics and promoting religious vocations in the United States required the church to build an authentic American presence, consistent with the country's values of freedom and governance. All of this called for American religious orders, American seminaries and universities, and less European influence. It also generated huge opposition from local ethnic groups and the foreign hierarchy. During the formation of the Paulists, Father Hecker had gone to Rome to plead the cause of the new order and was expelled from the Redemptorists for his seditious conduct. Pope Pius IX, however, eventually released Hecker and his associates from their vows as Redemptorists and suggested they form their own American house. Hecker not only successfully established the Paulists as a premier American religious order of the period but also founded the *Catholic World* and the Paulist Press, major communications media for the Catholic Church in America. The Americanism movement of the Catholic Church was championed by United States prelates such as Ireland and Gibbons during the ensuing years, leading to the establishment of the Catholic University of America in 1887.

Father Hecker died in December 1888 and was succeeded as superior general of the order by Augustine F. Hewitt. When Hewitt died in 1897, he was replaced by another of the founders, George Deshon. Deshon had been a roommate of Ulysses S. Grant at West Point, where he had graduated second in his class. He had taught at the academy after graduation and retained many of his military habits throughout his lifetime.[5]

In this setting the Paulists seemed to afford a safe harbor for Father Craft, who had been set adrift, as it were, by the church. Eventually, though, he decided it would be unfair to them and impractical for him to press the matter. Any talent he might bring to their fledgling publishing efforts would be seriously compromised by his reputation among the Chapelle and Sbaretti faction as being "dangerous, revolutionary, [and] ultra-American." He concluded that although Father Deshon may well have understood Craft's situation, his followers would not. Politically, they would "have to keep me out of sight. . . . It would also cut out of my life some years that I have not to spare, as it would be a long time before they would trust me with any work of importance."[6]

Through the efforts of Rev. J. W. Treis of St. Joseph's Church in nearby Matamoras, Craft was granted return of his clerical faculties by Bishop M. J. Hoban of Scranton, Pennsylvania.[7] On 4 July 1902 Hoban named Craft the first pastor of St. Matthew's Church in East Stroudsburg, Pennsylvania. The old frame church, atop a hill on Brown Street near a right-of-way of the Delaware, Lackawanna, and Western Railway, had been built in 1868 to provide a place of worship for the mostly Irish-Catholic railroad workers.[8] The bishop had concluded during the interim that not enough Catholic families had settled in the area to warrant a permanent parish. The area near the Pocono Mountains of Pennsylvania was a popular vacation spot, however, and the little village of Delaware Water Gap, four miles to the southeast, was a mecca for well-to-do-vacationers from eastern cities, especially New York and Philadelphia. Many of these visitors would spend entire summers at local resorts—the Castle Inn, Glenwood Hotel, Kittatinny House, Pocono Manor, and Reenleigh Hotel. Craft's initial assignment was to serve the needs of this influx of Catholic "boarders."

During the summer, though, he found more than sixty resident Catholic families who were eager to provide ongoing support for his rather meager needs. In November 1902, at age fifty, he set up housekeeping for the first time in his life. The women of the parish furnished the house near the church that served as the rectory. "The old army proverb holds good," he remarked, "Ladies can never do anything wrong."[9]

Perhaps it was this bucolic, invigorating environment that led Craft to spend the next eighteen years in relative anonymity as a parish priest; possibly he was squelched by the bishop as a condition of granting faculties; or maybe he was just burned out. He never returned to Indian Country, and he ceased writing for publication in the religious or secular press.

For his personal correspondence, though, Craft began using a letterhead embellished with a coat of arms bearing the motto ESSE QUAM VIDERI (To be rather than to seem). The shield was divided into quarters, with a lone passant lion in an upper quadrant. Above the aegis roamed a chimerical winged griffin with the head and tail of a dragon. Intriguingly, the griffin is a duplicate of that appearing on the Basset family crest, the side of his family that also provided his Indian blood. The motto "esse quam videri" appears on the Croft family crest, which may have been the closest he could find to his own family name.[10] The solitary lion certainly fits his personality. This was his personal stationery for at least sixteen years.

By 1906 the local press commented favorably on the growth of St. Matthew's under Father Craft's leadership. The resident parish population had grown to over three hundred, and together with the contributions of summer vacationers—the weekly mass at the Glenwood Hotel was regularly attended by more than three hundred communicants—easily covered his $900 annual salary. Any amount exceeding operating expenses and his salary was allocated to other church activities or charities. He prided himself on never having to ask for money, and he was popular with young and old. "Church and denominational lines are not observed by Father Craft when it comes to righting a wrong, lending a helping hand, or distributing charity," reported a local journalist.[11] Eighty years later, a few elderly parishioners still remember him fondly. When they were tiny children, the priest would extend the little finger of his right hand so they could grasp it in a greeting.

As the fiftieth anniversary of the Battle of Gettysburg neared in 1913, Craft's fragile health kept him close to home. He wanted to attend the reunion and its commemorative events, eager to meet with "old friends of both armies," but he was concerned about the strenuous trip in very hot weather at the time.[12]

However, a few years later, as a new war grew in Europe, Craft was once again seduced by the prospect of real combat. He wrote to his mother saying that the United States "*may* send some troops to France, more for the *moral* effect, but they won't be very many—at least for awhile. That German government has been acting like a pirate, and will have to be put out of business, for the peace and safety of the whole world."[13]

On 30 April 1917 he had attended a meeting of the Sons of the Revolution in New York City, where some three thousand members pledged their support for the country's entry into World War I. By June he had dropped all pretense about his plans. "Don't worry about my going to the war," he explained to his mother. "It is the duty of *every* American to offer his services at a time like this. My only fear is that they won't take me, at my age.[14] He registered his name and address at the United States Army Building on Whitehall Street "so that if . . . officers, who knew me in the 'old Army,' . . . would like to have me with them, they know where to find me. I speak French, and have been in France in war-times, and I can 'hold down a saddle.'" He hoped for a position as chaplain but was willing to accept practically any assignment: "I know that I could do more with troops than any who would not have the same experience that I have. Also, I speak the Sioux language, and could do good work with Indian troops, if they intend to use them. It seems a pity to let Uncle Sam lose the services of an experienced veteran, for the mere 'technicalities' of a few extra years, or a few 'battle-scars,' when experienced men, whom soldiers could feel they could rely on, are so much needed. I am waiting for a chance to get on the fighting line, and I hope Uncle Sam will use my services."[15]

True to his heritage, this aging veteran of five wars was trying to inveigle his way into a sixth one. The temptation is to dismiss his action as irrational, just another sign of mental instability. President Woodrow Wilson's desk, however, has been described as "piled high with petitions from former Indian fighters, Texas Rangers, southern 'colonels,' and other military adventurers." One of the more notable personages desperate to join the fighting was none other than Theodore Roosevelt: hero of San Juan Hill, twenty-sixth president of the United States. At the time, he was "fifty-nine years old, blind in one eye, and weakened by tropical fever."[16]

Father Craft never made it to a sixth war, and he turned his attention instead to expanding his parish. His legacy for many years was the construction of St. Mark's Mission in Delaware Water Gap, Pennsylvania. This small, friendly chapel served the "summer boarders" and the few permanent residents of the Gap for almost two decades.[17] As with many of his previous plans, however, poor timing and external factors shortened its life span. Vacation patterns changed drastically as the automobile opened more distant vistas to travelers from eastern cities, and the Great Depression of the 1930s closed the few old frame hotels that had not already been destroyed by fire. St. Mark's Church still stands today on Mountain Road in the Gap, but it has been converted to condominiums. On the right front behind some low bushes, however, the cornerstone still reads:

ST. MARK'S MISSION
ERECTED A.D. 1920
REV. FRANCIS CRAFT
RECTOR

St. Mark's opened on 30 May 1920. Not long after, Craft fell ill. He hemorrhaged and died on a Saturday evening, 11 September 1920. Bishop

Hoban delivered the eulogy in a service attended by priests from all around the state. A throng of mourners filled St. Matthew's, the overflow crowd extending down the entrance stairway and into the churchyard. However, even this final expression of respect from the church he had embraced so many years earlier was destined to be eclipsed. Soon after the funeral, a lengthy tribute appeared in the local paper. It concluded:

> Stroudsburg has lost a noble citizen, and his country a real Patriot, and the church of God a superb Christian minister and priest. God give his soul rest and light and peace in Paradise, and may the same God send us in this time of great need many many more (in all parts of His Church), of the same glorious type is the prayer of

REGINALD S. RADCLIFFE[18]

Like other prophets before him, Father Craft in the end found greater honor from quarters other than his adopted faith. Archdeacon Reginald S. Radcliffe was a prominent priest of the *Episcopal* Church.

Craft's most notable tribute in this life came some years later, in 1930, during the conversations of Black Elk and John G. Neihardt, which led to the classic biographical history of the Sioux Nation, *Black Elk Speaks*. Black Elk, a holy man of the Oglala Sioux, in describing the events just before the Wounded Knee tragedy, spoke these words: "There a Black Robe came and tried to coax us to return. Our people told him that Wasichu promises were no good; that everything they had promised was a lie. Only a few Oglalas turned back with the Black Robe. He was a good man and he was badly wounded that winter in the butchering of Big Foot's band. He was a very good man, and not like the other Wasichus."[19] To which Neihardt noted, "This was Father Craft."

†

EPILOGUE

In 1935, Father Sylvester Eisenman, O.S.B., the founder of St. Paul's Indian Mission at Marty, South Dakota, met with Mother Katharine Drexel to plan a community of Indian sisters. Bishop Bernard J. Mahoney of Sioux Falls gave his approval. Cautious provisions were made for a temporary rule to govern the order for at least five years; it was to begin as a "Pious Association."

Seven Native American women were invested into the Congregation of the Oblate Sisters of the Blessed Sacrament on 6 October 1935. The order's "Period of Essay" lasted from 1935 until 1943. On 25 April 1949 the Catholic Church at last fully recognized "the Oblate Sisters as a Religious Congregation, a red-letter day for the little community."[1] The order celebrated its sixty-fifth anniversary in 2000.

NOTES

Introduction

1. Francis M. Craft Journal, 11 July 1888, author's collection (hereafter Craft Journal).

1. The Formative Years

1. Sarah Craft to Craft, 27 January 1891, author's collection.

2. Francis M. Craft's application for membership, Society of the Sons of the Revolution, 5 November 1890, Fraunces Tavern Museum, New York.

3. Fannie F. Craft to Sister Mary Claudia Duratschek, O.S.B., 17 November 1945, Diocese of Sioux Falls, Sioux Falls SD.

4. Isaac B. Craft letter, 1 May 1863, copy in Craft Papers, Pike County Historical Society, Milford PA.

5. James Edward Kelley [*sic*], "Rev. Francis J. [*sic*] Craft Served Many Countries," *Scranton (PA) Catholic Light,* vol. 3 (October 1921); Diocesan Historical Series, Dual Jubilee Number, 6 October 1921, 39.

6. A. G. Craft to Craft, 1 December 1882, author's collection.

7. *East Stroudsburg (PA) Morning Press,* "Father Craft, Hero of Many Wounds, Quietly Dies Here," 8, no. 101 (13 September 1920).

8. Craft to Kelly, 16 and 26 January 1917, James Edward Kelly Papers (hereafter Kelly Papers), New-York Historical Society, New York NY.

9. *Stroudsburg (PA) Daily Times,* "Doctor, Soldier, Priest," 9, no. 139 (1 November 1902).

10. Craft to Kelly, 12 May 1910, Kelly Papers. Throughout the book, ampersands in quoted material have been converted to "and" for easier reading.

11. Craft Journal, 10 April 1890.

12. Rev. Harold G. Durkin to Doctor Dolan, 5 October 1945, Diocese of Sioux Falls. Durkin was pastor at St. Matthew's Church, 1943–61.

13. Craft to Isidore Daubresse, S.J., 25 November 1879, Lauinger Library, Georgetown University Archives, Washington DC.

14. Craft Journal, 21 March 1888.

2. Path to Priesthood

1. The Catholic religious order founded in 1540 by Ignatius Loyola, Basque soldier turned mystic.

2. Index Alphabeticus Sociorum, 1876, Jesuit Missouri Province Archives, St. Louis MO.

3. Craft Journal, 11 April 1889.

4. Catalogus Missionis, Neo-Eboracensis et Canadensis, 1877, 16; 1878, 15; and 1880, 32; and Catalogus Provinciae Belgicae, Societatis Jesu, 1879, 68, Jesuit Missouri Province Archives.

5. Craft to Daubresse, 25 November 1879, Lauinger Library, Georgetown University Archives.

6. Craft Journal, 16 April 1888.

7. Craft to Kelly, 7 November 1906, Kelly Papers.

8. Craft to Daubresse, 25 November 1879, Georgetown University Archives.

9. Craft Journal, 21 March 1888: "What Indian blood I have is not from these, and when with the Kalispels, I never thought to claim it."

10. Craft to George L. Willard, 27 January 1890, Bureau of Catholic Indian Missions Records, Marquette University Archives, Milwaukee WI (hereafter BCIM).

11. Alice B. Kehoe, *North American Indians: A Comprehensive Account,* 2d ed. (Englewood Cliffs NJ: Prentice Hall, 1992), 384. See also John R. Swanton, *The Indian Tribes of North America* (1952; reprint, Washington DC: Government Printing Office, 1968), 399–400.

3. Spotted Tail's Quest

1. The Sicangus, Lakota for "burnt thighs," were called Brûlé Sioux by the French.

2. Michael F. Steltenkamp, S.J., *Black Elk: Holy Man of the Oglala* (Norman: University of Oklahoma Press, 1993), 5.

3. Order of St. Benedict.

4. Francis Paul Prucha, *American Indian Policy in Crisis: Christian Reformers and the Indian, 1865–1900* (Norman: University of Oklahoma Press, 1976), 30–71. Religious denominations assigned to specific Indian agencies are listed in U.S. Commissioner of Indian Affairs, *Annual Report, 1872,* 461–62.

5. Society of Jesus (Societatis Jesu).

6. Sister Mary Claudia Duratschek, O.S.B., *Crusading along Sioux Trails: A History of the Catholic Indian Missions of South Dakota* (Yankton, SD: Benedictine Convent of the Sacred Heart, 1947), 39–59.

7. Robert F. Karolevitz, *Bishop Martin Marty: The Black Robe Lean Chief* (Yankton SD: Privately printed for the Benedictine Sisters of Sacred Heart Convent, 1980), 69–78.

8. George E. Hyde, *Spotted Tail's Folk: A History of the Brulé Sioux* (Norman: University of Oklahoma Press, 1961), 295.

9. Hyde, *Spotted Tail's Folk,* 322–25.

10. Prucha, *American Indian Policy in Crisis,* 57.

11. "Chief and Priest in One," *New York Sun,* 2 November 1890.

12. Hyde, *Spotted Tail's Folk,* 332–33.

13. Martin Marty to Indian Bureau, 15 June 1882, BCIM.

14. Marty to Frowin Conrad, 10 February 1883 (original in German), Conception Abbey Archives, Conception MO.

4. Conspiracy on Rosebud

1. James E. Kelly Papers, Archives of American Art, Smithsonian Institution, Washington DC.

2. William K. Powers, *Oglala Religion* (Lincoln: University of Nebraska Press, 1977), 100.

3. Florentine Digmann, S.J., Diary, 25, BCIM.

4. Royal B. Hassrick, *The Sioux: Life and Customs of a Warrior Society* (Norman: University of Oklahoma Press, 1964), 26.

5. Craft Answer to Charges, 10 July 1884, Record Group (hereafter RG) 75, National Archives, Washington DC.

6. Craft to Willard, probably 2 November 1888 (first page missing), BCIM.

7. James G. Wright, Reports of Agents in Dakota, 1883, 42–43, National Archives.

8. Craft Answer to Charges, 10 July 1884, RG 75, National Archives.

9. Craft Answer to Charges, 10 July 1884, RG 75, National Archives.

10. William J. Cleveland to Wright, 11 August 1883, RG 75, National Archives.

11. Francis Paul Prucha, *The Churches and the Indian Schools, 1888–1912* (Lincoln: University of Nebraska Press, 1979), 164–65.

12. The meeting is described in Craft's Answer to Charges, 10 July 1884, RG 75, National Archives.

13. Wright to Commissioner of Indian Affairs, 16 January 1884, BCIM.

14. James G. Wright, Reports of Agents in Dakota, 1884, RG 48, National Archives.

15. Mark G. Thiel, "The Omaha Dance in Oglala and Sicangu Sioux History, 1883–1923," *Whispering Wind,* fall–winter 1990, 5.

16. Thiel, "The Omaha Dance," 5. The charges against Craft were reconstructed from his Answer to Charges, 10 July 1884, RG 75, National Archives. The specific charges themselves are not contained there.

17. Lusk to Craft, 26 September 1884, BCIM. Charles S. Lusk was secretary of the Bureau of Catholic Indian Missions.

5. Conflicts on Standing Rock

1. Lusk to Craft, 26 September 1884, BCIM.

2. Katherine Burton, *The Golden Door: The Life of Katharine Drexel* (New York: P. J. Kennedy, 1957), 75–76. See also Rev. Anthony J. Prose, "Joseph Andrew Stephan: Indiana's Fighting Priest," *Social Justice Review* 69 (September–October 1976): 150.

3. Louis L. Pfaller, O.S.B., *James McLaughlin, the Man with an Indian Heart* (New York: Vantage Press, 1978), 59.

4. Joseph A. Stephan to John Brouillet, 13 September 1879 and 11 June 1881, BCIM.

5. Stephan to Gen. Charles Ewing, 31 March 1881, BCIM.

6. Marty to Craft, 13 February 1884, author's collection.

7. Pfaller, *James McLaughlin,* 3–4.

8. Pfaller, *James McLaughlin,* 169–70.

9. James McLaughlin to E. H. Bailey, 2 February 1889, McLaughlin Papers, roll 20, frame 806, Marquette University Archives, Milwaukee WI.

10. Stephan to Lusk, 22 July 1887, BCIM.

11. William T. Hagan, *The Indian Rights Association: The Herbert Welsh Years, 1882–1904* (Tucson: University of Arizona Press, 1985), 1–10.

12. Prucha, *Churches and the Indian Schools,* 5 and 219.

13. Report of Standing Rock Agency, 1888, National Archives, 59.

14. Pfaller, *James McLaughlin,* 100–102.

15. McLaughlin to [?], 13 September 1885, McLaughlin Papers, roll 2, frames 297–98.

16. Craft Journal, 10 April 1888.

17. Craft Journal, 22 June 1888.

18. Duratschek, *Crusading along Sioux Trails,* 94.

19. Joseph Epes Brown, *The Sacred Pipe: Black Elk's Account of the Seven Rites of the Oglala Sioux* (Norman: University of Oklahoma Press, 1953), 3–9.

20. Sister Mary Claudia Duratschek, *The Beginnings of Catholicism in South Dakota* (Washington DC: Catholic University Press, 1943), 108.

21. Craft Journal, 28 April 1888.

22. W. Fletcher Johnson, *The Red Record of the Sioux: Life of Sitting Bull and the History of the Indian War of 1890–91* (Philadelphia: Edgewood, 1891), 460.

23. Craft Journal, 28 April 1888.

6. Settling in on Standing Rock

1. Reports of Agents in Dakota, 1887, 51, National Archives.

2. Marty to Craft, 15 September 1886, author's collection. Father Wilhelm eventually succeeded Father Craft at the Fort Berthold mission in 1899.

3. *Hoffman's Catholic Directory* (Milwaukee: Hoffman Brothers, 1886), 332.

4. Craft Journal, 2 June 1888.

5. Craft Journal, 4 June 1888.

6. Craft Journal, 8 June 1888.

7. Marty to Craft, 17 December 1884, author's collection.

8. *Daily Press and Dakotaian,* 25 July 1885.

9. Craft Journal, 25 April 1888.

10. Craft Journal, 14 August 1888.

11. Craft Journal, 26 June 1888.

12. Walter Bower, *Scotichronicon,* ed. Walter Goodall (Edinburgh: R. Fleming, 1759), 2:292.

13. Craft Journal, 10 April 1888.

14. Craft Journal, 30 November 1888.

15. There are several D. F. Barry photographs of Gall, another Hunkpapa chief, wearing a large plain cross, possibly an Episcopalian response to this proliferation of crucifixes among the Sioux during the mid-1880s.

16. McLaughlin to Marty, 2 April 1885, BCIM.

17. Craft Journal, 5 June 1888.

18. Craft Journal, 5 April 1888.

19. Craft to Daniel E. Hudson, 8 November 1897, Daniel E. Hudson Papers, University of Notre Dame Archives, Notre Dame IN (hereafter Hudson Papers).

20. Craft to James R. O'Beirne, 26 August 1900, Kelly Papers.

21. Craft to Kelly, 29 June 1901, Kelly Papers.

22. "Yellowness" is an idiom Craft often used for such undesirable traits as malevolence, stubbornness, or cowardice.

23. Craft's verbal jab at "James the blacksmith" as a worthy successor to Alexander the coppersmith (the apostle Paul's accuser in 2 Tim. 4:14) is aimed at James McLaughlin.

24. Craft Journal, 23 March 1888.

25. "Father Craft's Statement," *New York Freeman's Journal,* 3 January 1891.

26. Craft Journal, 8 June 1888.

27. Craft Journal, 10 April 1888.

28. Craft Journal, 29 October 1888, and Craft to Joseph A. Stephan, 1 November 1888, BCIM.

29. Sister Mary Clement Fitzgerald, P.B.V.M., "Bishop Marty and His Sioux Missions, 1876–1896," *South Dakota Historical Collections* 20 (1940): 540.

30. Last Will of Two Bears, author's collection.

31. Craft to *North Western Chronicle,* 29 November 1885, author's collection.
32. Pierre J. DeSmet to Chiefs and Braves, 16 March 1871, author's collection.

7. Missionary Labor and Sacrifice

1. Craft Lecture Notes, about 1890, author's collection.
2. Craft to Conrad, 29 May 1888, Conception Abbey Archives.
3. Handwritten note, 23 August 1886, author's collection.
4. Craft to Kelly, 12 July 1895, Kelly Papers.
5. Ibid.
6. Craft Journal, 25 March 1888.
7. Craft Journal, 25 December 1888.
8. Craft Journal, 23 March 1888.
9. Craft Journal, 10 June 1888.
10. Craft Journal, 28 December 1888.
11. Craft Journal, 24 March 1888.
12. Craft Journal, 5 December 1888.
13. Craft Journal, 18 May 1888.
14. Craft Journal, 15 January 1889.
15. Craft Journal, 16 January 1889.
16. Craft Journal, 11 February 1889.
17. Craft Journal, 20 November 1889.
18. Craft Journal, 23 May 1889.
19. Craft Journal, 3 January 1889.
20. Craft Journal, 10 and 11 January 1889.
21. Craft Journal, 1 May 1888.

8. Humor and Whimsy

1. Marty to Frowin Conrad, 10 February 1883, Conception Abbey Archives.
2. George Gordon Lord Byron, *Childe Harold's Pilgrimage,* canto 1, stanza 9.
3. *Ho-bu* means a wild young man.
4. Craft Journal, 3 April 1888.
5. Craft Journal, 4 April 1888.
6. Craft Journal, 14 April 1888.
7. Craft Journal, 28 March 1888.
8. Craft Journal, 10 April 1888.
9. Craft Journal, 16 March 1889.
10. Craft Journal, 10 April 1888.
11. Craft Journal, 29 December 1888.
12. Ghost Feast, or the Dance of the Ghosts.
13. A mixture of marrow and cherries.
14. Craft Journal, 8 April 1888.

15. Craft Journal, 9 May 1888.

16. Craft Journal, 9 September 1889.

17. Craft Journal, 10 September 1889.

18. Craft Journal, 31 March 1888. The anniversary is based on the liturgical calendar.

9. The Land Boomers

1. Richard H. Pratt to Craft, 4 August 1888, author's collection.

2. Craft Journal, 6 August 1888.

3. Craft Journal, 7 August 1888.

4. Craft Journal, 23 June 1889.

5. Craft Journal, 1 August 1889.

6. Craft Journal, 2 August 1889.

7. Craft Journal, 3 August 1889.

8. James McLaughlin, *My Friend the Indian* (Boston: Houghton Mifflin, 1910), 285.

9. McLaughlin, *My Friend the Indian,* 286–88.

10. Martin F. Schmitt, ed., *General George Crook: His Autobiography* (Norman: University of Oklahoma Press, 1946), 288.

10. Fort Berthold

1. Craft to Hudson, 30 September 1897, Hudson Papers.

2. Craft Journal, 15 May 1889.

3. Craft Journal, 21 May 1889.

4. Craft Journal, 22 June 1888. The quotation is from Hos. 2:1.

5. Craft Journal, 18 August 1888.

6. Craft Journal, 5 September 1888.

7. Craft Journal, 14 September 1888.

8. Craft Journal, 24 September 1888.

9. Hermann Koneberg, O.S.B., *Blessed Ones of 1888,* trans. Eliza A. Donnelly (New York: Benziger Brothers, 1888), 149–80.

10. Hovering Eagle.

11. Craft Journal, 14 November 1888.

12. Craft Journal, 15 March 1889.

13. Craft Journal, 9 April 1889.

14. Craft Journal, 21 April 1889.

15. "Diocesan News," *Dakota Catholic,* 1 June 1889.

16. Emma Halsey's name in religion.

17. The mass text "on the day of burial."

18. Craft Journal, 18 August 1889 to 27 August 1889.

19. Craft Journal, 2 July 1889 and 3 July 1889.

11. A Special Envoy

1. Willard to Craft, 3 November 1889, BCIM. Father George L. Willard was vice director of the Bureau of Catholic Indian Missions.

2. Craft to Willard, 14 November 1889, Sacred Heart Monastery Archives, Richardton ND.

3. Burton, *Golden Door,* 73–108.

4. Burton, *Golden Door,* 130.

5. Burton, *Golden Door,* 252.

6. Craft Journal, 19 December 1889.

7. Craft Journal, 20 January 1890.

8. Craft to Willard, 17 January 1890, BCIM.

9. Marty to Bishop John Shanley, 1 March 1890, Diocese of Fargo, Fargo ND.

10. Craft Journal, 24 March 1890.

11. Craft Journal, 9 February 1890.

12. Craft Journal, 19 February 1890.

13. Charles Lavigerie (1825–92), cardinal and archbishop of Carthage, founder of the Society of Missionaries of Africa (the White Fathers), whose mission was to adapt themselves to the lives of African natives.

14. Craft Journal, 25 February 1890.

15. Craft Journal, 1 and 2 April 1890.

16. F. X. Weiser, S.J., *Kateri Tekakwitha* (Caughnawaga PQ: Kateri Center, 1972).

17. Craft Journal, 26 April 1890.

18. In 1943 Pope Pius XII elevated Kateri Tekakwitha to the status of "venerable servant of God," placing her at the threshold of sainthood along with Sister Josephine Mary of Saint Agnes.

19. Prucha, *American Indian Policy in Crisis,* 293–95.

20. "The Poor Indians: A Catholic Missionary's Fifteen Years' Experience with Them," *New York Freeman's Journal,* 21 June 1890.

21. *Irish World,* 16 August 1890.

22. "The Catholic Indian Missions," *Irish World,* 20 January 1891.

23. Lusk to Shanley, 28 August 1890, BCIM.

24. Stephan to M. Farrell, 28 August 1890, BCIM.

25. *New York Freeman's Journal,* 15 November 1890.

26. Document in Craft's handwriting, 4 December 1890, BCIM.

27. O'Beirne to Redfield Proctor, 24 November 1890, RG 75, National Archives.

28. Proctor to O'Beirne, 27 November 1890; Proctor to Craft, 3 December 1890; Proctor to Noble, 4 December 1890, author's collection.

29. Emil Perrig, S.J., Diary, 86–87, BCIM.

30. James M. Mooney, *The Ghost-Dance Religion and the Sioux Outbreak of 1890,* Fourteenth Annual Report of the Bureau of American Ethnology, 1892–93 (Washington DC; Government Printing Office, 1896), 928–52.

31. O'Beirne to Craft, 17 December 1890, author's collection.

32. *New York Freeman's Journal,* 3 January 1891.

12. Wounded Knee

1. Draft of Craft's affidavit, undated, author's collection. This is substantially the same as a typed copy in RG 75, National Archives.

2. Craft to Kelly, 13 March 1891 and 12 February 1892, Kelly Papers.

3. "Correcting His Own Obituary," *Milford (PA) Dispatch,* 19 February 1891.

4. Craft to Kelly, 12 February 1891, Kelly Papers.

5. Craft to Kelly, 13 March 1891, Kelly Papers.

6. Stephan to Shanley, 23 January 1891, Assumption Abbey Archives, Richardton, ND (letter in Shanley File, Diocese of Fargo Archives).

7. For other descriptions of the encounter, see Richard E. Jensen, R. Eli Paul, and John E. Carter, *Eyewitness at Wounded Knee* (Lincoln: University of Nebraska Press, 1991); William Coleman, *Voices of Wounded Knee* (Lincoln: University of Nebraska Press, 2000); Mooney, *Ghost-Dance Religion;* and Robert M. Utley, *The Last Days of the Sioux Nation* (New Haven: Yale University Press, 1963).

8. *Milford (PA) Dispatch,* 19 February 1891. See also Perrig Diary, 11, BCIM.

9. James H. Cook, *Fifty Years on the Old Frontier* (New Haven: Yale University Press, 1923), 236.

13. Bitter Aftermath

1. Thomas J. Morgan to Craft, 14 January 1891, author's collection.

2. "A Word from Father Craft," *New York Freeman's Journal,* 31 January 1891.

3. Stephan to Shanley, 23 January 1891, BCIM.

4. Stephan to Craft, 5 January 1891, author's collection.

5. *New York Sun,* 5 February 1891.

6. James M. King to Proctor, 6 February 1891, RG 094, Adjutant General's Office, National Archives.

7. Morgan to E. W. Halford, 7 March 1891, BCIM.

8. Eugene T. McAuliffe to Craft, 30 March 1891, author's collection.

9. Finley's Hotel, operated by trader James A. Finley, was at Pine Ridge.

10. "Letter to the Editor," reprinted in *New York Freeman's Journal,* 7 February 1891.

11. Gilbert Bailey, newspaper reporter for the *Chicago Inter-Ocean* and *Denver Rocky Mountain News.*

12. "A Word from Father Craft," *New York Freeman's Journal,* 7 March 1891.

13. Craft to Lusk, 25 April 1891, BCIM.

14. Prucha, *Churches and the Indian Schools,* 20.

14. The Origins of the Indian Sisterhood

1. Novices to Craft, 25 January 1891, author's collection.
2. McLaughlin to Herbert Welsh, 12 June 1891, BCIM.
3. McLaughlin to Sister Superioress, 17 June 1891, BCIM.
4. Novices to Craft, 21 July 1891, author's collection.
5. Mother Gertrude to Craft, 21 July 1891, author's collection.
6. Sister Mary Ewens, O.P., "The Native Order: A Brief and Strange History," in *Scattered Steeples—the Fargo Diocese: A Written Celebration of Its Centennial,* ed. Jerome D. Lamb, Jerry Ruff, and Father William Sherman (Fargo ND: Burch, Londergan and Lynch, 1988), 13.
7. Craft to Kelly, 17 November 1891, Kelly Papers.
8. Mother Mary Catharine to Mother Gertrude, 10 December 1891, Sacred Heart Monastery, Yankton ND.
9. Craft to Rev. F. B. Luebberman, 9 January 1892, author's collection.
10. Ibid.
11. John S. Murphy to Morgan, 7 March 1892, RG 75, National Archives.
12. Craft to Kelly, 12 February 1892, Kelly Papers.
13. Craft to Herman J. Heuser, 25 July 1892, Archdiocese of Philadelphia Archives, Overbrook PA.
14. Theresa Tegaiagonta, a widow befriended by Kateri Tekakwitha two years before her death in April 1680.
15. *Poor Souls' Advocate* 4 (July–August 1892): 389–92, 428–32.
16. Craft to Kelly, 12 February 1892, Kelly Papers.
17. Craft to Kelly, 6 May 1892, Kelly Papers.
18. Murphy to Morgan, 31 August 1892, McLaughlin Papers, Marquette University Archives.
19. Shanley to Katharine Drexel, 3 November 1892, Archives of the Sisters of the Blessed Sacrament, Bensalem PA (hereafter SBS Archives).
20. Shanley to Drexel, 13 November 1891, SBS Archives.
21. Sister Mary Angela Schier, S.S.N.D., "The History of Indian Missions in North Dakota (1874–1938)" (M.A. thesis, Catholic University of America, 1938), 73.
22. *Irish World,* 23 July 1893.

15. The Death of Sacred White Buffalo

1. James H. Moynihan, *The Life of Archbishop John Ireland* (New York: Harper, 1953), 39.
2. Gerald P. Fogarty, *The Vatican and the American Hierarchy from 1870 to 1965* (Stuttgart: Anton Hiersemann, 1982), 120.
3. James H. Moynihan to Craft, 3 February 1893, author's collection.

4. Drafts of letters from Mary Liguori to Francesco Satolli, 11 February and 17 March 1893, author's collection.

5. Craft to Kelly, 6 February 1893, Kelly Papers.

6. Frank Wells to Shanley, 18 March 1893, Archdiocese of Fargo.

7. John Tracy Ellis, *The Life of James Cardinal Gibbons*, ed. Francis L. Broderick (Milwaukee: Bruce, 1963), 122.

8. Craft to James Gibbons, 22 March 1893, Archdiocese of Baltimore Archives, Baltimore MD.

9. Murphy to Shanley, 6 April 1893, Diocese of Fargo.

10. Gibbons to Craft, 7 April 1893, author's collection.

11. Written vows of Mother Catharine, 12 March and 21 April 1893, author's collection.

12. Many centuries earlier, Saint Benedict had asked his monks to bring him into the oratory to die.

13. Craft to Kelly, 18 May 1893, Kelly Papers.

14. Ibid.

15. Gibbons to Craft, 12 May 1893, author's collection.

16. Craft to Kelly, 8 July 1893, Kelly Papers.

17. Craft to Kelly, 10 July 1893, Kelly Papers.

18. Craft to Kelly, 8 July 1893 and 16 June 1899, Kelly Papers.

19. Ewens, "Native Order," 17.

20. Craft to Stephan, 6 February 1896, BCIM.

21. Bernard Strassmaier to Shanley, 4 December 1893, Diocese of Fargo.

16. Illusions of Success

1. Interior to Agent W. H. Clapp, 3 October 1893, RG 75, National Archives.

2. Craft to Kelly, 11 September 1894, Kelly Papers.

3. Undated letter by Father Fintan Wiederkehr, probably between November 1897 and March 1898, St. Meinrad Archabbey Archives, St. Meinrad IN.

4. Craft to Stephan, 2 June 1895, BCIM.

5. Craft to Stephan, 2 July 1895, BCIM.

6. Craft to Stephan, 2 June and 20 August 1895, BCIM.

7. Craft to Kelly, 5 September 1895, Kelly Papers.

8. Craft to Kelly, 13 December 1895, Kelly Papers.

9. U.S. Commissioner of Indian Affairs, *Annual Reports, 1896,* 230.

10. Craft to Stephan, 6 February 1896, BCIM.

11. Craft to Kelly, 16 April 1896, Kelly Papers.

12. Elbow Woods was apparently the original spelling. It has since evolved to Elbowoods.

13. Craft to Kelly, 21 September 1896, Kelly Papers.

14. Craft to Frank Philbrick and reply, 28 September 1896, author's collection.

15. Canceled checks of the Congregation of American Sisters, 1897, author's collection.

16. Sister Mary Aloysia to James McLaughlin, 8 September 1894, author's collection.

17. A Malicious Assault

1. *Hoffman's Catholic Directory, 1897*, 295.

2. *Irish World*, 3 April 1897.

3. Telegram from F. Glenn Mattoon to Commissioner, 8 April 1897, RG 75, National Archives.

4. Telegram from Commissioner to Mattoon, 8 April 1897, RG 75, National Archives.

5. Craft to Kelly, 10 April 1897, Kelly Papers.

6. Craft to Hudson, 2 April 1897, Hudson Papers.

7. Telegram from Cornelius Newton Bliss to Mattoon, 17 April 1897, RG 75, National Archives. Bliss served as President McKinley's secretary of interior during 1897 and 1898.

8. Craft to Stephan, 20 April 1897, BCIM.

9. Telegram from Shanley to Bliss, 28 April 1897, RG 75, National Archives; Craft to Kelly, 30 April 1897, Kelly Papers; Stephan to Craft, 25 April 1897, BCIM.

10. Craft to Kelly, 30 April 1897, Kelly Papers.

11. Craft to O'Beirne, 20 October 1899, Kelly Papers.

12. Craft to Stephan, 2 May 1897, BCIM.

13. Stephan to Shanley, 22 May 1897, BCIM.

14. Craft to Hudson, 30 September 1897, Hudson Papers.

15. Wiederkehr to Abbot, 30 October 1897, St. Meinrad Archabbey Archives.

16. Marty died in September 1896.

17. Wiederkehr to Abbot, 30 October 1897, St. Meinrad Archabbey Archives.

18. Thomas O'Gorman to Wiederkehr, 9 March 1898, St. Meinrad Archabbey Archives.

19. Peter Couchman to Commissioner of Indian Affairs, 17 March 1898, RG 75, National Archives.

20. Martin Kenel to Frowin, 4 April 1898, Conception Abbey Archives.

21. Wiederkehr to Sisters, 5 April 1898, St. Meinrad Archabbey Archives.

22. Couchman to Craft, 7 April 1898, RG 75, National Archives.

23. The Sons of the Revolution is a membership of direct lineal descendants of those who helped establish American Independence during the Revolutionary War. Its current headquarters are at the Fraunces Tavern Museum in New York City. Craft first joined the organization on 5 November 1890 and formed the North Dakota State Society of the Sons of the Revolution on 12 February 1897. He was listed on the letterhead as president of the state society.

24. Craft to Bliss, 7 April 1898, RG 75, National Archives.

25. Craft to Hudson, 15 April 1898, Hudson Papers.

26. Craft to Bliss, 19 April 1898, RG 75, National Archives.

27. Black Tomahawk to O'Gorman, 14 May 1898, author's collection.

28. Thomas Ryan to Craft, 3 June 1898, RG 75, National Archives.

29. Ellen Clifford and Ellen Clark are the same person. She was the first half-blood Sioux to enter the Benedictine convent at Zell, South Dakota, making her profession as Sister Mary Gregory, O.S.B., in 1886. She joined Father Craft's community as Sister Mary Gertrude. See Jerome D. Lamb, Jerry Ruff, and Father William Sherman, *Scattered Steeples—the Fargo Diocese: A Written Celebration of Its Centennial* (Fargo ND: Burch, Londergan, and Lynch, 1988), 10 and 23, and Terrence Kardong, *Catholic Life at Fort Berthold, 1889–1989* (Richardton ND: Assumption Abbey Press, 1989), 33.

30. James E. Jenkins to Superintendent at Pierre School, 10 October 1898, RG 75, National Archives.

18. A Strategic Retreat

1. *Harper's Pictorial History of the War with Spain* (New York: Harper, 1899), 453.

2. *Irish World,* 23 April 1898. This and subsequent confused news accounts apparently counted Craft as one of the sisters.

3. William M. Fisk to Craft, 27 April 1898, author's collection.

4. O'Beirne to Monsignor [Donato Sbaretti?], 17 January 1900, author's collection.

5. Anita Newcomb McGee to Craft, 8 October 1898, author's collection.

6. Craft to O'Beirne, 29 October 1898, Kelly Papers.

7. Testimony of Dr. Anita Newcomb McGee, 56th Cong., 1st sess., 1899–1900, S. Doc. 23, 3170.

8. John Ireland to Craft, 3 January 1899, author's collection.

9. *New York Times,* 15 March 1899.

10. Craft to O'Beirne, 30 January 1900, Kelly Papers.

11. Congressman John Francis Fitzgerald of Massachusetts introduced H.R. 379 on 28 February 1899, conveying the "thanks of Congress [to] the Sisters of American Congregation who, bravely and heroically, in the hospital and on the field, ministered to the wants of the soldiers in the Spanish-American War" (*Congressional Record* [4 December 1899], 33:12).

12. Craft to Kelly, 25 May 1899, Kelly Papers.

13. Craft to Kelly, 16 June 1899, Kelly Papers.

14. The quotation is from Lord Byron's *Childe Harold's Pilgrimage,* canto 3, stanza 57. Craft substitutes "her" for "his" and "soldier" for "stranger."

15. Craft to O'Beirne, 20 October 1899, Kelly Papers.

16. C. F. Humphrey, Deputy Quartermaster General to Craft, 26 December 1899; 4th Indorsement, War Department, Quartermaster General's Office, Washington, 5 February 1900, author's collection.

17. Note attached to endorsement of A. N. McGee, 29 February 1900, author's collection.

18. Annie Pleets to Wiederkehr, 7 December 1899, St. Meinrad Archabbey Archives.

19. Craft to O'Beirne, 12 January 1900, Kelly Papers.

20. Ewens, "Native Order," 23.

21. Maj. E. Greble to Craft, 16 June 1900, Kelly Papers.

22. Craft to O'Beirne, 27 July 1900, Kelly Papers.

23. Craft to O'Beirne, 3 November 1899, Kelly Papers.

24. Bishop Donato Sbaretti, who in 1901 replaced Archbishop Placide L. Chapelle as apostolic delegate to Cuba, Puerto Rico, and the Philippines. Before his assignment as bishop of Havana, he had been Cardinal Francesco Satolli's secretary in the apostolic delegation in Washington DC.

25. Maj. Gen. Leonard Wood, who served as military governor of Cuba from 1899 to 1902.

26. Craft to O'Beirne, 26 August 1900, Kelly Papers.

19. Was Father Craft Insane?

1. McLaughlin to Welsh, 12 June 1891, BCIM.

2. Morgan to Halford, 7 March 1891, BCIM.

3. Shanley to Drexel, 19 August 1899, SBS Archives.

4. Thomas Richards to W. A. Jones, 12 March 1901, RG 75, National Archives. See also Kardong, *Catholic Life at Fort Berthold*, 34.

5. Shanley "Diary," BCIM, 53.

6. Wells to Shanley, 18 March 1893, Diocese of Fargo.

7. Hunt to Shanley, 2 August 1893, Diocese of Fargo.

8. Murphy to Shanley, 6 April 1893, Diocese of Fargo.

9. Kenel to Conrad, 4 April 1898, Conception Abbey Archives.

10. Shanley to Drexel, 3 November 1892, SBS Archives.

11. Wiederkehr to Conrad, 30 October 1897, St. Meinrad Archabbey Archives.

12. Ewens, "Native Order," 18.

13. Craft Journal, 14 April 1888.

14. Issued 25 May 1899.

15. Undated manuscript written by Fintan Wiederkehr, O.S.B., probably between November 1897 and March 1898, St. Meinrad Archabbey Archives.

16. Congregation of Sainte-Croix, or Holy Cross.

17. Craft to Kelly, 11 September 1894, Kelly Papers. If Craft's name was ever on a list of candidates for bishop of Sioux Falls, it never got beyond the apostolic delegate in Washington DC. Such lists are even now cloaked in secrecy; however,

the official ternae of episcopal candidates for the Sioux Falls diocese that reached Rome for the appointments of 1889 and again in 1896 did not include his name. Letter of Crescenzio Cardinal Sepe, Prefect, Congregation Pro Gentium Evangelizatione, Rome, to author, 16 May 2001.

18. [Francis M. Craft], "Native Indian Vocations," *Catholic World Magazine,* June 1897.

19. Frederic Eberschweiler, S.J., "An Indian Clergy Impossible," *Catholic World Magazine,* September 1897.

20. Katharine Drexel was beatified by Pope John Paul II on 20 November 1988 and canonized on 1 October 2000.

21. Prose, "Joseph Andrew Stephan," 188.

22. Burton, *Golden Door,* 74.

23. Stephan to Drexel, 11 June 1885, SBS Archives.

24. Karolevitz, *Bishop Martin Marty,* 100.

25. James O'Connor to Drexel, 26 May 1883, SBS Archives.

26. Karolevitz, *Bishop Martin Marty,* 99.

27. O'Connor to Drexel, 29 August 1885, SBS Archives.

28. O'Connor to Drexel, 21 April 1887, SBS Archives.

29. O'Connor to Drexel, 16 May 1888, SBS Archives.

30. Drexel to O'Connor, 15 December 1888, SBS Archives.

31. Craft Journal, 14 January 1889.

32. O'Connor to Drexel, 16 February 1889, SBS Archives.

33. Drexel to O'Connor, 24 February 1889, SBS Archives.

34. O'Connor to Drexel, 28 February 1889, SBS Archives.

35. O'Connor to Drexel, 16 March 1889, SBS Archives.

36. Marty to Drexel, 6 April 1889, SBS Archives.

37. Craft Journal, 8 and 9 April 1889.

38. Drexel to O'Connor, 12 May 1889, SBS Archives.

39. O'Connor to Drexel, 16 May 1899, SBS Archives.

40. Craft Journal, 2 and 3 July 1889.

41. Craft to Willard, 19 July 1889, BCIM.

42. O'Connor to Drexel, 20 July 1889, SBS Archives.

43. Craft Journal, 1 October 1889.

44. Drexel to O'Connor, 28 October 1889, SBS Archives.

45. Craft to Willard, 17 January 1890, BCIM.

46. Shanley to Father J. Williams, 7 March 1890, author's collection.

47. Willard to Craft, 23 January 1890, author's collection.

48. Lusk to Shanley, 28 August 1890, BCIM, and Stephan to Farrell, 28 August 1890, BCIM.

49. Sister Consuela Marie Duffy, *Katharine Drexel:A Biography* (Bensalem PA: Sisters of the Blessed Sacrament, 1966), 160.

50. Ryan to Drexel, 29 May 1890, SBS Archives.

51. Stephan to Shanley, 23 January 1891, BCIM.

52. Lou Baldwin, *A Call to Sanctity: The Formation and Life of Mother Katharine Drexel* (Philadelphia: Catholic Standard and Times, 1988), 52.

53. *Irish World*, 21 February 1891.

54. Shanley to Drexel, 3 November 1892, SBS Archives.

55. Sister Mary Catharine (Crowfeather) and others to Mother Gertrude Leupi, 10 December 1891, in Lamb, Ruff, and Sherman, *Scattered Steeples*, 14–15.

56. Craft to Heuser, 28 June 1892, Archdiocese of Philadelphia Archives.

57. Craft to Kelly, 28 June 1892, Kelly Papers.

58. Craft to Heuser, 25 July 1892, Archdiocese of Philadelphia Archives.

59. Shanley to Drexel, 3 November 1892, SBS Archives. A more extensive quotation from this letter appears on pp. 104–5.

60. Baldwin, *Call to Sanctity*, 74.

61. Sister Maria E. McCall to author, 21 October 1998, SBS Archives.

62. Gibbons to Craft, 7 April 1893, author's collection.

63. "Sisters Must Quit Cuba," *New York Times*, 15 March 1899.

64. Craft to Stephan, 2 July 1895, BCIM.

65. Craft to Stephan, 20 August 1895, BCIM.

66. Craft to Stephan, 6 February 1896, BCIM.

67. Stephan to Craft, 10 July 1888, author's collection.

68. Karolevitz, *Bishop Martin Marty*, 133–34.

69. Craft Journal.

20. Homecoming

1. James Kelly sketched Mother Joseph's portrait in New York on 4 April 1901.

2. Ewens, "Native Order," 23.

3. Burton, *Golden Door*, 167.

4. Ibid.

5. Joseph McSorley, *Father Hecker and His Friends* (St. Louis: Herder, 1952), 274–75.

6. Craft to Kelly, 29 January 1902, Kelly Papers.

7. J. W. Treis to Craft, 13 June 1901, author's collection; also Craft to Kelly, 10 July 1901, Kelly Papers. Unfortunately, the records of the Diocese of Scranton contain no files on Craft that would shed light on his acceptance by Bishop Hoban or his assignment to St. Matthew's Church.

8. Marie Summa and Frank Summa, *The Stroudsburgs in the Poconos* (Charleston SC: Arcadia, 1998), 35.

9. Craft to Kelly, 14 November 1902, Kelly Papers.

10. *Fairbairn's Book of Crests of the Families of Great Britain and Ireland* (London: T. C. and E. C. Jack, 1905).

11. "St. Matthew's Prospers," *Stroudsburg (PA) Daily Times*, 18 January 1906, 1.

12. Craft to Kelly, 5 July 1913, Kelly Papers.

13. Craft to his mother, 7 May 1917, Kelly Papers.

14. Craft to his mother, 20 June 1917, Kelly Papers.

15. Craft to Kelly, 6 November 1917, Kelly Papers.

16. Nathan Miller, *Theodore Roosevelt: A Life* (New York: William Morrow, 1992), 555.

17. In the late 1930s and early 1940s my brother Bob and I served as altar boys at daily summer masses.

18. *Stroudsburg (PA) Record,* 2 October 1920.

19. John G. Neihardt, *Black Elk Speaks* (Lincoln: University of Nebraska Press, 1979), 252.

Epilogue

1. *A Celebration of Praise* (Chamberlain SD: St. Joseph's Indian School, Tipi Press, 1995).

BIBLIOGRAPHY

Manuscript and Research Sources

Archdiocese of Baltimore Archives, Baltimore MD
Archdiocese of Philadelphia Archives, Overbrook PA
Archives of American Art, Smithsonian Institution, Washington DC
Archives of the Oregon Province of the Society of Jesus, Spokane WA
Assumption Abbey Archives, Richardton ND
Catholic Indian Mission, Fort Yates ND
Conception Abbey Archives, Conception MO
Diocese of Fargo, Fargo ND
Diocese of Scranton, Scranton PA
Diocese of Sioux Falls, Sioux Falls SD
East Stroudsburg University, East Stroudsburg PA
Georgetown University Archives, Lauinger Library, Washington DC
Georgia Historical Society, Savannah GA
Jesuit College Archives, Leuven, Belgium
Jesuit Missouri Province Archives, St. Louis MO
Katholieke Universiteit Leuven, Leuven, Belgium
Marquette University Archives, Milwaukee WI
National Archives, Washington DC
Nebraska State Historical Society, Lincoln NE
Newberry Library, Chicago IL
New-York Historical Society, New York NY
North Dakota Heritage Center, Bismarck ND
Pike County Historical Society, Milford PA
Red Cloud Indian School, Holy Rosary Mission, Pine Ridge SD

Sacred Heart Monastery Archives, Richardton ND
Sacred Heart Monastery Archives, Yankton SD
St. Matthew's Catholic Church, East Stroudsburg PA
St. Meinrad Archabbey Archives, St. Meinrad IN
St. Peter's Catholic Church, Fort Yates ND
Sisters of the Blessed Sacrament Archives, Bensalem PA
Sons of the Revolution Archives, New York NY
United States Military History Institute, Carlisle Barracks PA
University of Notre Dame Archives, Notre Dame IN

Newspapers

The Catholic Light
The Catholic Mirror
The Daily Press and Dakotaian
The Dakota Catholic
The East Stroudsburg (PA) Times
The Irish World and American Industrial Liberator
The Milford (PA) Dispatch
The Stroudsburg (PA) Morning Press
The New York Freeman's Journal and Catholic Register
The Northwestern Chronicle
The New York Sun
The New York Times
The Omaha Bee
The Stroudsburg (PA) Daily Times
The Stroudsburg (PA) Record

Secondary Sources

Baldwin, Lou. *A Call to Sanctity: The Formation and Life of Mother Katharine Drexel*. Philadelphia: Catholic Standard and Times, 1988.

Bantin, Philip C., with Mark G. Thiel. *Guide to Catholic Indian Mission and School Records in Midwest Repositories*. Milwaukee: Marquette University, 1984.

Brown, Dee. *Bury My Heart at Wounded Knee*. New York: Holt, Rinehart, and Winston, 1970.

Brown, Joseph Epes. *The Sacred Pipe: Black Elk's Account of the Seven Rites of the Oglala Sioux*. Norman: University of Oklahoma Press, 1953.

Bruce, Robert. *Art and Sculpture of James Edward Kelly, 1855–1933*. New York: George Hope Ryder, 1934.

Buechel, Rev. Eugene. *A Dictionary—Oie Wowapi Wan of Teton Sioux*. Edited by Rev. Paul Manhart, S.J. Pine Ridge SD: Red Cloud Indian School, 1983.

Burns, Robert Ignatius, *The Jesuits and the Indian Wars of the Northwest.* New Haven: Yale University Press, 1966.

Burton, Katherine. *The Golden Door: The Life of Katharine Drexel.* New York: P. J. Kennedy, 1957.

Butler, Anne M. "Mother Katharine Drexel: Spiritual Visionary for the West." In *By Grit and Grace: Eleven Women Who Shaped the American West,* edited by Glenda Riley and Richard W. Etulain. Golden CO: Fulcrum, 1997.

Catlin, George. *North American Indians.* Edited by Peter Matthiessen. New York: Penguin Books, 1996.

Coleman, William. *Voices of Wounded Knee.* Lincoln: University of Nebraska Press, 2000.

Congressional Record, 56th Cong., 1st sess. Vol. 33. Washington DC, 1900.

Cook, James H. *Fifty Years on the Old Frontier.* New Haven: Yale University Press, 1923.

[Craft, Francis M.], "Native Indian Vocations." *Catholic World Magazine,* June, 1897.

DeLand, Charles Edmund. "The Sioux Wars: Red Cloud Wars; Little Big Horn and Other Battles of 1876; Wounded Knee." *South Dakota Historical Collections* 17 (1934).

Duffy, Sister Consuela Marie. *Katharine Drexel: A Biography.* Bensalem PA: Sisters of the Blessed Sacrament, 1966.

Duratschek, Sister Mary Claudia. *The Beginnings of Catholicism in South Dakota.* Washington DC: Catholic University Press, 1943.

————. *Crusading along Sioux Trails: A History of the Catholic Indian Missions of South Dakota.* Yankton SD: Benedictine Convent of the Sacred Heart, 1947.

Eastman, Elaine Goodale. *Sister to the Sioux:, The Memoirs of Elaine Goodale Eastman.* Edited by Kay Graber. Lincoln: University of Nebraska Press, 1978.

Eberschweiler, Frederic, S.J. "An Indian Clergy Impossible." *Catholic World Magazine,* September 1897.

Ellis, John Tracy. *The Life of James Cardinal Gibbons.* Edited by Francis L. Broderick. Milwaukee: Bruce, 1963.

Ewens, Sister Mary, O.P. "The Native Order: A Brief and Strange History." In *Scattered Steeples—the Fargo Diocese: A Written Celebration of Its Centennial,* edited by Jerome D. Lamb, Jerry Ruff, and Father William Sherman. Fargo ND: Burch, Londergan and Lynch, 1988.

Fairbairn's Book of Crests of the Families of Great Britain and Ireland. London: T. C. and E. C. Jack, 1905.

Fitzgerald, Sister Mary Clement, P.B.V.M. "Bishop Marty and His Sioux Missions, 1876–1896." *South Dakota Historical Collections* 20 (1940): 525–54.

Fogarty, Gerald P. *The Vatican and the American Hierarchy from 1870 to 1965.* Stuttgart: Anton Hiersemann, 1982.

Freidel, Frank Burt. *The Splendid Little War.* Boston: Little, Brown, 1958.

Gallagher, John P. *A Century of History: The Diocese of Scranton, 1868–1968.* Scranton PA: Diocesan Guild Studios, 1968.

Hagan, William T. *The Indian Rights Association: The Herbert Welsh Years, 1882–1904.* Tucson: University of Arizona Press, 1985.

Harper's Pictorial History of the War with Spain. New York: Harper, 1899.

Hassrick, Royal B. *The Sioux: Life and Customs of a Warrior Society.* Norman: University of Oklahoma Press, 1964.

Heski, Thomas M. *The Little Shadow Catcher.* Seattle: Superior, 1978.

Hinton, May E. *South of the Cannon Ball: A History of Sioux, the War Bonnet County.* Grand Forks ND: Washburn Printing Center, 1984.

Hoffman's Catholic Directory. Milwaukee: Hoffman Brothers, 1886–99.

Holy Bible. Chicago: Catholic Press, 1955.

Hyde, George E. *Red Cloud's Folk: A History of the Oglala Sioux Indians.* Norman: University of Oklahoma Press, 1937.

———. *A Sioux Chronicle.* Norman: University of Oklahoma Press, 1956.

———. *Spotted Tail's Folk: A History of the Brulé Sioux.* Norman: University of Oklahoma Press, 1961.

Jensen, Richard E., R. Eli Paul, and John E. Carter. *Eyewitness at Wounded Knee.* Lincoln: University of Nebraska Press, 1991.

Johnson, W. Fletcher. *The Red Record of the Sioux: Life of Sitting Bull and the History of the Indian War of 1890–91.* Philadelphia: Edgewood, 1891.

Kardong, Terrence. *Catholic Life at Fort Berthold, 1889–1989.* Richardton ND: Assumption Abbey Press, 1989.

———. *Prairie Church: The Diocese of Bismarck, 1910–1985.* Richardton ND: Assumption Abbey Press, 1985.

Karolevitz, Robert F. *Bishop Martin Marty: The Black Robe Lean Chief.* Yankton SD: Privately printed for the Benedictine Sisters of Sacred Heart Convent, 1980.

Kehoe, Alice B. *North American Indians: A Comprehensive Account.* 2d ed. Englewood Cliffs NJ: Prentice Hall, 1992.

Kelley, William Fitch. *Pine Ridge 1890: An Eye Witness Account of the Events Surrounding the Fighting at Wounded Knee.* Edited and compiled by Alexander Kelley and Pierre Bovis. San Francisco: Pierre Bovis, 1971.

Kingsbury, George W. *History of Dakota Territory, South Dakota, Its History and Its People.* Edited by George Martin Smith. Vols. 1–5. Chicago: S. J. Clarke, 1915.

Kolbenschlag, George R. *A Whirlwind Passes: Newspaper Correspondents and the Sioux Indian Disturbances of 1890–1891.* Vermillion: University of South Dakota Press, 1990.

Koneberg, Hermann, O.S.B. *Blessed Ones of 1888.* Translated by Eliza A. Donnelly. New York: Benziger Brothers, 1888.

Lamb, Jerome D., Jerry Ruff, and Father William Sherman. *Scattered Steeples—*

the Fargo Diocese: A Written Celebration of Its Centennial. Fargo ND: Burch, Londergan, and Lynch, 1988.

Liguori, Sister Mary. "Indian Vocations." *Poor Souls' Advocate,* July–August 1892.

McGregor, James H. *The Wounded Knee Massacre.* Rapid City SD: Fenske, 1940.

McLaughlin, James. *My Friend the Indian.* Boston: Houghton Mifflin, 1910.

McSorley, Joseph. *Father Hecker and His Friends.* St. Louis: Herder, 1952.

Miles, Nelson A. *Serving the Republic.* New York: Harper, 1911.

Miller, David Humphreys. *Ghost Dance.* Lincoln: University of Nebraska Press, 1959.

Miller, Nathan. *Theodore Roosevelt: A Life.* New York: William Morrow, 1992.

Mills, Anson. *My Story.* Washington DC: Byron S. Adams, 1918.

Mooney, James M. *The Ghost-Dance Religion and the Sioux Outbreak of 1890.* Fourteenth Annual Report of the Bureau of American Ethnology, 1892–93. Washington DC: Government Printing Office, 1896.

Morgan, H. Wayne. *America's Road to Empire: The War with Spain and Overseas Expansion.* New York: John Wiley, 1965.

Moynihan, James H. *The Life of Archbishop John Ireland.* New York: Harper, 1953.

National Cyclopaedia of American Biography. New York: James T. White, 1930.

Neihardt, John G. *Black Elk Speaks.* Lincoln: University of Nebraska Press, 1979.

Nelson, Bruce O. *Land of the Dacotahs.* Minneapolis: University of Minnesota Press, 1946.

Oblates of the Blessed Sacrament. *A Celebration of Praise.* Chamberlain SD: St. Joseph's Indian School, Tipi Press, 1995.

Pfaller, Louis L., O.S.B. *James McLaughlin, the Man with an Indian Heart.* New York: Vantage Press, 1978.

Powers, William K. *Oglala Religion.* Lincoln: University of Nebraska Press, 1977.

Prose, Rev. Anthony J. "Joseph Andrew Stephan: Indiana's Fighting Priest." *Social Justice Review* 69 (September–October 1976).

Prucha, Francis Paul. *American Indian Policy in Crisis: Christian Reformers and the Indian, 1865–1900.* Norman: University of Oklahoma Press, 1976.

———. *The Churches and the Indian Schools, 1888–1912.* Lincoln: University of Nebraska Press, 1979.

———. *The Great Father: The United States Government and the American Indians.* Lincoln: University of Nebraska Press, 1984.

———. *Indian Peace Medals in American History.* Madison: State Historical Society of Wisconsin, 1971.

———. *United States Indian Policy: A Critical Bibliography.* Bloomington: Indiana University Press for the Newberry Library, 1977.

Reily, John T. *Collections and Recollections in the Life and Times of Cardinal Gibbons.* Martinsburg VA: Herald Press, 1892.

Robertson, James I., and the Editors of Time-Life Books. *Tenting Tonight; The Soldier's Life.* Alexandria VA: Time-Life Books, 1984.

Robinson, Doane. *A History of the Dakota or Sioux Indians.* Minneapolis: Ross and Haines, 1967.

Schier, Sister Mary Angela, S.S.N.D. "The History of Indian Missions in North Dakota (1874–1938)." M.A. thesis, Catholic University of America, 1938.

Schmitt, Martin F., ed. *General George Crook: His Autobiography.* Norman: University of Oklahoma Press, 1946.

Smith, Rex Alan. *Moon of Popping Trees.* New York: Reader's Digest Press, 1975.

Steltenkamp, Michael F. *Black Elk: Holy Man of the Oglala.* Norman: University of Oklahoma Press, 1993.

Stewart, George C., Jr. *Marvels of Charity: History of American Sisters and Nuns.* Huntington IN: Our Sunday Visitor, 1994.

Summa, Marie, and Frank Summa. *The Stroudsburgs in the Poconos.* Charleston SC: Arcadia, 1998.

Swanton, John R. *The Indian Tribes of North America.* 1952. Reprint, Washington DC: Government Printing Office, 1968.

Thiel, Mark G. "The Omaha Dance in Oglala and Sicangu Sioux History, 1883–1923." *Whispering Wind,* fall–winter, 1990.

U.S. Commissioner of Indian Affairs. *Annual Reports.* Washington DC: Government Printing Office, 1881–1900.

U.S. Department of the Interior. *Biographical and Historical Index of American Indians and Persons Involved in Indian Affairs.* Boston: G. K. Hall, 1966.

U.S. Senate Committee on the Judiciary. *Wounded Knee Massacre: Hearings on S. 1147 and S. 2900.* 94th Cong., 2d sess., 1976.

Utley, Robert M. *The Lance and the Shield: The Life and Times of Sitting Bull.* New York: Henry Holt, 1993.

———. *The Last Days of the Sioux Nation.* New Haven: Yale University Press, 1963.

Vestal, Stanley, ed. *New Sources of Indian History, 1850–1891.* Norman: University of Oklahoma Press, 1934.

———. *Sitting Bull: Champion of the Sioux.* Norman: University of Oklahoma Press, 1965.

Weiser, F. X., S.J. *Kateri Tekakwitha.* Caughnawaga PQ: Kateri Center, 1972.

Zens, Sister M. Serena, O.S.B. "The Educational Work of the Catholic Church among the Indians of South Dakota from the Beginning to 1935." *South Dakota Historical Collections* 20 (1940).

INDEX